Life After Death

Life After Death

Surviving Suicide

RICHARD
BROCKMAN, MD

Arcade Publishing · New York

Arcade Publishing books may be purchased in bulk at special discounts for sales promotion, corporate gifts, fund-raising, or educational purposes. Special editions can also be created to specifications. For details, contact the Special Sales Department, Arcade Publishing, 307 West 36th Street, 11th Floor, New York, NY 10018 or arcade@skyhorsepublishing.com.

Arcade Publishing® is a registered trademark of Skyhorse Publishing, Inc.®, a Delaware corporation.

Visit our website at www.arcadepub.com.

10 9 8 7 6 5 4 3 2 1

Library of Congress Cataloging-in-Publication Data is available on file.

Cover design by Brian Peterson
Cover image by Susan Brockman

Print ISBN: 978-1-68099-805-4
Ebook ISBN: 978-1-68099-806-1

Printed in the United States of America

For Ruth

Once we had a language that included a past and a present and the future, once we could think about what happened and transfer information to people about what might therefore happen, we were going to be telling stories.

—Margaret Atwood

Foreword

Two Stories

I WAS BORN ON DECEMBER 15. THAT IS A NARRATIVE TRUTH.

I was born seven years, two months, two days earlier on October 13. That is a biologic fact.

Story has narrative. Story has biology.

Life After Death tells two stories.

One is the story of my mother's suicide—the devastation that her suicide brought to our family and to me. The other is the story of story itself—how story is biologically laid down, assembled, expanded. How it comes apart; dies, regenerates.

One is narrative. The other biologic.

The narrative has beginning, middle, and end.

The biology has birth, growth, and death.

When my mother killed herself on December 15, she ended the biology of her life. When my mother killed herself on December 15, she ended the narrative of mine. Her suicide ended the narrative of who I was. The narrative of who I wanted to be. When my mother killed herself, she ended the narrative of her seven-year, two-month, two-day-old boy.

How does one continue a narrative when all has been lost?

One doesn't. One can't.

The narrative can't go on because narrative is only part of the story. Story has a biologic as well as a narrative arc.

The biology of story begins with a synapse. A synapse connects neurons. When neurons connect, memory is formed. When memories overlap, they form assemblies that connect various parts of the brain. When various parts of the brain connect, story begins.

Thus when asked, "Who are you?" one might say, "I am an adventurer," or "I am a conquistador," or—if asked by a hookah-smoking caterpillar—one might reply, as Alice did, "I, I hardly know, Sir, at present. At least I know who I was when I got up this morning." And from that response one would surmise that since that morning, Alice's story had been "challenged," perhaps overwhelmed, and was disorganizing.

Being an assembly, story can be put together. Being an assembly, it can come apart. And when the biology of assembly comes apart, story comes apart.

So there is biologic reason why Alice did not know who she was. There is biologic reason why overwhelming experience disorganizes narrative. There is biologic reason why my mother's suicide overwhelmed. Overwhelming experience assaults the biologic organization of story which puts the integrative action of narrative at risk—"I, I hardly know, Sir, at present—"

Like Alice, I too knew "who I was when I got up" that morning—but by that afternoon, my story had come apart, my sense of time destroyed, my narrative had collapsed.

In order for narrative to be regenerated, biology must be restored. Only then can narrative progress.

Life After Death tells two stories. One is the narrative of my mother's suicide. The other is the biology of story. To understand how overwhelming trauma affects story one must understand how story is born, assembled, how it grows, dies, and how—with time, work, love, and the recreation of safety—it can be restored.

One's story, the story of who you are, of who I am, is both an abstract truth and a biologic fact.

I was born on December 15. That is a narrative truth.

I was born seven years, two months, two days earlier on October 13. That is a biologic fact.

Life After Death tells two stories.

Chapter 1

"What Are You Thinking?"
Take One

Those who seek revenge must dig two graves.
—Chinese proverb

"WHAT ARE YOU THINKING?" THE PSYCHIATRIST ASKED HIS PATIENT lying supine on the couch—as he took a drag on his Parliament cigarette, leaned back in his worn leather chair, exhaled.

She stared at the ceiling. A thin puff of smoke drifted above and dissolved. Her hand moved toward the wall. There was another long pause. Another puff. Another—

"What are you thinking?"—after which she uttered the start of a thought that just hung in the air as fragile as smoke.

"I can't. I—"

He took another drag.

And when she went no further, he repeated, "What are you thinking?" crossing and uncrossing his legs.

But there was another question, one he never asked. A question that should have been addressed not to her, but to himself: "What am I going to do about her thinking?"

And the failure to ask that question is why I hold him guilty of murder, and why my life has been lived seeking some form of justice—or revenge.

Chapter 2
"What Are You Thinking?" Take Two

"WHAT ARE YOU THINKING?" THE PSYCHIATRIST ASKED HIS PATIENT lying supine on the couch—as he took a drag on his Parliament cigarette, leaned back in his worn leather chair, exhaled.

She stared at the ceiling. A thin puff of smoke drifted above and dissolved. Her hand moved toward the wall. There was another long pause. Another puff. Another—

"What are you thinking?"—after which she uttered the start of a thought that just hung in the air as fragile as smoke.

"I can't. I—"

He took another drag.

And when she went no further, he repeated, "What are you thinking?" crossing and uncrossing his legs.

"I, I just can't—"

He shifted in his chair. His shoes were wingtipped. Socks, blue diamonds on a background solid black. His suit was gray. His tie was dark with bold stripes. He had full, heavy lips. He took another drag, cleared his throat, "'What can't you do?'" Flicked the ash into the tray on the table beside him. His eyes were dark, not really brown, not really gray, not really green. He was a Jew, but that I'm sure was something you already knew. "What can't you—?"

"I cannot advise my colleagues too urgently to model themselves during psychoanalytic treatment on the surgeon, who puts aside all his feelings, even his human sympathy, and concentrates his mental forces on the single aim of performing the operation as skillfully as he can."[1]

"What can't you do?" uttered again, this time more forcefully, the way a soldier or cop, the way Freud, or an analyst under the influence of—

"What can't you—?"

—because it is common knowledge that "Patients consciously and intentionally keep things back that are perfectly well known because they have not gotten over their feelings of timidity and shame."[2]

"What can't you do?" he sent into the smoke filled air, then as if to clarify what was already there.

And thus Freud in discussing a new case of an eighteen-year-old girl named "Dora," "a case that has smoothly opened to the existing collection of picklocks."[3]

"What can't you—?"

Freud had used "picklocks" to overcome her timidity and shame, the repression and "amnesia" of a girl who had seen "what useful things illness could do" for a wife when her husband, Dora's father, came home from his travels "to find his wife in bad health, although, as Dora knew, she had been quite well only the day before." All spelled out quite clearly in *The Complete Psychological Works*, Volume Seven, pages thirty-eight and -nine, how she, that is to say how "Dora realized that the presence of the husband had the effect of making his wife ill, that she was glad to be ill so as to be able to escape the conjugal duties which she so much detested."[4]

"I, I—" she said. "I just can't."

Most psychiatrists, certainly one as well schooled as Stein, had read the passages on pages thirty-eight and thirty-nine, and thus he was fully aware of the power of resistance and the need for "picklocks" to overcome amnesia, timidity, the forces of repression and shame.

She covered her eyes with her hand as if to shield her mind from the light.

He leaned back in his chair, a well-crafted genuine Stickley, in fact, that he had bought at a shop on the Lower East Side. Stein was proud of the purchase. It had been on sale, a steal. On the back of the chair, there was a marker that read "Als ik kan" and the name Gustav Stickley. After finalizing the deal, he asked the shopkeeper the meaning of "Als ik kan." "'To the best of my ability.' Stickley's parents were Dutch," the shopkeeper explained.

On the table beside him there was a phone, a pad of paper, a Parker T-Ball Jotter pen which he sometimes clicked as if to mark the passage of time. Stein liked to keep track of things—time, money.

"I—" she uttered. "I just—"

And he repeated, "What can't you do?"

And the answer that couldn't be found, words refusing to align the way words usually do—under the weight of repression, amnesia, and the failure of—

"I, I—"

—mind.

"The second assertion (after the fact of the unconscious) which psychoanalysis puts forward is that instinctual impulses which can only be described as sexual, play an extremely large part in the causation of mental disease."[5]

Lying there, fully clothed, yet feeling exposed.

"I—"

"An extremely large part in the causation of mental disease is—"

"Sexual?" he said—more a statement than a question.

"What do you mean?"

"What you can't do, what you can't do for your husband—"

She lowered her hand.

There was another long pause.

Then she said, "Yes," almost in tears. "I cannot—" Then added, "I cannot give—"

"Give—?"

Her hand went back to her face.

"Joy," she said in a voice that was louder than she had expected. Louder than anything she had said in that room in a very long time.

"Joy," she said, lying on her back, staring at the ceiling, she knew she was incapable of bringing—

"Cannot or will not?" Stein asked, then waited. The analyst assumes that when he asks a question, the patient will surrender. All he has to do—

And that is what Stein did.

He waited.

"The patient must be left to do the talking and must be free to choose at what point he or she shall begin."[6]

A click of the pen. Another puff of smoke.

And as she lay there, thoughts filled her as if from a trough. *I hate everything about myself. I bring unhappiness. To my husband, my children, my home. I am more than miserable. I—*

"What are you thinking?" he asked, interrupting her thinking.

—am obscene.

He coughed.

She lowered the hem of her dress to cover her calf.

"Nothing," she said.

"Nothing?"

"Nothing."

Stein lit another cigarette, leaned back in his chair. There was a dark purple sore at the corner of his mouth, a memento of the many Cuban cigars he had brought back just before the revolution, just before the war. *A lucky purchase. A guilty pleasure. I miss*—he thought as his tongue licked the purple sore at the corner of his mouth. His tongue often went back to that spot. *Cuba—The Hotel Nacional.* And the beach a short ride away where he had been approached by a young Cuban girl, *surely a whore,* he thought, as his tongue moved over the sore.

"*Quieres?*"

He took another drag wondering why these thoughts were coming to him now, thoughts of that girl as her thigh moved slightly forward through the slit down the side of her dress.

"*Quieres?*"

Part of his reaction—*countertransference*, it's called.

Her hand moved to the wall.

He took another puff, satisfied with that bit of self-analysis—as palm trees swayed gently on that distant beach. Children approached—selling anything they might have. Cigars. Cheese. A sister. A Coke. He never returned to Cuba. It was just too—

"*Quieres?*"

—louche.

He smiled—

Louche.

—leaning back in his chair. He liked the feel of the word, the way it played in his mouth—*a louche association* he thought, slightly amused with himself.

"I cannot—" she said.

"Cannot—?" he said, leaning forward, returning to the pathological process as the image of palm trees drifted like smoke. He was a superior analyst despite or perhaps because of his ability to drift.

Scratches. She turned to the wall. She stared at the wall thinking she heard sounds—faint scratches like the ones an animal might make, an animal trapped inside the wall.

"You cannot have sex? Is that what you are saying?"

She was still focused on the sounds, the scratches, coming from the wall.

He waited, then asked, "Are you angry with your husband?"

"Am I—?"

"Angry?"

"No. I, I am not. You see he, he, he—"

7

"So that is why you cannot have sex with your husband, because he—"

"—because he deserves someone who, who—"

"Someone who is better than you?"

"Yes. Someone who is better," she said as the first finger of her left hand rubbed in small circles on the wall.

"So we perceive that the self-reproaches are reproaches against a loved object. . . . The woman who loudly pities her husband for being tied to such an incapable wife as herself is really accusing him, her *husband* of being incapable, in whatever sense she may mean."

"He deserves happiness. He deserves joy. He deserves better—"

"Everything derogatory that she says about herself is at bottom really being said about someone else."[7]

"He is a good man. He deserves to be happy, but all that I bring is unhappiness. All that I bring is, is—"

She continued to rub her finger on the wall.

"You love your husband?"

"Yes."

"With whom you do not have sex."

"Because I am unworthy."

"Unworthy—?" he asked.

"Yes," she replied.

"—of sex?"

"—of love," she said in a voice that he didn't hear.

Stein made a note on his pad, "Cannot have sex—" He clicked his Parker T-ball pen, then clicked it again "—because she is unworthy."

"The complex of melancholia behaves like an open wound, drawing to itself energies from all directions, emptying the ego until it is totally impoverished."[8]

She continued to rub her finger in circles on the wall. Tiny flecks of plaster fell to the floor—"I have lost happiness. I have lost joy. I have lost—"

"Please don't do that."

She looked back, confused, almost frightened.

"The wall," he said.

She withdrew her hand, "The wall?"

"You are rubbing plaster off the wall."

"I'm sorry. I wasn't aware," she said as she brought her hand to her side.

"It's all right."

"I'm sorry."

"Your husband—"

"I wasn't aware that I was—"

"Does your husband try to make you happy—?"

"My husband—?"

"—with sex," he said.

She stared.

"Does he try?" Stein asked. "With sex?"

"Yes," she said, "he tries, but I—I am sorry if I—"

"Yes?"

"Please understand—"

She paused because she heard it again.

The sound. The sound a small animal would make. She looked at her hand, her finger indeed was close to the wall, but it was not touching, not scratching, not rubbing. Not making the sound.

And then she heard the click of Stein's pen.

And then again. There. The sound.

"My imagination?" she thought. But then she remembered something she had discovered not so long ago, "I hear voices." She closed her eyes. "There are voices calling from inside my head. Sometimes I hear my name—"

"Ruth—?"

"Sometimes a voice inside of my head—"

"Ruth—"

There. She heard it again and then she realized—

"—I'm sorry to interrupt—"

—it was Stein. Calling her name. He rarely called her by her name. He rarely ever said—

"Ruth, I think there is a sound."

Then she heard the click of his Parker T-ball pen.

She twisted round and looked back over her head.

"A sound coming from the other side of the wall," Stein said as he stood. "I'm just going to check, just going to see—"

She swung her legs to the floor and sat facing Stein.

Stein moved to the first door. He opened it very slowly making almost no noise. "I'm just going to open. I think there is someone. There are sounds—" he said as he moved his hand to the knob of the second door, turned, then pushed with sudden force.

The room was empty. There was nothing, no one. "I must have been wrong."

Then he looked down, and addressed someone she could not see.

"And just what do you think you are doing?"

Chapter 3

Herbs

I OPENED THE DOOR TO ENTER THE HOUSE, AND MY MOTHER WAS THERE, searching the hall closet. When she heard the door, she turned and shielded her eyes as if she couldn't see through the glare of sunlight from the street. She stared at me for a moment as if trying to make sense of what she saw, then said, "Why aren't you in school? Aren't you supposed to be in school? You're supposed to be—"

"I know, but they said, and so—"

"Who said?" She took her dark green jacket from the closet. She wore that jacket a lot. And her green hat.

"I got a shot."

"A what?"

"In my arm."

"Get your coat."

She put on her dark green jacket. I was already wearing my coat.

"They should have told me."

"But Mommy—"

"Never mind," she said, straightening her hat.

She wore her dark green jacket and hat when it was cold. It was October. It was cold. They said a piece of polio was in the shot. I don't know what piece but it hurt a lot. A lot of kids cried. I didn't, but it was close. I wasn't sure what polio was but I was pretty sure it was bad because it hurt. "Mommy, what's polio?" I followed her out

11

the door, across the yard, into the garage. She walked fast. She used to play tennis. I think she used to play pretty good. When I get older, I want to play—

"Mommy?" I called. It was hard to keep up.

Every kid got a shot—every kid except Alan Fisher because he was allergic to eggs. I didn't see what eggs had to do with it. I followed her into the garage. My bike was there against the wall. I loved my bike. I loved it a lot. It had blue and red streamers, and if you pinned baseball cards in the wheels, it hit the spokes and made lots of noise.

"Get in the car."

"Where are we going?"

We had a car. It was a Cadillac. I hated that car. When we drove along the street, I'd slink down. I didn't want the kids to know that my father had a Cadillac. I don't think we were rich but my father had a Cadillac so I guess he didn't care what others thought—or maybe he did. The very day I saw it in the driveway, I asked my father what a Cadillac car was doing in the driveway, a car he must have known I hated. "I'd never buy a Mercedes," he said, "not after what they did."

"What did they do?" I asked.

"And anyway, it's better than a Mercedes." My father was a Jew. I guess that meant I was one too. "It's a beautiful car."

I hated the car.

"Where are we going?" I asked once more as she backed out of the driveway. "Mommy?" Once she hit the stone post. My father got so mad that I thought he was going to tear the post down with his bare hands.

"I have an appointment."

"What for?"

We drove down Falmouth Street then up Orient Avenue onto Shore Parkway, past Sheepshead Bay where sometimes I'd go fishing off the blue wooden bridge—porgies and flounders were fish that

I never caught. I once caught a fish that was black. I threw it back because I hate to eat fish, and it was slimy. "Mommy?"

We drove past Ebinger's Bakery where she went when it was my birthday. I loved presents, but mostly I loved Ebinger's cake. I wanted a dog; I got a bike. I also wanted a bike, so that was okay. "Mommy?" She just drove.

She drove past the turn to Neptune Avenue and Coney Island. We drove down a street where my mother said I should never ride my bike, then she turned onto the Belt Parkway. "Where are we going?" She just drove. All I wanted to know was—

"Richard, sit back."

She just drove, and then she turned onto Ocean Boulevard. And there it was. Dead ahead. And suddenly I knew where we were going.

In 1927, Ivan Pavlov published *Conditioned Reflexes*,[1] which established the experimental basis for associative memory. One of the classic experiments was learned fear. Pavlov placed a dog in a cage, rang a bell and a few seconds later, administered a shock which the dog could not escape. After a few repetitions, Pavlov could ring the bell and the dog would exhibit a fear response—with cowering, whimpering, sometimes it would urinate or defecate—in anticipation of the shock. The bell had become the conditioned stimulus (the CS) associated with the shock itself which was the unconditioned stimulus—(the US). Fear of a painful shock is an unconditioned response, which is innate. Fear in response to a bell is a conditioned response, which is learned. Associative learning is one of the most basic forms of learning. A mollusk, a mouse, a man—are all capable of associative learning. The amygdala—a group of neurons in the medial part of the temporal lobe—is critical for conditioned fear learning in a mammal.

A neurophysiologically more complicated conditioned fear response is when the animal is placed in a box where it had previously been shocked. The recognition of the place is enough to elicit fear. A rodent will freeze when placed in such a box because it has learned to associate the place with a shock. Place recognition, a form

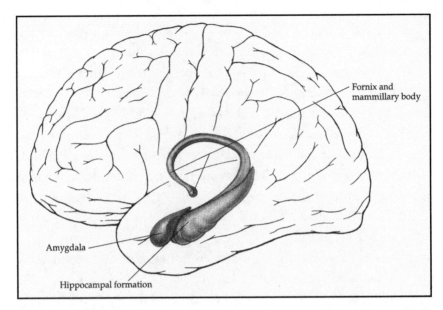

The amygdala and hippocampus are both in the temporal lobe. The amygdala responds to and records emotionally charged memory—especially fear. The hippocampus integrates memory from multiple parts of the brain into long-term memory.

of conditioned learning, requires that the hippocampus, also part of the temporal lobe, be intact. I guess my hippocampus was intact because when I saw the Dime Savings Bank Building, I froze.

The Dime Savings Bank Building, the one with the clock where Alan Fisher's father, the dentist, had his office, was like one of those boxes for me. When I saw the clock, tears welled in my eyes. I started to shake. I had trouble breathing. I thought about jumping out of the car onto Ocean Boulevard where I figured I would be run over and die. The hippocampus, and the rest of my temporal lobes, must have been working just fine.

I was still whimpering in the back of the Cadillac when my mother pulled into the lot. She got out of the car. The parking lot man ripped the yellow sticker apart, handed one half to my mother, and placed the other under the wiper. As he was doing that, he saw me in the back curled like a petrified rat. He called after my mother,

"Hey lady, you can't leave the kid. They got rules." She paused, nodded, seemed to recall that I was still in the car. She walked back and opened the door,

"Richard, you can't stay there. They've got rules."

"I'm not going. It's not fair. You never said."

"Fine." Then she turned and started to walk away.

I got out of the car. I ran past the parking lot man. I caught up to my mother.

"It's not fair."

She kept walking.

"I hate the dentist." I had to skip-run to keep up. "I really, really do." She kept walking. I caught up again, "After, can I get a BLT with mayo on toast?" The only good thing about the dentist was that after, I got a bacon, lettuce, and tomato with mayo on toast, at Junior's Luncheonette. If it weren't for Junior's, I would have killed myself long ago on Ocean Parkway.

"No," she said.

"Why?" I stomped both my feet, then ran to catch up.

"Because we are not going to the dentist."

"We're not?" I said, suddenly feeling a lot better. "Then where are we going?" I asked as she disappeared through the revolving doors.

Those were the only revolving doors I had ever been through. They were made out of glass and steel, and said "Dime" right there on the bar where you pushed on the way to Dr. Fisher.

"Mommy?" She looked at her watch even though there were clocks on the walls. I could read a clock. It was two things before noon. "Then where are we going?" I followed her into the elevator.

"Eight," she said to the elevator man. He was a black man wearing a dark blue suit that said, "Dime" on the collar. He closed the doors.

"What's on eight?" I asked. Dr. Fisher was on eleven. She was staring in the glass—like she was staring at something I couldn't see.

My mother was beautiful. I'm pretty sure she was beautiful. Sometimes when I didn't have school, like after June when it's July, she'd let me play with my soldiers as she got ready to take a bath. My father was at work; my sisters were both grown. I loved cowboys. I loved Indians. I loved watching my mother.

"You shouldn't let him see you like that," my father said one morning as he left for work, which was in a factory that made fans. That's what my father did. He went to a factory that made fans.

"Oh, Dave," she said as she kissed him goodbye, "I'm old. What's to see?" She wasn't old.

"Mommy—?"

I had cowboys and Indians. My mother had bottles and creams. I'd play just inside the door as she ran the water for her bath. Even though I had more Indians, the cowboys won. That was how it was done.

"So what are you doing today?" she asked as she poured something from a purple bottle into the water. The steam rose and clouded the mirror.

"What makes it smell like that?" I asked.

"Like what?"

"Like that," I said.

She sat in the chair by the bath, "It's got herbs." I nodded. "Herbs," she said.

"What are herbs?" I asked.

"Lavender, sage—those are herbs," she said.

"Odors are critical for learning and memory about events and places and constitute efficient retrieval cues for the recall of emotional episodic memory."[2]

"Oh," I said, "That's an herb."

"Yes," she said, stirring the water with her hand. "Maybe you can go fishing," she said. We lived in Manhattan Beach—which was between the ocean where there were waves and Sheepshead Bay where there were fish. "Mommy?" I asked as she took off her robe.

She stood up and lay her robe over the back of the chair, "What?" Her robe was white. My eyes just followed from the white of the robe on the chair to her hand, to her arm, her shoulder, her back, to her skin.

She wasn't wearing any clothes.

"Richard—?"

Freud would have said it was oedipal. I would have said it was my mother.

"Richard—?"

"What?"

"What are you doing?"

"Watching."

Then she just smiled, and as she pulled her hair back from her face and held it up with a clip, she said, "You've seen enough," and stepped into the bath, "Go fishing," she said as she lowered herself into the water, and as she did the smell of herbs rose like fish. "Richard?"

"What?"

"Ask Michael."

Michael Starr was my best friend who lived around the block next to my cousins, Susan Margo and Judy. "Now go." I stood there. "Go." I gathered my cowboys, my Indians. This time the Indians won. As I walked out, she was settling in the bath. She seemed kind of pleased. I turned to her, and asked, "Mommy, are you beautiful?"

She smiled as she stirred the water. "Ask your father," she said.

In his work, Pavlov discovered the rudiments of learned fear. But he also discovered the rudiments of learned safety—which, as it turns out, is not the mere opposite of fear. There is learning that predicts danger. There is a learning that overrides the fear associated with danger. And then there is learning that predicts safety. Each has its own neurophysiology. The fear system predominantly involves learning in the amygdala. The overriding of fear predominantly involves learning in the prefrontal cortex.

The learning of safety predominantly involves the nucleus accumbens, which is a part of the system that predicts reward.

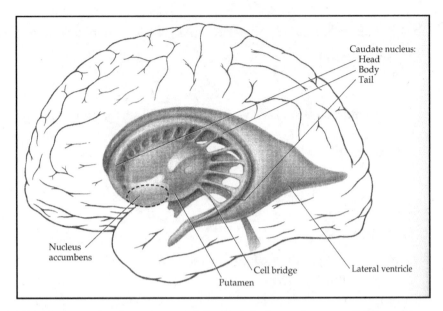

Caudate nucleus:
Head
Body
Tail

Nucleus
accumbens

Cell bridge

Putamen

Lateral ventricle

The nucleus accumbens is one of the brain's "reward centers." The nucleus accumbens does not respond to the attainment of reward but rather to the anticipation of reward.

Learned safety involves more than the absence of fear. It involves the anticipation of reward.

Lavender. Sage.

Herbs.

Rewards. Like the sight of my mother. Herbs are rewards.

The most interesting thing about the nucleus accumbens—a small group of cells in the ventral striatum, a subcortical part of the mammalian brain, is that it doesn't respond to the gratification of reward. It responds to the anticipation of reward.

Herbs.

The elevator man moved the crank to the right then back around to the left. "Eight," he said and then he opened the metal frame door, and there we were. On eight.

My mother didn't move, just kept staring deep into the glass. "You did say eight?" the elevator man asked.

Then she turned to the elevator man and said, "Yes. Thank you. Eight."

I followed her out. When I looked back, the elevator man was watching. He nodded. I nodded.

Right then and there I knew that when I grew up, I was gonna be an elevator man.

I ran to catch up to my mother. She walked down the long stone floor to another door. In the Dime Savings Bank Building, every hallway door was made of glass with silver round the sides. She stopped in front of one that said "Dr. David J. Stein," written in black. She stared at the glass. "Who's Dr. Stein?" I asked. She didn't answer. She just stared. "Mommy—?"

"I know."

"What—?"

We went inside. There was no one. No desk. No nurse. No doctor. No one. Two chairs. A table. A picture on the wall of a train that said "Sud."

"What's Sud?" I asked.

Another door opposite the one we had come in was dark and brown and old. "Is Dr. Stein a dentist?" The only other doctor I knew in the Dime Savings Bank Building was Dr. Fisher, the dentist. She looked at me as if trying to decide what to say. Then she said, "He's a specialist."

"Oh," I said. She sat down. "What's a specialist?" I asked.

She opened her purse, took out a Kleenex. She blotted her lips, leaving red streaks in the white tissue. She tossed the Kleenex into the waste bin next to the chair. "A specialist is someone you see when there's nothing wrong." Her purse snapped shut. "Or when you're incurable."

"What does that mean?"

She lay her head back and closed her eyes.

There were two chairs in the room, each against opposite walls. I moved the one chair closer to where my mother was sitting. For a while I just stared at the wall with the picture of "Sud." Then I asked, "Am I sick?" She opened her eyes. "Mommy?" Her hands were folded neatly on her lap.

I looked around the room. The room was quiet like in a movie when something bad is about to happen. But nothing was happening so I asked,

"Mommy, after I see Dr. Stein, can I get a BLT with mayo on toast at Junior's?" I waited, "Mommy?"

"No."

"Why not?"

She didn't say, and then she said, "Because you're not seeing Dr. Stein."

"Oh." That also made me feel better. "Then what am I doing here?"

I stared at the old door as if the answer lay just behind. Like on one of those TV shows I sometimes watched if no one was around I'd just sneak down to the basement and turn it on—my father had bought us a Philco, and I loved it.

"So will it be door number one, door number two, or door number—?"

But there was only one door—and it was dark and brown and old. The kind of door that would never have a washing machine or a car or a dog behind it. I wanted a dog.

I stared at the door trying to figure out what might be behind it, when I heard a sound, the kind a door makes—but the door was still closed.

I stared at the old, dark, brown door trying to figure why it was still closed, and then it opened. I was thinking how that was weird—how first I heard a door open and then the door actually opened—and then I realized—

Two doors!

Chapter 4

Two Doors

THE CANADIAN PSYCHOLOGIST DONALD HEBB WROTE A BOOK IN 1949, *Organization of Behavior*, in which he elaborated some of the most influential neuropsychological arguments of the twentieth century. The arguments were based on theory not fact. Hebb recognized the dangers he faced. "Theorizing at this stage is like skating on thin ice—keep moving, or drown."[1] He kept moving—and elaborated two hugely consequential theories, "cell assembly" and "lasting cellular change."

Of the first, Hebb wrote, "Any frequently repeated particular stimulation will lead to the slow development of a 'cell-assembly,' a diffuse structure comprising cells in the cortex and diencephalon (thalamus and related structures)."[2]

Hebb reasoned that repeated synaptic communication between neurons did something to the synaptic connection between the neurons that was strengthened by the very interaction, creating loops that were capable of supporting reverberating activity. He was arguing that repeated interaction between neurons enhanced those interactions. But how were these connections "strengthened"? How were neuronal networks formed?

Hebb had predicted that some form of a "coincidence detector" had to exist in the core biology of the neuron for learning, that is to say, for memory to occur. He offered a theory as to how that

21

"coincidence detector" might work, a theory that would become known as "Hebb's Law."

> Let us assume then that the persistence or repetition of a rever-beratory activity (a memory "trace") tends to induce lasting cel-lular changes that add to its stability. This assumption can be precisely stated as follows: *When an axon of cell A is near enough to excite a cell B and repeatedly or persistently takes part in firing it, some growth process or metabolic change takes place in one or both cells such that A's efficiency, as one of the cells firing B, is increased.*[3]

Hebb conjectured that when neurons discharge simultaneously, the synapses joining those neurons are biologically facilitated by the dis-charge itself, and as a result communication between simultaneously firing neurons is strengthened. Hebb anticipated that the facilitated synaptic communication through simultaneous neuronal discharge was key to neuronal connection, and thus key to an understanding of how a biological "coincidence detector" worked. And thus key to understanding how a neuronal network—how a "cell assembly"—was formed. He did not know the biology of this facilitation, but he hypothesized that it had to exist—theories that decades later would be proven correct.

Thus he argued that synapses are strengthened when juxtapos-ing neurons fire simultaneously ("Neurons that fire together, wire together" is the mantra medical students all learn). And further that when a great number of neurons fire simultaneously, the connec-tions between neurons, the synapses, are strengthened. And when many synapses from many neurons are strengthened (hundreds, thousands—millions in fact), the communication between these neu-rons is facilitated and cell assemblies are formed. And when cell assemblies are formed, the neurons from one cell assembly overlap with neurons from another cell assembly. And when the neurons of cell assemblies overlap, the action of one cell assembly leads to another, creating communication between diverse cell assemblies and diverse parts of the brain.

It explains, for example, why when neurons compromising the visual memory of an "old door" in one cell assembly overlap with neurons compromising the visual memory of an "old door" in another cell assembly, the two cell assemblies interact. It explains how the activation of the neurons of one cell assembly can activate the neurons of a second cell assembly. It explains how memories interact—

Two doors!

—and how story starts.

"Memory . . . is an action; essentially it is the action of telling a story."[4]

I stared at the old brown door trying to figure why it was still closed, and right then and there it opened. I was thinking how that was weird—how first I heard a door open and then the door actually opened—and then I realized—

Two doors!

—when a man in a gray suit entered the room. My mother stood up. I stood up. "Wait here," she said.

"I don't like it here."

"Richard, you'll be fine."

"I don't like it here."

"Just wait."

"But, Mommy—"

The man in the gray suit removed his glasses, rubbed the sides of his head with his fingers and thumb. He was wearing a tie. He half smiled as he looked at me. He seemed surprised. There was a little purple lump in one corner of his mouth.

"Is this your son?" he asked. My mother nodded her head.

He turned to me. "Hello," he said. "How do you do?"

I held onto my mother's leg. Then he turned to my mother and said, "Please come in."

My mother looked at me. "Richard, be a good boy and just sit. I won't be long."

"Where are you going?"

"I'll just be in the next room."

"What room?"

"I won't be long."

She removed my arm from her leg. "You'll be fine." She opened her purse. "Here," she said and gave me a Life Saver. Then she said, "Here," and gave me the whole roll.

She walked through the door, and he followed her, closing the old brown door behind him. And then I heard it again, and when I did, I thought, *Two doors.*

I looked around the room. There was nothing. Nothing to do. Nothing to touch. Nothing to play with. Nothing. Just some magazines, a picture of "Sud." And a wastebasket. Then I remembered the roll of Life Savers that was in my hand. The first was pineapple. But the second was cherry. Cherry was my favorite. That helped. I tossed the pineapple Life Saver into the wastebasket and sucked on the cherry. I never liked pineapple.

I walked around. The room was real small. There was nowhere to go. Nothing to explore. I went to the wastebasket. It was empty—only the pineapple Life Saver and the Kleenex that my mother had thrown in. I picked up the Kleenex. It was white except for the red where she had left the mark of her lips. I put my mouth on the mark her lips had left. Tissue stuck to my teeth. And then I heard something I hadn't heard even though it had been there all along.

There was a machine on the floor that made noise—like the noise of a huge gray and white cat—like the noise from Mr. Palowski's, the neighbor whom I hated, gray and white cat.

A machine that made noise. This was the worst room. I hated the room. Why would my mother bring me to this room? What did the room do? What kind of a doctor has a room with nothing but

24

a machine that makes noise like Mr. Palowski's gray and white cat—and two doors?

I went to the machine. I got down on my knees and pushed the machine to see what it would do. It did nothing. It just lay there curled on the floor and made noise. Then I saw a button. I pushed the button. The noise stopped. I pushed it again. The noise came back. I pushed it once more. The machine was boring. It did nothing. And then I remembered the doors.

I crawled over. The door was old and dark and brown like the one in my grandmother's house, down the hallway in Williamsburg, Brooklyn, that smelled like chicken fat and old age. My bobe, which is grandmother in Yiddish, smelled like chicken fat and old age—just like the hall. Whenever I went to see her, there were teeth by her bed in a jar. Usually she'd forget about her teeth, and would just mouth with her gums and kiss me and say things I couldn't understand because I wasn't born where she had been born, somewhere far, it never made sense, then she'd say, "You want I should make *zup*? *Hindl zup* I make just for my Malki."

"My name isn't Malki," I'd say to myself, knowing it didn't matter, knowing she never listened or heard. I think she was deaf.

"Malki you think your *savta* forgets her *boobalah's nomen*, my *bisl* Malki?"

When she talked to me like that, I'd turn to the teeth to see if they were moving.

"So Malki, you want the *hindl zup* your *savta* makes just for you?"

Always "*hindl zup*." Never cupcakes. Never brownies. Never Pez from one of those really cool Pez dispensers that Michael Starr had. Like there was nothing in the world except "*zup*."

Once my grandfather, my zayde, took me to where he bought chickens. You had to walk under the tracks of the train which ran by their house. They called it "the L"—which made no sense until you understood what the L really meant. When the train went past, huge sparks fell from above. I was afraid sparks would fall on my head and set me on fire.

It was a long walk to a place where there was a door—a door on the street that was old and dark and peeling and brown. No pictures, no signs. "Are we going to a store?" I asked. "No store," he said. Just a door.

My grandfather went to the door. Straightened his long black coat. Looked up and down the block, and then knocked. One, two. Then he knocked again, one, two, three. And then a man opened the door.

The man who opened the door had a beard, an apron covered with blood, and a voice like a cantor, which was what my zayde said he was. He laughed at everything and puffed fat cigars—like Uncle Cookie who wasn't really my uncle but whom we all called Uncle Cookie.

Always in Yiddish.

My zayde said things I didn't understand. Then the man would say things and then they would both say things and then they'd both laugh and say more things.

Inside there was a wooden table, a pail, and endless strips of flypaper like candy, only covered with flies, sometimes dead, sometimes buzzing. But the weirdest thing—behind my zayde and the man and the table and the flypaper and the flies, there was a door and behind the door there was a plastic curtain, and behind the plastic curtain there were chickens—clucking and scratching—walking back and forth as if they were lost or frightened or shopping.

And then the man picked up a pot and banged it against the table. I grabbed my zayde by his black coat, and he laughed, and explained something in Yiddish, and laughed some more. So I guess it was funny, and I guess all the chickens were scared because they all moved away from the door and the plastic curtain. And then the man with the beard and the apron and the pot parted the curtain and walked through. Just like that. He walked through the two doors.

"Like Moses," my zayde said.

"Who's Moses?" I asked.

My zayde looked up and said, "'Who's Moses?' *Got mukhl im er iz nor a eyngl.*"

The man with the beard and the apron and the pot was gone for a minute. Then two. Then the clucking just got louder until the curtains parted again and he walked back holding a chicken by its feet.

The man took the chicken to my grandfather, and said things in Yiddish as he poked the bird and then my grandfather poked the bird, and nodded, smiled, and then the man said something again as he lay the bird on the wooden block and chopped off its head. Just like that.

And then blood. Over the side of the table, into the pail, onto the floor.

Blood.

The man wrapped the chicken in a newspaper written in what must have been Yiddish because I couldn't read it, then handed it to my grandfather. Then they talked. On and on.

The chicken's head lay on the table, its eyes wide, still trying to understand what had happened. I wanted to explain that it had just been chopped off. I wanted to let the chicken know, but I didn't speak Yiddish which I figured was something a chicken living in that place might understand. And so I just stood there as the man and my grandfather continued to talk. Also when you talk Yiddish, you use hands. When you are dead, you stare. My grandfather talked Yiddish. The chicken stared. The blood that poured off the table was red. The smell that filled the room was old. Everything seemed to be happening in Yiddish.

I just stood there for a while staring at the head—for a while it was like I was that head trying to understand what had happened. For a minute I was unable to move or to speak as Yiddish swirled around me like the buzzing of flies.

I thought of my mother's lipstick-stained Kleenex that I had pulled from the trash—I guess because of the red.

"*Lamir aheym geyn,*" my grandfather said, then added, "Let's go home." Yiddish was the language my grandfather spoke since he was a boy, the language I never learned, the language that he brought with him from Poland. After leaving Poland and coming to America, he never really learned English, never really left "home," was somehow in his head still just outside of Cracow. "Grandma is waiting." He took my hand. Never really left after coming all that way. "She is waiting."

I went to the door.

Then I realized it wasn't quite closed.

"You will bring her the *hindl*," he said handing me the headless chicken wrapped in Yiddish. "She is waiting." I never quite understood how he decided when to speak Yiddish, which I didn't understand, or when to speak English. Or when to use both, "Malki, she is waiting for the *hindl*."

And then I heard a man's voice. Then I heard it again.

He held the chicken. "Here," he said. "Show Grandma. Then bring it back. Better I should make the *zup*."

And that's when I realized—Grandma never let Grandpa make "*zup.*" Grandma never let anyone in her kitchen. Not even me. "Enough. It's not ready. Ya, ya, ya, not ready the *zup*." And that's when it hit me—

It wasn't old age I was smelling. It was blood.

In 1906 Charles Sherrington proposed that simple reflexes—stereotyped movements elicited by activation of receptors in skin or muscle—are the basic units of the reflex-arc. A reflex-arc, or stimulus-response system, moves in one direction—from the incoming stimulus to the outgoing response. If one's knee is tapped (the incoming sensory stimulus), it responds (the contraction of the quadriceps muscle). The direction is from stimulus to response. It is a feed-forward, unidirectional, cause-and-effect system that is "inactive until stimulated by the outside world."

"Your bobe is waiting," he said.

Beginning in the early twentieth century, it became clear that a feed-forward, unidirectional reflex-arc failed to account for what was becoming known about memory. Memory does not need an external stimulus. It can start by itself. It can arrive unannounced. Memory can change direction. Unlike the reflex-arc, memory has no beginning nor end, it can move backwards or forwards. Memory can linger in the past. It can reach to the future. It can bring hope. It can kill time. Memory is its own mind.

"By itself a single neuron is not intelligent. But a vast network of neurons can think, feel, remember, perceive, and generate the many remarkable phenomena that are collectively known as 'the mind.'"[5]

To account for these observations, several hypotheses emerged. In 1938 the Spaniard Rafael Lorente de No argued that the reflex arc with its unidirectional, feed-forward path failed to explain most mechanisms of memory. He proposed the theory of synaptic loops where the impulse could begin and end in the same place and thus the idea that a neuron assembly could feed back as well as forward, and thus could be recurrent, self-sustaining. Memory could go back to where it began and start all over again. No feed-forward reflex-arc could account for that.[6]

In 1950 Karl Lashley tried to induce memory deficits in monkeys and rats by removing larger and larger areas of the cortex.[7] His efforts failed. The animals could remember most tasks even after large areas of their cortices had been removed. As a result of this experimental failure, he dropped the idea that memory is localized, and laid the groundwork for the idea that memory must exist in a distributed network of "cell assemblies," in multiple areas of the cortex, where neurons of one cell assembly can be a part of, and thus bridge, to another. So a rat, for example, may remember where it had found some food by memory stored in sight, by memory stored in touch, by memory stored in smell—and if any one of those systems remains, the rat will find its way to the cheese. Memory is distributed in a network. Memory is an assembly of distributed networks of cells.

"It is commonly assumed that reorganization of neural networks in the brain is a decentralized process in which synapses are modified as a result of the interaction of neurons rather than in response to signals from some central authority. A consequence of such localized self-organization is that one synapse on a neuron can be modified while another remains unchanged."[8]

Memory is not located in one place, or in one neuron. It is an assembly of neurons, an assembly of cells—a cell assembly—joined by synapses that are a product of learning.

Memory in this light is not so stable, predictable, polite as the more localized notion that had been envisioned in the reflex arc. Memory, having no king, can be as free and unruly as any healthy democracy.

"Cell assemblies are the neural basis of concepts. The cell assembly is a set of interconnected neurons that can persist without external stimulus, is learned, and is supported by synchronous firing."[9] Unlike the reflex arc, which requires an external stimulus, the cell assembly can be generated from within—by another memory, by another thought, by an idea, or by sensation from within or without.

And then I heard my mother's voice, but I couldn't make out the words. All I heard were the sounds.

And when I heard the sound of her voice coming from the other side of the door, two doors, I knew I was hearing something I wasn't supposed to hear, so I opened the first door a little more so I could get my ear closer to the second door. To the door that wasn't old and dark and brown. I crawled a little farther into the space between the two doors. And then I heard her voice again and then I heard another voice, a man's voice. I guess it was the voice of the man in the gray suit with the glasses and the purple sore at the side of his mouth. I crawled in a little more. And I heard him again, and then I heard my mother's voice, "I can't. I just can't." Which I had heard her say once before but I didn't know what she meant or why she said it, so I crawled till my ear was touching the door inside the door when I heard, "Please—understand—" Then I didn't hear anything. It got real quiet. The way it does before rain, or in the scary movie before someone gets shot.

And when we got home, standing outside the old, dark, door, Zayde said, "Bring it to Bobe," nodding at the chicken in the Yiddish paper stained with blood, "It will make Bobe happy." I was afraid, afraid to see, afraid of the smell, afraid of Bobe, like Hansel and Gretel, which I had just read—I was afraid that she might cook me in her zup.

"Richard," Zayde said, suddenly speaking like he'd been born in Bay Ridge, "Bring the chicken to Grandma." Then he pushed me a little toward the door, his strong hands on my back, his voice loud and clear. "Now," he said. "Bring her the chicken," he said first in English then in Yiddish, "*Brengt ir dos hun.*" And then he pushed me harder. "*Mahkn ir gezunt.*" And then with one last push I was inside the room. "Make her happy," he said. "Show her the chicken."

All I could think of was the smell in the room and the teeth in the jar. "Go on," he said. "Go on. *Mahkn ir tsufridn, Malki. Mahkn ir tsufridn.*" And I just stood there just inside the door filling with smell.

"Grandpa I—"

"Make her happy."

And then I heard her say, "Please understand I can't. I just can't."

And then I heard, "Can't what?"

And then I heard it again, "Can't what?" first in a whisper, then out loud, "Can't what?" in a voice that sounded like mine—and then I realized it was my voice, and I started to tremble, there on the floor between the two doors. I was afraid. Afraid for my Mommy. "Can't what?" still louder until it was loud, "Can't what?"—which was when the door opened—and when I was afraid to look up because some- how I knew what was going to be there.

"*Mahkn ir tsufridn!*"

Cell assembly thus creates large networks of interconnected neurons. Firing of neurons within the network leads to activation of other neurons. This spreading of activation from one memory trace to another is an example of "pattern completion"—an idea that has been applied to very large networks. The activation can be connected by an overlapping sensation, thought, the sight of an old door, or of words overheard. It has to do with the fact that memory is distributed in large networks of neurons—hundreds, thousands, millions of neurons—that overlap. And thus memory traces can spread from one assembly to the next. Patterns can move forward or back. The pattern anticipates what is missing and thus what comes next. And when something is anticipated or gets filled in—

"Can't what?"

—you have the action of story.

"I, I, I—"

"With the extraordinary development of the prefrontal cortex, the human brain has gained the capacity to make future predictions far beyond that of any other animal species. . . . The evolution of the prefrontal cortex has endowed humans with a sense and command of their future."[10]

Memory creates the past. By creating the past, memory creates time. By creating time, memory creates the future. And by creating the present, the past, and the future, memory creates story, and by creating story, memory anticipates—

"I, I, I—"

—what comes next.

"*Mahkn ir tsufridn!*"

Chapter 5

What Comes Next

BOBE WAS LYING IN BED. SHE WAS BREATHING THROUGH HER MOUTH. Her lips were purple-blue. Dry air passed back and forth through the space where her teeth used to be—her teeth now in the jar on the table by her bed. "Grandma—" I said standing a few feet inside her room. I was holding the chicken, unable to move.

I stared at the teeth. I stared at her lips. And then I heard it again, "*Mahkn ir tsufridn!*"

The teeth on the table chattered as the elevated train rumbled just outside, overhead. I stared at the teeth. "*Mahkn ir tsufridn!*" The teeth seemed to talk. They seemed to have eyes that stared like the eyes of the chicken. It was as if the teeth and the chicken had something in common, something they both understood. It was as if—

"*Mahkn ir tsufridn!*"

I was afraid to look up.

"*Mahkn ir tsufridn!*"

All I could see were dark shoes and gray pants.

And then I heard it quite clearly, "What are you doing?" The shoes were dark, almost black. The laces were tied in neat little knots. Whenever I tied my shoes—

"Did you hear what I said?"

I was afraid of her lips. Afraid of her teeth. Afraid of the chicken wrapped in Yiddish.

33

"Did you hear what I said?" he repeated.

I shook my head.

"You were eavesdropping. Do you know what this is?"

I didn't move.

"What you were doing was wrong!"

I stared at his shoes.

"Look at me!"

I lifted my eyes as far as the pair of glasses he held in his hand, a finger looped in his belt. "Did you hear what I said?" The glasses stared at me the same as Bobe's teeth.

He turned toward my mother who was sitting on a couch against the wall in that room. "Are you all right?" he asked.

"I'm sorry," she said, "It was my fault. I, I forgot—"

Zayde's hand touched my shoulder. When it did, I startled, confusing his touch for Bobe's teeth, which I always felt might jump out of the glass and—

"Forgot?"

"The school didn't tell me, or maybe they did."

"I don't understand," he said.

"Polio," she said. "Today was the day when he got his first—"

"Right, right. That's all right," he said. "All kids today—"

"They get a shot."

"You forgot?"

"I'm sorry," she said.

Alan Fisher didn't get a shot because he was allergic to eggs. I didn't see what eggs had to do with it.

"Go on," Zayde said, pushing me further into the room. The room smelled like Bobe. The smell made me scared that at any moment Bobe might rise up like—

"*Mahkn ir gezunt*,' Zayde said. "Make her better," he said. "Make her happy."

I stood there staring, waiting for Bobe to speak. The smell of her filled me. I couldn't think. I couldn't move. I couldn't breathe.

"You are old enough to know that you shouldn't do that. You know it's not right," he said.

I kept staring at my sneakers. The laces were undone. They were Keds, red and white US Keds.

"It was wrong," he said, cleaning his glasses and then holding them up as if there were something on them. "You are old enough to know better," he said as if to remind me I was almost seven, putting his glasses back on. The dark mark on the side of his mouth was like blood, which reminded me of the–

"What do you have to say?"

I stood quiet and still. Everything was quiet and still. Even the machine that made noise. I couldn't think what to say, my mind went blank and then out of nowhere, I said, "Does that mean I'm not gonna get a BLT with mayo on toast at Junior's Luncheonette?"

Dr. Stein cleared his throat, kind of licked the dark spot on the side of his mouth, "If it were up to me, it means 'yes.' You are *not* going to get a BLT with mayo on toast at Junior's Luncheonette. Not after what you did."

Then he turned to my mother and said, "I think the session is over for today." She nodded. Then he nodded back, "I will see you on Friday." She moved toward the door, "I'm sorry," she said to Dr. Stein, as she took my hand and walked toward the door. "I'm sorry."

"Go on," my zayde said.

"Thank you," she said.

I never understood why she would say–

"Mahkn ir gezunt."

I moved closer to the bed.

Then my grandfather said to his wife, "Bobe, *kuk ver iz do.*"

Bobe smiled and reached out with her hand. I took a step back but Zayde pushed me forward.

Her fingers touched my face the way a blind man's touch food.

Once when I was at Lundy's, I saw a blind man who–

"*Mahkn ir gezunt.*"

35

Bobe just stared. Then she asked, "Malki?"

"*Ya es i rus s kleyn eyngl.*" And then he said, "Ruthie's little boy."

And then Zayde pushed me closer. Bobe took my face to her lips. They were dry. They were cold. I didn't know what would happen when you were kissed by lips that were purple and dry and cold.

"*Adank,*" Bobe said. "*Adank.*"

"This spreading of activation from one neuron to others is an example of pattern completion. Such a neural process is thought to be responsible for the psychological phenomenon of memory retrieval. Partial information triggers recall of more information based on the completion of a neural activity pattern. Symmetric pattern completion is possible for a cell assembly because . . . activity can spread in any direction."[1]

"*Adank,*" she said as her cold purple lips began to smile.

"Thank you," my mother said to Dr. Stein as we walked past the two doors, past the machine that made noise—but it wasn't making noise. Then I remembered—I had pushed the button.

"Show her the chicken," my zayde said. "Let her see."

I held up the chicken, the one with no head. Blood no longer dripped. It was stuck in the neck.

Memory is ongoing, fluid. It opens, like water flowing over stone.

"*Adank,*" she said. "*Adank.*"

"The complexity of the functions involved in reproductive memory implies that every instance of recall requires the activation of literally millions of neurons. The same neurons which retain the memory traces of one experience must also participate in countless other activities."[2]

"Thank you," my grandfather said.

"What did I do?"

"You brought her zup," my zayde said.

Memories share neurons. One neuron is incorporated into multiple memories because of cell assembly.

"*Adank*," Grandma said.

Cell assembly.

"You brought her zup," Grandpa said.

"Zup."

Chapter 6

DeKalb Avenue

WE WALKED OUT OF THE ROOM PAST THE MACHINE THAT MADE NOISE. We went out into the hall past all the glass doors with the black and silver frames. My mother was holding my hand. "Mommy?" I asked when we got to the elevators. I looked up at her. She opened her purse, took out some Kleenex.

The elevator door opened. I tripped over my laces.

The elevator man nodded, then closed the door. He turned the crank to the left, and we started down. My mother kept holding my hand. We got out in the lobby, past the big clocks. Then we went out onto Jefferson Place. She was still holding my hand. "Mommy—?" She kept walking right past the parking lot. "I think I better tie my—"

We got to the corner then turned onto DeKalb. "Where we going?"

We walked further. My sneakers had both untied. And then she stopped. And there it was. I almost cried.

She let go of my hand.

The neurons of my nucleus accumbens (the part of the brain that anticipates reward) were on fire. We were standing on DeKalb Avenue in front of my favorite place in the whole world.

Junior's Luncheonette!

Then my mother just walked to the door and held it open for me. Junior's!

We sat at a booth that was vinyl and red. All the booths were vinyl and red. My feet swung back and forth—not quite touching the floor. There were menus on the table that I never read. I knew what I wanted. I knew by heart.

Stacey, the waitress, the one with blond hair and bad teeth, like the woman I had seen on *Queen for a*—

"So how was the dentist? I know, I know I should go, that's what they all say, but hey what can I get you? Mom, you want coffee, that much for sure," she said to my mother, turning the cup and filling it up without even waiting for my mother's reply. Then she turned to me, "And you? Let me guess, I bet you'd like a BLT with mayo on toast. Am I correct?" She started writing in her pad, "I am correct."

My mother said, "Thank you, Stacey."

"How 'bout a cruller?" Stacey asked.

My mother smiled and shook her head.

"I really love that show," Stacey said staring off at the TV at a woman who was praying for a washing machine and a winter coat. "Me, I'd pray for a new mattress." Stacey winked. "And a divorce." She turned to me and winked again. Whenever I tried to wink, both of my eyes would just close.

Stacey moved toward the back, then called to the cook in a voice loud enough to be understood by someone who didn't understand English.

I just sat there and stared at my mother. She looked at me. "I'm sorry if—" then she stopped, looked out the window. She ran her hand through her hair. It was long and dark.

"Thank you—for coming with me," she said.

"Who is he?" I said kicking the side of the booth.

"I'm not sure," she said, which seemed odd. She took a sip of coffee. She really liked coffee. Even though I liked the smell, I never understood how come grown-ups could spend so much time sipping coffee.

And then Stacey came back to our table. "Here it is!" she said,

"Brooklyn's best BLT." It came with a side of slaw and a pickle. Everything at Junior's came with a side of slaw and a pickle. I stared at my BLT. It was the greatest thing!

"What do you say?"

"Wow!"

"Thank you, Stacey," my mother said.

I picked it up. I looked at my mother. She stared at me. I took a bite—mayo oozed out the sides, onto my hands, down the lines of my palms.

"*Aqui*, see this," she said. I looked into my hand. "*Hay tormentas*," she said shaking her head. "*Aqui—*" the fortune teller at a booth down the ramp from the boardwalk at Coney Island had said to me as my cousins Susan Margo and Judy ate their cotton candy. "*Aqui esta ligna—*"

"Thank you," my mother said, taking my hand from the fortune teller. "We have to go." The fortune teller looked up, "*Pero, señora—*"

"We have to go," my mother said.

I put the BLT on the plate, licking my fingers flooded with mayo. I turned to my mother. "If you want a bite, it's okay," I said hoping that she would say "no," and when she said, "No," I felt my heart in my throat. I almost choked.

"It's yours," she said.

"All of it?"

She nodded, then smiled. It was the first time I'd seen her smile since my birthday—the one she remembered.

"All of it," she said as she sipped coffee.

"All of it," I thought as I lifted the BLT, paused for a breath. Then I opened my mouth as wide as I could.

"*Hay tormentas*," the fortune teller said. "*Pero, el destino es el destino*" she said in case there were doubt. "*Algodon de azucar*," she called out.

"What does that mean?"

"It means you will have a long and happy life," the fortune teller said.

40

My mother handed me my cone of cotton candy.

I took another bite.

"*Una vida larga y feliz,*" she smiled at my mother, who smiled back.

"*Dos pesos,*" she said.

"All of it," she said.

Chapter 7
The Big Orange

BABAR WAS THE BIG ORANGE.
Whenever my mother asked what story I wanted to read, more than any other the one I'd pick was the Big Orange. It's the book I "read" before I could read. It's the book I knew from one orange cover to the other.

"'In the great forest a little elephant is born,'"[1] my mother read as I lay on the bed. If a car passed on the street, lights would cross on the wall. "'His mother loved him very much,'" she read, and I would recite alongside because I knew the Big Orange by heart, "'She loved her baby Babar.'"

And I would ask "Did she love him more than Zephyr?"—jumping ahead a book or two just to make sure (we had read them all). "More than that rascal monkey Zephyr," she said, undoing the clip that held her hair. "More than Zephyr." It was long. It was dark. It fell down her back.

"More than Zephyr," she said, "That's how much she loves her baby Babar." I loved to hear that. I loved to hear how much she loved her baby Babar.

She turned the page. And I would study the pictures and it would all come back, every sound, every feeling, every word. Like a fortune teller reading a palm. It came back. "*El destino es el destino,*" the fortune teller had said, but I didn't know what that meant.

"Babar has grown bigger," I'd say, then I would add to show that I knew what came next, "See him digging in the sand with his shell."

"Here is Babar," she would say, holding the book up for me, and I would point to Babar—"There he is digging in the sand." And then she would turn the page, and I'd continue to read from memory—

"Babar is riding on his mother's back."

"Yes," she'd say, "Babar is riding on his mother's back." I'd love that, I loved it when she read, when I could be alone with her and Babar. It was magic. Lights passed on the walls. Sometimes she would lie down next to me and spoon, front to back. It was magic like that. I'd close my eyes, "Babar is riding on his mother's back."

And then I heard, "Ruth, it's late," from the far end of the hall. "The boy has school."

She looked at me, and smiled without saying a word.

"Ruth!"

"We're reading Babar," she yelled back.

"Here is Babar digging in the sand."

"Ruth, are you coming to bed?" He was standing right there at the door.

"I'm almost finished," my mother said.

"Do you know what night this is?" he asked moving toward the bed.

"Yes, I am totally aware—"

"Good," he said as he pulled the Big Orange from her hands and tossed it to the floor—

"Dave!"

—and walked out of my room down the hall.

My mother just stared—sitting on the edge of my bed. She didn't say anything and her lip started to quiver the way it sometimes did when she was about to cry. And so I started to "read," "'Here is Babar digging in the sand.'"

"I'm sorry," she said.

"Babar is riding happily on his mother's back when—"

"I'm sorry."

I'd seen him throw things before. Books, clothes. He once threw a glass that smashed against the wall and all over the floor. He once stormed out of the house, breaking a door. I once saw him—

"Turn over," she said.

"What for?"

"Turn over."

I sat up.

"On your stomach."

I lay on my stomach. And when I did, she pulled my pajama top over my head.

"Mommy—?"

"Shh."

"Mommy—?"

"Put your head down!" I put my head down. She ran her fingers on my back, like pins, fine pins. "The little men are running," she said. I lay there as her fingers ran up and down my spine.

"The little men are running."

"Mommy?"

First slowly, very slowly, "The little men are running," then a little faster. Her fingers up to my shoulders, then down my back so I almost cried out in the tingle of pleasure and pain, then over to one side, "The little men are running. They are running and running over here, over there, up and down all around," her fingers, like pins, like fires. Like, like, like—

"Cellular function can only be understood in terms of the constant dialogue that occurs between the genome and its environment—"

"Ruth—?"

"The environment regulates the cellular signals that control the operation of the genome. . . . Epigenetic mechanisms are an ideal candidate mechanism for the effects of environmental signals including such events as social interactions, on the structure and function of the genome. Cellular signals, referred to as transcription factors, regulate the activity of a gene."

"The little men are running," she said. "The little men. The little men, the little men are running and running and running—until they are far, far, far—"

"The biological primacy of gene-environment interactions is apparent from the simple realization that the levels and the activation of these transcription factors is controlled by environmental signals. The operation of the genome is dependent upon context."

"The little men are running far, far from home."

"Ruth?"

"Mommy?"

And then she leaned down and kissed the back of my neck. And that's when I realized what they were—

"Tactile stimulation by the dam's licking and grooming of her pup increases serotonin activity. Maternal behavior activates the cellular signal in the pup."

"Ruth—?" he yelled from down the hall. "Ruth, I'm waiting."

—that's when I realized the drops on the back of my neck were tears.

"Such effects underlie the dynamic interdependence of gene and environment."[2]

"The little men are running. The little men, the little men. Good night, my little man."

"Why did he do that?"

"Running and running and running."

"Ruth—?" he called again from the hall.

She picked the book up off the floor, put it back in the shelf, turned out the light, "Sleep, my little angel, you sleep."

Then she walked out of my room. I could tell she was just about at their door when I heard him say, "Do you know what night it is?" And then I heard the door close.

I lay on my bed, staring in the dark thinking about the little men running as the lights of a car crossed over the wall. It was night. They were running—

Running, and running, and running.

"Where are you going?" I asked the lights of the cars crossing the wall.

It was quiet. "Where are you going?" I listened but there were no answers, no sounds.

"Mommy?" I called.

I didn't know where they were going.

Chapter 8
Troubled Sleep

SOMETIMES I'D STARE AT THE BIG ORANGE ON THE SHELF, WAITING FOR the car lights to come back to my walls as I watched the baby elephant riding through the jungle on his mother's back. I think that's when I loved Babar most. Before he grew up. When he was little riding on his mother's back.

Babar's mother rocked him to sleep with her trunk while she sang. Her toes were too big to play "little men." There, see over there, I could see over there where Babar lay in the hammock as his mother rocked him. I could see in the dark. In the dark. In the dark. The elephants, the monkeys. There was no father. I never asked where he was or why he wasn't there. Just Babar and his mother—and bananas and monkeys and shells to dig in the sand. I never asked how shells got to the jungle—maybe birds brought them. "See him digging in the sand." I could see the butterflies. I could see the monkeys playing in the high grass. I could see the elephants bathing.

I could see Babar riding on his mother's back. I could see the hunter hiding in the bushes. I could see Babar's mother. I could see the barrel of the hunter's gun. I could see—

"Mommy!?"

That's when the night terrors began.

My bedroom was at one end of the hall. My parents' was at the other. My two sisters' were in between. They were both lots older than

47

me, both gone. Jolie was fifteen years older than me. She was in Boston with Sid. I loved Sid. My sister Susan was at Cornell—somewhere cold. She hated the cold. I don't know why she chose to go there.

I had trouble sleeping ever since Jolie left. Maybe it's because Jolie was old enough to be my mother.

I woke up a lot. I had trouble with sounds, far off sounds kept calling.

In 1953 Eugene Aserinsky and Nathaniel Kleitman, physiologists at the University of Chicago, discovered rapid eye movement, or REM sleep. They hypothesized that this phenomenon might be associated with dreams.

"To confirm the conjecture that this particular eye activity was associated with dreaming, 10 sleeping individuals in 14 experiments were awakened and interrogated during the occurrence of this eye motility."[1] The researchers found that the recall of dreams was indeed associated with REM sleep as opposed to non-rapid eye movement (NREM) sleep from which dream recall was much less likely. This led to the identification of three distinct patterns of brain activity: wakefulness, REM sleep, and NREM sleep.

Cars crossed on the walls and sped overhead. They were welcome intruders. I had trouble with sounds. Words. Voices. Calls from under the bed. Things that made noise. I welcomed the lights that crossed overhead.

Sometimes I'd hear my mother's voice late at night.

Parasomnias are disorders of "partial awakenings" where one part of the brain is functionally awake while another part is functionally asleep. These disorders of sleep arousal, or *parasomnias*, are confined mostly to non-rapid eye movement, non-REM, sleep.

"Please understand I, I—"

"Ruth—"

"Please—"

I got up from bed. I'd walk down the hall dragging my blue blankie—

"But don't you see, I just can't—"

—drawn to the sound, as if I had been called, my head cocked like a dog's, past my sisters' bedroom to my parents' bedroom door—

"Ruth—"

—where I'd curl on the floor with my blue blankie as the sounds kept going round.

"Ruth—"

"Please."

I had trouble with sounds.

"State dissociation describes the capacity of the brain to be both asleep and awake at the same time, to straddle NREM sleep and wakefulness with deactivation of higher cortical areas and the simultaneous activation of motor pathways. These mechanisms permit the expression of complex behaviors without conscious control, and are manifest in the form of night terrors, sleep talking, and sleep walking."[2]

"Dave, I can't. Please understand—"

"You can—"

"Don't do this to me—"

Curled in my blue blankie. It was warm and wet—wet from my mouth.

"Dave—"

"Ruthie, you can. You must. We both need—"

"Please—I, I—"

"Ruthie—"

"Please—"

I listened at the door like a duck to a hunter's call.

But somehow each morning I'd find myself back in my bed, not sure where I had gone or how I'd returned, what I had seen or what I had heard. It wasn't exactly clear whether I had been lost or been found.

"Disruptions of the NonREM sleep characterized by recurrent arousals, are thought to serve as the initiating source of these disorders."[3]

I was also known to talk in my sleep, walk in my sleep, scream in my sleep.

"Ruthie!" he said.

Once they found me in the kitchen yelling at the light bulb in the back of the refrigerator: "Wake up! Wake up! Wake up!" Soon the whole house was awake. Or at least that's what my father said, laughing as he drank his coffee, reading the paper before leaving for work. "You were standing right there," he said pointing at the refrigerator, "naked as the day you were born."

"Dave, you've told him three times," my mother said. I didn't remember. I couldn't believe I was really—

"—yelling at the light bulb to 'wake up'!"

I really couldn't believe that I was—

"Naked," he said, as he put down the paper. "You woke up the neighborhood," he said as he took a last gulp of coffee, laughing so hard it spilled on his shirt.

I remembered none of it. Not a word. Not a bit.

"Ruth, I've got to go." Still laughing, "'Wake up!'" He moved toward the door. "I'll see you tonight."

"What time—?"

"Pray for heat," he said as he kissed my mother goodbye. "And thank you," he said, patting her where she sat. "Was it really so bad?" he asked as he adjusted his hat, kissed her again. "Six-thirty, maybe seven." My father was going to the factory where they made fans. There was a white bear on the wall standing on a block of ice and underneath it said, "Frigid Fans." It was the factory that he ran with Uncle Cookie who wasn't really my uncle.

"Naked," he said, shaking his head as he turned back to my mother. "You'll feel better. You'll see. It's medicinal," he said but I didn't know what that meant. "Just what the doctor ordered," he said, patting her again. "Pray for heat," then he headed for the door, laughing, straightening his tie, readjusting his hat, trying to wrestle the stain from his shirt.

I sat at the kitchen table finishing my Rice Krispies. I could hear the engine of the Cadillac start. My mother cleared the plates from the table.

"Mommy?"

"Go and get dressed," she said.

I nodded. I would. Then I said, "I want a dog."

And then there was a knock on the door.

Chapter 9

A Knock on the Door

FIRST ONE, THEN ANOTHER. LIKE SOMEONE TRYING TO BREAK IN—OR break out. One, two, then—

A light turned on from upstairs—

—three, four, five.

—and then the light in the downstairs hall.

Finally I heard my father's voice through the door, "Who is it? And what the hell do you want at this hour of the night?"

"Dave, it's me. Open the goddamn door. It's Katie, Katie Galst."

My father opened the door. He was wearing pajamas. His feet were bare. Katie was wearing a bathrobe, slippers, and socks. "Katie, what are you doing at this hour of the—?" And then he saw me, standing behind Katie. "Richard—? Why aren't you in bed?"

"Dave," Katie said stomping her foot. "Do you have any idea? How dare you leave a little boy all alone?!"

"What are you talking about?"

"And middle of the night! Dave, it's not *what*, it's *who* I am talking about. You and Ruthie, that's who, that's what—leaving a little boy!" I was standing there holding Katie's hand, barely awake. "You should be ashamed," Katie yelled and then took out a pack of Camel unfiltered cigarettes from the pocket of her robe. She always carried a pack in her—

"I need a light."

"I don't know what you are talking about," my father said.

Katie found matches in the other pocket. "There I was watching *Lucy*—the time when she and Ricky trade places. She goes to the factory and he stays home cleaning the house when —"

After two tries she lit her cigarette, blowing smoke over my head.

"—so I'm in my chair, and there's this knock, this knock, knock, knocking—and I'm thinking 'must be the wind,' I don't know—But then I realize—and so I go—look out and there he is—no slippers, alone and scared, repeating over and over, 'They left me!' 'Who left you?' I ask, bringing him inside. 'They left me,' he keeps saying."

"Richard was on the street—?" my father turned to me. "Why did you go to Katie's house? Why would you do that when your mother and I were both in our room, just down the hall."

I didn't remember. I didn't remember getting up from bed. I didn't remember walking down the stairs. I didn't remember going out the door. I didn't remember walking to Katie Galst's house. I didn't remember banging on her door. I didn't remember Katie opening the door. I didn't remember saying, "They left me." I didn't remember Katie asking me, "Who left you?" I didn't remember repeating, "They left me" over and over and over. I didn't remember.

"He told me you left him," Katie said.

"Richard, your mother and I would never leave you. Why would you say such a thing?"

I didn't know what to say because I couldn't remember. "I don't know," I said.

"Richard?"

"I don't know—"

"Why did you go to Katie's?"

"I don't know." I was tired and almost in tears.

And then he realized what it was. "You were walking! Like that time in the kitchen. You were walking."

"I don't know."

"Sleepwalking," he said.

My father and Katie exchanged looks of "Oh, so that's what it was" as they both realized that's what it was. Katie took a drag on her cigarette.

"Did Ruthie tell you about the time when he—?"

"No, Dave. You did," enjoying the full gravel of her voice. She had the voice of a man who drank. Her doctor told her she had the voice of a woman who smoked.

Sleepwalking.

After saying thank you and good night to Katie Galst, my father picked me up and carried me up the stairs. I was half asleep. Nothing made sense. "So where did you go?" I asked my father.

"We didn't go anywhere. We were here all along."

"But how did I get to Katie's house?" I asked as we got to the top of the stairs.

"You walked to her house in your sleep."

"In my sleep?" I thought about that. "How did I do that?" I asked.

"I don't know," he said. "Just don't do it again."

My father kissed my head as he tucked me in. "Get some sleep. And this time, stay in your bed." He walked out of my room, and down the hall, I heard him say to my mother, "You'll never guess what our boy did." Then I heard the door close.

I lay in bed in the dark, waiting for car lights to pass on the wall. I turned to my bookshelf. I stared at the Big Orange.

I found my blue blankie on the floor by my bed. I picked it up, held it to my face.

"Perhaps some soft object or type of object has been found and used and then this becomes what I am calling a transitional object."[1]

I lay there in the dark holding my blue blankie, staring at the Big Orange, and then all of a sudden, I heard, "In the great forest a little elephant is born." I sat up and stared at the Big Orange. The window was open. The pages of the book seemed to be turning on their own. "His name is Babar." Another page turned. "His mother loves him very much." I could see Babar. I could see his mother. I could see the great forest. I held my blue blankie.

"She rocks him to sleep with her trunk while singing softly to him." I could feel her trunk on my face. It was wet. It was strong. It was soft. I could smell the earth. I could hear her voice: "His name is Babar. His mother loves him very much."

The lights of a car crossed the walls of my room.

She loves her Babar very much. She would never leave him.

"Patterns set in infancy may persist into childhood so that the original soft object continues to be absolutely necessary at bed-time or at time of loneliness or when a depressed mood threatens."[2]

I turned onto my stomach.

She would never leave him. She would never leave her Babar.

I lay there and waited. For something. I didn't know what. I waited and waited and waited. And then from far off I heard, "The little men are running. The little men are running. The little men are running and running and running." I lifted my head. The room was dark. It was quiet. Another car's lights crossed on the wall. I lay my head down on the pillow. I started to drift. And then I heard the whispers again, "The little men are running and running and running."

I didn't know why I walked in my sleep. I didn't know why I had walked down the hall, down the stairs, across to our neighbor, Katie Galst. Why I banged on her door while repeating, "They left me." All that I knew was that alone with my blue blankie, I felt safe. "The little men are running." I heard her voice. It was as if she were there, all around. The sound of her. The touch of her. The sight of her. The smell of her. "The little men are running," I whispered as the lights of a car passed overhead. "Running, and running, and running."

"The child's attachment to the mother appears before birth, when the baby learns about the mother's voice and odors. . . . The maternal odor produces orienting responses and mouthing and soothes a crying infant."

I put a corner of my blue blankie in my mouth—

"The little men are running."

—and sucked hard.

It was dark.

I felt safe.

Running, and running, and running.

As I fell asleep, it was her voice I was hearing, not mine.

"His mother loves him very much. Your Mommy loves you very, very—"

Another set of lights crossed on the wall.

"I love you very, very much."

"It is quite possible that this neonatal learning (about the caregiver) is the first postnatal expression of learning within the attachment system and perhaps one of the first ways in which our sense of safety is constructed."[3]

And then as I was drifting to sleep, I started to sing, singing a song I didn't remember ever hearing, didn't remember ever learning. Singing a song I didn't know that I knew.

Too-ra-loo-ra-loo-ral

Too-ra-loo-ra-li

"An older child goes over a repertory of songs and tunes while preparing for sleep."

Hush now, don't you cry.

Too-ra-loo-ra-loo-ral

Too-ra-loo-ra-loo-ral

Too-ra-loo-ra-li

"The need for a specific object or a behavior pattern that started at a very early date may reappear at a later age when deprivation threatens."[4]

I felt safe in the dark.

"This attachment system evolved to ensure altricial animals (animals born helpless) form a repertoire of proximity-seeking behaviors to the caregiver—

I felt safe.

—regardless of the quality of care-giving received."[5]

Too-ra-loo-ra-loo-ral

That's an Irish lullaby.

We weren't Irish. I had two zaydes and two bobes who spoke Yiddish. We were Jewish. But I loved the song that was Irish.

Chapter 10
His Mother's Voice

MY PARENTS HAD A RECORD PLAYER THAT PLAYED RECORDS IN A DARK wooden box. It was called Victor. They listened to Ella Fitzgerald, Lionel Hampton, Benny Goodman, Beethoven, and Bach. And on every record, there was a dog with its head cocked to the side. Under the dog it read, "His Master's Voice," and then it said Victor—RCA Victor. It was a long time before I understood that the dog was listening to the voice as if his master were calling from inside the dark box. It took me a while before I realized the dog was recognizing the voice. And that's what I wanted. A dog that would recognize my voice.

"The first strong evidence for fetal learning came from studies on early voice recognition . . . in which it was found that babies recognize and prefer their own mother's voice—"

Obviously I do not have conscious memories of the time I spent in my mother's womb, but during that time I learned quite a lot—about her fears, her joys, her smell, her taste, her voice. I learned quite a lot.

"Newborns prefer human voices, female voices to male, their own mother to another mother reading the same Dr. Seuss story."[1]

When I was learning these things—my mother's fear, joy, smell, taste, voice—I was getting pretty close to where story starts. Story starts in the womb,

I know some new tricks
Said the Cat in the Hat
A lot of good tricks
I will show them to you.

I don't think my mother read to me from *The Cat in the Hat*—at least not while I was a fetus. The book wasn't published until 1957, and she would have been dead too soon after that. No, I don't think my mother read to me from *The Cat in the Hat*. I did not learn about her from that. But I did learn quite a lot about her while still in her womb.

There is compelling evidence that the fetus begins to learn about his mother from the first beats of the fetal heart. That is to say, I was becoming aware of my mother more or less when she was becoming aware of me. First bonds are like that. They are sensual and fierce—in almost every sense. For a human those senses of earliest attachment are sound, smell, taste and for the neonate, sight. For a rat, the mammal on which the most research on intrauterine attachment has been done, smell and taste are the senses that guide the pup to the dam, to her ventrum, to her teats. The infant or pup that fails to find that path fails.

"I once said: There is no such thing as an infant, meaning of course, that whenever one finds an infant one finds maternal care, and without maternal care there would be no infant."[2]

I found my way to my mother's ventrum. I found my way to her breasts and her teats. And when I got there, there was evidence that she wasn't ready. There was evidence that she wasn't ready to keep her side of the bond.

Rat pups, before they reach postnatal day ten—that is to say when they are very young and still totally dependent on the dam—can be abused, with for example a tail shock, and if the tail shock is paired with a smell, they will become attached to that smell even if it is a predictor of pain. Because the pup—and by extension the infant—is totally dependent on the dam for survival, the pup learns to approach whatever its senses find in the nest; that is to say, will approach whatever is associated with the dam—for good or bad, for better or worse.

"This special early learning process, which strongly favors preference learning and inhibits avoidance learning, may well be the basis by which infant mammals from puppies to humans, form strong attachments to even abusive caregivers."[3]

My mother wasn't abusive. She just wasn't ready for what lay ahead when she was forced by my conception and then by my birth to be a mother once again. In two words, she was bipolar depressed.

Because of her emotional state, the depressed mother fails to respond to her infant's other-directed distress signals, and thus fails to provide the infant with appropriate regulatory help. "Emotional unavailability is more distressing to the infant than simply being left alone to rely on his/her own resources."[4]

I have pictures of my mother from before I was born. There is one picture in particular. My mother is standing on a tennis court, wearing a short skirt revealing strong, shapely legs. She holds a racket in one hand, about to bite into an apple that she holds in the other. She stares straight into the camera with a wry smile that is as tempting as the apple, as seductive as Eve. It is the image of an athlete who, with the slightest tilt of her head, makes you forget you've just lost the first set.

My mother had a younger sister, my Aunt Fran, and a younger brother, my Uncle Al. They were both ordinary in every sense of the word. My mother was rare. Fran and Al fawned over her as if she were a flower that had to be watered, to be watched. Watered lest she wither. Watched lest she run off with a good-looking man whom she had just met at a dance.

My mother wasn't a slut. That's not an easy thing to say about one's mother. But in 1950's Brooklyn, a woman who showed too much calf, knee, or thigh risked being called a slut. My mother wasn't a slut. She was bipolar. And when she wasn't depressed, she was lively—lively like the life of the party, lively like a fish on a line. Bipolar lively cuts both ways.

And as the picture shows, my mother was an athlete. She could run. She could jump. She could swim. She could dance. She was comfortable in her body. And a young woman back then in the "shtetls" of Brooklyn—long before Brooklyn was "hip"—a woman wasn't comfortable *in* her body unless she was comfortable *with* her body—playing tennis or not. And when she wasn't depressed, that is to say when she was those few precious steps ahead of despair, she was comfortable with dance, song, tennis, sex. When she wasn't depressed, she was comfortable with joy. When she wasn't depressed, she was hot.

"Come on, Dave, it's early. Let's go," she said to my father after an elegant dinner at Luchow's, the one that once was on 14th and Third, where Christmas was celebrated every month of the year. "Let the sitter sit. I want to swing. I want to sweat. I want to feel my body wet."

"Ruthie, people are watching."

She stared at my father—

"Dave, I am waiting."

—extending first an arm, then a long, shapely leg, "It's either you," she looked straight ahead, "or the man standing behind," still staring at my father, both threatening and flirting with one flick of her head. There was no one behind her. There was only my father, staring straight ahead—amazed at his wife, at his luck, at this woman whom he adored.

"Kiss me," she said.

My father looked to see who might be watching.

Uncle Cookie turned to his wife, Jeanie, then looked at my father, took the cigar out of his mouth. "Even money—" He said taking two Hamilton's out of his wallet. He put the money on the table. "My money's on Ruthie."

My father watched his wife—one hand reaching for him, the other on her hip. The hour was nine. The month was May. The day was the tenth. "Dave—?" she said. My father stared at this woman, this beauty, his wife.

She moved her dress just a little up higher on her thigh, then said with both a threat and a sigh, "Don't make me, or the Hamiltons, wait."

Chapter 11

The Savoy Ballroom

THE SAVOY BALLROOM WAS ON LENOX AVENUE BETWEEN 140TH AND 141st Streets in Harlem. The clientele was mostly black. The northeast corner of the Ballroom, called "Cat's Corner," was reserved for dancers who knew how to Lindy, for those who knew how to hop, for those who were hot. And on the night of May 10, 1952, story has it, my mother walked into Cat's Corner to be thrown, spun, slid across the floor by a man dressed all in black. My father was nervous and proud. My mother was sexy and hot.

When the bandleader paused, she walked off the floor, to general applause. This was, after all, a place that was three-quarters black, and no white woman, or very few, could dance the Lindy like that, not back then, not in May of '52. When she got to my father, she looked at him straight, "Kiss me," she said. This time, he did not hesitate.

"Dave," Uncle Cookie said, "you owe me twenty dollars." My father took out a Franklin from his wallet, handed it to Uncle Cookie. "Keep the change," then kissed his glorious wife, my mother, again as she kissed him back, her lips hard against his. She was comfortable with her body. She was comfortable with dance. She was comfortable with sex. She was comfortable with joy. She was lively like that, bipolar lively. She was lively and hot.

Meanwhile back at 169 Falmouth Street a block from the ocean, two from the bay, I was asleep beside Katie Galst who was asleep in front of the TV. It was 11:00 at night, May 10, 1952.

At 11:00 on the morning of October 29, 2012—Hurricane Sandy was still gathering strength in the mid-Atlantic before making a turn toward New Jersey. At 8 p.m. that night, Sandy came ashore around Atlantic City as a Category 3 hurricane with sustained winds of 115 mph. The winds, high tide, and full moon generated a storm surge powerful enough to send flood waters as far inland as Metuchen, inundating the warehouse of Oz Moving and Storage.

I got a call later that week, informing me that my sister Susan's belongings—that had been in storage since her death in September of 2001—had been damaged or destroyed. I was asked to triage. I was there the next day.

Going through the remains, soaked with seawater and sewage, I found letters. I found notes. I found a necklace of pearls. I found a sheet of paper with handwritten words.

And I found pictures of my mother that I had never seen.

In one she stood in profile. Her gaze cast down. Her hair cut short. She was wearing a necklace of pearls.

The one I held in my hand.

She was wearing a pale "flapper" dress. I turned the picture over and on the back was a stamp, "The Savoy Ballroom." Underneath was a date, "May 10th, 1952."

Aunt Fran was not much of a dancer. To say she was a wallflower implied that she showed up. She was younger, shorter, not much of a looker. When she was born, her grandfather turned to her father (my grandfather) and said, "*Ikh bin zikher zi vet zeyn klug*" ("I'm sure she'll be very smart").

Aunt Fran adored my mother. She envied my mother. It's what the ordinary do. What Aunt Fran did. She adored and envied the ones who could dance, who could love, and who were loved in return—and when she learned that her older, more beautiful, adored sister was dead—when she learned that her wish had come true—she buried the thought as deep as she could. It's what the ordinary do.

Aunt Fran kept things buried except when she'd pull them out and show them to me. I was just a kid and didn't know what they meant and it was always confusing whether Aunt Fran was telling me things to keep me informed or telling me things because she couldn't keep them down any more.

There is another picture of my mother. This one from before I was born. She is on a boat. You can see the rigging. Her lips are parted. Her hair is pulled back. You can sense the wind in her face. She is staring at someone just outside the frame. There is both longing and pain. Hunger and hope. Sadness and lust. It could have been she was staring at my father. It could have been the first mate.

Is that a bad thought for a son to have of his mother? Is this where preoedipal pathology starts? Is this the tip of the "borderline" iceberg that will rip at my heart?

Maybe it was my father who took the picture. Maybe he was the one whom she always wanted. He was, after all, the one she took.

"Lundy's? Shall I take you to Lundy's?" Aunt Fran asked, knowing how I felt about Lundy's.

When it opened, Lundy's was the biggest restaurant in New York City. It was right next to Sheepshead Bay. "Let's go to Lundy's," she said making sucking sounds from the back of her mouth.

Aunt Fran was the one who put gossip in my head. After her sister, my mother, was dead. When she was no longer around. When Fran's envy had been quenched by her sister's "sudden" death. People always asked "Was it sudden?" when what they were really asking was, "Was it suicide?"

"It was sudden," Aunt Fran said.

I loved my Aunt Fran—even though she was so much less than her sister, my mother, Ruth. Even though she was the one who put rumors in my head sipping coffee at Lundy's once or twice every month.

"I had to buy Similac," Aunt Fran said. "Similac—can you imagine?"

According to Aunt Fran my mother failed the test where "the mother helps her infant find her ventrum and teats."

"She didn't have milk," Aunt Fran said stirring cream into her coffee, emphasizing the contrast, the point. "How is your chocolate egg cream?" she asked. I loved chocolate egg creams.

"I had to buy Similac—'as good as the breast'—that's what they said, but between you and me, it is not," she said with a laugh, sipping coffee as I slurped my chocolate egg cream. "It looks very good," she said and then more to herself, "I don't think she was ready. I don't think she wanted. But your father, ah your father," she said, taking another swirl of coffee. "It was your father who wanted. 'Six inches,' he'd say. 'Six inches'—he thought it was so funny. Darling, how is your chocolate egg cream?"

It was at Lundy's where Fran told me that my mother had had a lover. It's hard for me to totally understand why she felt it necessary to "confess" her dead sister's sins, unclear just what a "confession" or a "lover" really was. "He was a journalist," she said.

Slightly before the photo of "Eve on the tennis court"—the one where she's holding an apple, slightly before any "respectable" woman would show so much thigh—"there was a journalist," a man who had died somewhere in France during or soon after the Second World War—the man, according to Aunt Fran, whom my mother had loved more than any other, "more than your father, more than Dave," she said under her breath, an aside as I thought about asking for another chocolate egg cream.

Maybe she was staring at that man when the picture was taken. Maybe he had been on the boat, sailing to France, a journalist who would die during or just after the Second World War. Maybe that's why she looked both happy and sad, showing both hunger and pain. Maybe it wasn't two sides of bipolar. Maybe it was two sides of love.

According to Aunt Fran that man, whose name was Jacob, she

said, loved my mother and met her passion with the fury and abandon of a man about to ship off to war. My father, whom she had married years before, was steady and predictable, a "breadwinner." She ate from your father's table, drank from her lover's glass—according to my Aunt Fran. It was a lot for a kid to handle even though I didn't really understand. "During the war, while your father patrolled the quiet streets of Brighton Beach, Jacob patrolled the battlefields of France."

"I'll take you to Lundy's—just the two of us—you and me." I knew there was something a little weird about it all—but I really loved chocolate egg creams. She took me to Lundy's, and told me things as though she were talking to herself. Both before and after my mother was gone. The "before" as if to inform me, to lessen her envy, to answer questions I never asked. The "after" to undo whatever damage she imagined she had done with what she had told me "before."

But then any story about Mother from Aunt Fran was suspect. Any story coming from someone who envies is suspect. I trusted Aunt Fran to be generous, attentive, loving—and dishonest with both herself and with me. I trusted Aunt Fran's story about a lover who died somewhere in France a few years before or after I was conceived. I also trusted that the man who had been her lover had not been my father. I never doubted the source of my genes.

Chapter 12

Paternity

THE HAIR ON THE HEAD OF THE MAN WHOM I ALWAYS KNEW TO BE MY father went from brown to silver and from thick to thin the instant he turned forty. He never went bald. My thick brown hair turned silver and fine the instant I turned thirty-nine. It's still mostly there—silver and fine.

My father had eyebrows that were as wild as a saint's. Once when I was walking down Seventh Avenue toward Pennsylvania Station in New York, two delightfully plump teenage girls walking toward me, burst out, "Oh my God, it's Captain Eyebrows!"

No, I never doubted my paternity. I never thought I was conceived by a man who died somewhere in France despite the stories that Aunt Fran kept tossing like seed to see where they might land. I never doubted. She never stopped tossing.

"Waiter," she called out.

"What is it, ah, sugar?" he said with a smile.

"The coffee is cold."

But one story Fran told me, sitting by a window at Lundy's. Aunt Fran was smoking her unfiltered Chesterfield. I was sipping a chocolate egg cream. I was eight years old. My feet were close but still not quite touching the ground. I had a two-wheeled bike. I had a dog. My mother was dead. The waiter seemed deaf.

"Waiter!"

The waiter walked right past focused on something that must have been left—a scarf, an earring, hope. As he walked his hands kept moving as if instructing marionettes.

"Waiter—?" Aunt Fran called as he walked by.

"Italians," she said as she lit another cigarette. She blew out smoke then stared past the arches over our table into the main empty hall where the waiter disappeared in the rows of tables set with red and white checkered cloth that seemed to extend into Queens.

Aunt Fran shook her head, then as if addressing an audience that had left long ago, "Your mother wasn't ready to be a mother." I watched as she picked a leaf of tobacco from her teeth.

"When you were born—"

"When was that?" I asked slurping my chocolate egg cream.

Aunt Fran told me there was a lot of trouble when I was born as I watched the first boats come back from the sea with fish and old men. I loved chocolate egg cream. Aunt Fran loved cigarettes. "Your mother," she began once again, "wasn't ready to be a mother. It was different with your sisters—" She took another drag on her Chesterfield unfiltered. I waited. After an exhale that took a long time, she added, "How is your chocolate egg cream?"

Aunt Fran married Manny—Uncle Manny—who spent every day in front of the TV. He wasn't really watching. The TV was just there as he lay like a beached walrus on a couch in a room that smelled faintly of sewage.

On the wall there was a painting of an orange stripe on a background of brown. Aunt Fran said it was a masterpiece.

Everyone thought Aunt Fran was crazy when she hung the orange stripe on a background of brown. "Who would buy such crap?" my father rhetorically asked. "Your Aunt Fran—that's who." Once on a path, he couldn't stop. "That's not a painting. It's an orange stripe on a brown piece of crap."

Much later I learned "the orange stripe" was by Barnett Newman. Aunt Fran had also bought early drawings by Chagall and earthenware by Picasso. She had bought them before she had met Uncle Manny, long before anyone in Brooklyn knew the names Newman or Chagall. Everyone knew Picasso's name.

Aunt Fran and Uncle Manny never had kids. Judging from Uncle Manny, it would be a good bet that they had never tried—though I don't think that was the whole story. But still they never had kids.

They lived around the corner from my mother and father on Ocean Avenue. So when—after two sisters, Jolie and Susan, and five miscarriages, Fran's sister Ruth gave birth to a son, it was another moment for Aunt Fran to feel cheated by fate. Another reason for Aunt Fran to drag on her Chesterfield and to blow smoke over my head as I sucked on the straw for the dregs of my chocolate egg cream. "Can I have another?" Another reason for Aunt Fran to feel envy. "Of course you can," she said. "Really?" I said, totally caught off guard. Lundy's was quite the place.

Two years before I was born, Aunt Fran and Uncle Manny adopted Susan Margo. Two years later, they adopted Judy.

"Waiter," Aunt Fran called out. When she yelled, "Waiter," the sound echoed through Lundy's vast, empty hall. He smiled and approached the table, his hands just finishing a thought.

"What can I ah do for ah you, ah sugar? Such a pretty face. Just like a yours."

"This coffee is cold, and another chocolate egg cream for my nephew."

The waiter smiled, "So what is ah your ah name?" the waiter asked, squeezing my head like a fruit.

"My coffee is cold," Aunt Fran said.

"Ah scuza, sugar, scuza," he said grabbing the pot.

Susan Margo and Judy had been adopted from somewhere in the Midwest—and cousin Alan, who was adopted by my Uncle Arthur and his hugely overweight wife, Pearl, from somewhere in Jersey. The four of us played "doctor" quite a lot in the playhouse behind Aunt Fran's house.

"So pretty I thought must be ah girl."

"Thank you," Aunt Fran said. "My nephew is not a girl."

Uncle Manny, when not on the couch in front of the TV, lavished gifts on Susan Margo. Everyone loved Susan Margo, maybe because she was "outspoken" and "foreign" ("I'm from Nova Scotia," she would say for no reason except that she knew that Nova Scotia was far from Brooklyn). The rest of us were dark and Sephardic, having been driven to this place courtesy of the Anschluss and the Third Reich. But Susan Margo was different. She was blonde and ornamental. It was as if she had been offered to make up for the ordinariness of the rest. She was special like my mother was special even though Susan Margo was the only blonde anyone knew. She was that kind of special. Special for Uncle Manny, special for Aunt Fran, special for me. Special the way a sacrifice is special.

"Such ah pretty ah boy," the waiter said.

Susan Margo was the first girl who ever kissed me. She was the first girl ever who ever opened my pants. The first girl ever who touched between my legs. The first girl ever who put her finger in my ass.

"Curiosity about gender difference is visible in childhood sexual-explorative play."[1]

After Susan Margo did all that to me, I would do exactly as Susan Margo had done, to Judy. Then Judy would do it to Alan. Then Susan Margo and I would do it to Alan, because he was the youngest. That's how doctor was played in the playhouse that Uncle Manny had bought for Susan Margo in the yard behind Aunt Fran's house—a block from the sea, two blocks from the bay.

"Brooklyn has everything," Aunt Fran used to say, "Why would anyone leave?"

"Children, children—time for milk and cookies," Aunt Fran called from the porch by the kitchen door. Susan Margo told Alan to pull up his pants. "We're coming," she yelled.

In the playhouse, Susan Margo was the guide. She was only two years older, but already budding in ways I didn't understand. We all loved Susan Margo, only I loved her in a way that was hidden, forbidden. I didn't know if Brooklyn had everything, but it had Susan Margo which was more than enough for me.

"Did you have fun?" Aunt Fran asked.

Susan Margo spoke for us all. "Yes. We had fun."

One day Susan Margo didn't come to school. That day turned into two, then three. She had pains in her belly. Aunt Fran assumed it was the curse, and slapped her, then hugged her.

Being from the Midwest (not Nova Scotia despite what she had said), Susan Margo hit back.

The pains didn't stop. It wasn't the start of her "flow." Aunt Fran called Uncle Al's wife, Aunt Pearl, who didn't know what to do. "It's not 'the curse.'" Aunt Pearl suggested Aunt Fran call my father's brother, Uncle Lou, who was a doctor. He had an office in the basement of his house in the Midwood section of Brooklyn. He came to 4152 Ocean Avenue where he examined Susan Margo. He took his stethoscope from his black bag and listened to her heart, then her lungs. "It must be something she ate," he said after squeezing her belly, reassuring himself that it was soft. "Have her take one of these," he wrote out a prescription. "She'll be fine." Aunt Fran thanked Uncle Lou.

Susan Margo died of non-Hodgkin's lymphoma. My guide to the netherworld was no more. When my sister Jolie told me, I didn't fully understand because she was so young. "Was she cursed?" I asked.

"No," Jolie said. No one could explain.

So I asked, "When will she come back to school?"

She was buried at Green-Wood Cemetery. It was the first time I had ever been to a cemetery. You could see Manhattan and the upper New York Bay. You could see boats, ferries, and cranes. You could see the Statue of Liberty. You could see Ellis Island on the other side of the Bay.

There were trees. There were birds. There was a hole in the ground. A big hole with dirt all around and next to the hole, there was a long wooden box. That's where they said Susan Margo was. In that box.

There were no other kids at the cemetery—just Judy and me—and then I remembered Susan Margo. We were there. "When will she come out?" I asked. I remembered our games. "Children, children—time for milk and cookies."

There was a service. Aunt Fran was there, Uncle Manny, Uncle Al, and Aunt Pearl. Others I didn't know. My father said he couldn't go because he had work. People said things, but how much can be said about a girl who died before starting the seventh grade?

When Uncle Manny stood up to speak, he just cried.

I thought maybe I should say something—something about what we did in the playhouse. How she touched me, made me feel things I had never felt—and now that she was gone, how would I ever again do the things we had done? I didn't understand.

"Are you okay, sugar?" my sister Jolie asked. I thought of the waiter at Lundy's. Susan Margo had called me sugar—maybe it was because when she had gone to Lundy's with her mother, my Aunt Fran, the waiter must have called her "sugar," the way Jolie sometimes called me.

"Are you okay, sugar?" Jolie asked leaning down. My hands shook. My eyes welled with tears. "Sugar," she rubbed my shoulders, my face, my back, my neck. "Sugar, do you want to cry?"

Just a little over there, a little past the hole they had dug for Susan Margo, was a stone marker that read, "Loving wife, mother, sister, friend." I read it again, "Loving wife, mother—"

"What's she doing here?" I yelled. "This is for Susan Margo. It isn't fair. What is she doing here?"

"Sugar—" Jolie said.

I was upset. I guess Susan Margo, the way she had died, what we had done. I looked over at the stone marker, "What is she doing here? This is for Susan Margo."

"Ruth," Jolie said.

"I don't know anyone named Ruth!"

"That's Mother," Jolie said. "Your mother, my mother, our mother—"

I looked over the pile of dirt, past Susan Margo. To the headstone—

"Her name was Ruth," Jolie said.

"Loving wife, sister, mother, friend," the words read.

"What is she doing here?"

"Resting," Jolie said. "She's resting."

And that's when it hit me. That's where we were—where dead people rest, where dead people live. I had never been. After she died, they never brought me. I had never known. Where they took her. Here. This is where—Loving wife. Mother. Susan Margo was buried right next to Ruth.

"Oh Richard, oh sugar."

And that's when the trees and the boats started to shake.

That's when I started to cry.

"Oh, sugar," she said holding me tight. "Oh sugar—"

"Memory networks overlap and interlink profusely with one another by common nodes whereby a cortical neuron or neuronal assembly practically anywhere in the cortex, can be part of multiple networks."[2]

Lashley was right, and Lashley was wrong. Memory was stored in a distributed network as Lashley had reasoned, but it was not universally distributed over the entire neocortex.[3] Memory was stored in specific neuronal networks related to their perception. Memory and perception make use of some of the same neurons. The neurons that hear a sound, for example, are the same neurons that store the memory of that sound. Memory and perception overlap.

"The capacity to store information is present throughout the nervous system. Almost all regions of the brain store memory of one kind or another. Available evidence indicates that memories subsist in networks—interconnected and distributed neocortical networks."[4]

"Ah so ah sugar, can I get you anything else? Blueberry ah

pie—baked ah just for ah you," the waiter asked Aunt Fran as he hovered with the pot of coffee. "This coffee, sugar, is ah very hot just ah for ah—"

"Sugar." He called us all "sugar."

"—and for you one ah more chocolate egg ah cream."

"Is there really an egg?" I asked.

He poured Aunt Fran another cup. "Hey for you they put ah two."

On his chest there was a pin that said, "Vinny." On his face, there was a wine-dark blotch just under his eye. "And what more can I get ah for you ah sugar besides the ah coffee?" The waiters at Lundy's addressed all unaccompanied women as "sugar," "sweetheart"—even waiters like Vinny who had a wine-dark blotch under his eye. Maybe it's because he was Italian. All waiters at Lundy's were Italian—especially those from Mexico, Honduras, Guatemala.

"And for ah sugar?"

"More cream," Aunt Fran said.

"More ah cream," Vinny said as he went off like a man endlessly trying to remember a dream, "More cream—ah coming ah right up."

Uncle Manny used to drink coffee with cream—he'd pour in lots of cream—and stir it with strips of matzo. Then he'd eat the matzo, and coffee would drip on his chest, which was why, I figured, he was almost never dressed.

Sometimes I think Aunt Fran took me to Lundy's so she could get away from Uncle Manny.

"Thank you," Aunt Fran said to the waiter as he struck a match for her Chesterfield unfiltered cigarette. She put her hand on his to keep the flame close enough to the tip of her cigarette. Vinny's hands shook.

"Molto bene," Vinny said walking down the long empty hall of Lundy's at a quarter past four with his red cloth draped over his arm like a matador in search of a bull.

"This time don't slurp," Aunt Fran said as I unwrapped the straw. She took another drag, "So when you were born—"

Chapter 13

So When You Were Born

"So when you were born," Aunt Fran said making that sucking sound from the back of her mouth. I moved my lips to the straw. "Your mother complained because you cried. She said you were 'a difficult child.' Cried all the time. She never got sleep. You were always wanting to be held. 'You clung to her breasts,' that's what she said."

I sucked on the straw.

"In rhesus monkeys there is a basic clinging reflex which leads the neonate to attach to the ventral surface of the mother and orally to the mother's breast."

"You know, your mother had beautiful breasts," taking another drag on her cigarette, "Who can blame you?" she said with a laugh.

"Stimulation of the baby's face causes the infant to rotate its head until the nipple is touched. The nipple is then orally engulfed—"

"Always crying—except when you were fed." Aunt Fran took a tube of lipstick out of her purse and circled it thick round her mouth, applying a stroke between each word, "Or when you were held." She looked at herself. "There," she said returning the lipstick and mirror to her purse.

"If you weren't in her arms, you'd crawl. Once you fell—right off her chest. You don't remember. You were too young. You hit your

76

head. I remember." She sat back and smiled. "You loved to climb. You loved to crawl. You hit your head."

"Another reflex that may be related to the act of nursing is that of upward climbing."

I loved to climb. Over fences. Over walls. Over the gate to the carpenter's shop where they repaired the carousel horses from Steeplechase Park. There was nothing that I couldn't climb.

"If a neonatal monkey is placed on a wire ramp, it will climb up and over the end and fall to the floor unless it is restrained."[1]

"Richard, be careful—"

My mother used to iron our clothes in the basement while I'd play on the floor.

One day I heard a loud voice coming from the TV.

"Hear all that clapping—?" the voice said.

I climbed up onto the back of the couch.

"—they're clapping for you."

There was a man talking to a lady standing beside him. Another voice came on and said, "And this is the star of our show, Jack Bailey." Jack Bailey held a microphone in his hand that he moved from his mouth to the lady who was standing beside him.

My mother was hanging laundry to dry. There was a line between the water pipes.

"So tell me your name," Jack Bailey said. The lady turned to the tag pinned to her chest a little like the one Vinny wore.

"You need to look at the tag to remember your name?" Jack Bailey said.

"Well no, you see, it's just—" the lady said.

"Surely you knew your name before you came to the show."

"Well yes, of course," she smiled, then moved her feet back and forth, her eyes all the while on Jack Bailey as if to keep from falling. "I'm Mrs. Claudia Hall," she said.

"And what was it before it was *Mrs.* Hall?"

"Schneider."

"And where are you from, Miss Schneider?"

"Van Nuys."

"A local girl."

"Well yes—we live not too far, pretty close by—"

"So tell us what it is you want and tell us why."

"Well yes, I've got seven children—"

"Seven?"

"Un hunh."

"And how old is the oldest?"

"Eleven."

"Any twins?" She shook her head.

"Triplets?"

"No."

"Quadruplets?"

She shook her head.

"So they all came one at a time."

"Well, yes," the lady said, forcing a smile as Jack Bailey moved the microphone closer to her chest.

"And you were there for each and every one," he said as if suggesting—

She had a large chest.

"Well yes—I mean, what do you mean?"

Jack Bailey smiled, paused. Then he just said,

"And so tell us just what is it that you want."

"Mmm, well yes—I need to go into the hospital for, you know, an operation."

"An operation?" things suddenly got calmer between Jack Bailey and Miss Schneider. He moved the microphone a little back.

"Well yes." She started a lot of her sentences with "well yes."

"Well yes, they say it will take fourteen days. So what I need is a replacement for me—for well, yes, two weeks."

"Sounds kind of serious," Jack Bailey said.

"Well yes. And since my husband is in the service—"

"The Army?"

"The Navy."

"So he won't be able to care for six children—"

"Seven."

"Seven kids can send a lesser woman to an early grave. We'll need to find you a really tough one."

"Well yes—but the kids aren't that bad."

"Well no," Jack Bailey said, "I'm sure they're very well behaved. And wouldn't it be wonderful to have your seven kids taken care of while you're in the hospital getting better?"

"Well yes—"

"And that is just what you will have if our audience elects you Queen Claudia—"

I climbed up onto the couch riding its back like a horse.

"—Queen for a Day."

Aunt Fran said that I cried and crawled. Cried and crawled. That's why she said my mother never slept. I just cried and—

—fell to the floor smashing against the ironing board. The iron fell on my head, then on my right wrist. I screamed as it burned into my skin. For years I knew left from right because of that scar.

"You know she was not a very good mother," Aunt Fran said perhaps forgetting whose child I was. "It never came natural. It was almost like—" Aunt Fran cut off the thought as she took a sip of her coffee—

"—uncomfortable," she said as the rest of the thought got lost in the coffee that swirled in her mouth.

"—strong infant-mother ties are essential to survival. This system is so binding that many infants can survive . . . in the face of unfeeling mothers."[2]

"She never had the 'feeling.' I don't think she ever really wanted—more concerned with," Aunt Fran leaned back as if trying to remember. "She was beautiful." Aunt Fran took another gulp of coffee. "Still is," she said as if she were alive, as if more than remembering, as if she were seeing.

"Well yes."

Aunt Fran took her compact mirror out of her purse again. She looked at herself. "But she got better don't you think?" looking a little sad and far off like one of those ladies on *Queen for a Day*—about how she had a sister with whom she didn't compare, couldn't compete. As if she were explaining to Jack Bailey how she had been cursed from the start. "Your mother was beautiful," Aunt Fran said as she put her compact mirror back in her purse.

"Well yes."

I stood up to reposition the straw.

"Do you remember how you cried? Well no, of course you don't. You were just a child—'a difficult child,' she said. But she was wrong. Do you want to know what it was—?" I sat down. "A hole."

I slurped up the last of my second chocolate egg cream.

"A hole in your belly."

I wanted another but I didn't think she'd ever get me a—

"When you lay on your back—a hole would open down there," I looked up. She looked down. She went on,

"—and then you know, your little insides would slide, and get stuck in the hole, and then you would cry. You would cry like a turtle on its back. Cry, cry, cry. But when I picked you up, the insides would slide out, and—"

"More coffee, sugar?" The waiter walked up to the table wiping the clean surface with his dusty cloth.

"—you'd stop."

"Stop what?"

"Can I bring you ah more ah coffee or maybe a piece rugelach. Fresh they made ah Jewish ah food—rugelach? So, sugar, what do you say?"

She looked at the waiter, dabbed her lips with the striped napkin that said Lundy's right on it, "Thank you, I've had quite enough—'Jewish food.'" She took two dollars from her purse. "And my name is not 'sugar,'" she said.

"*Prego,*" he replied just like he was still in Palermo or Naples, Chiapas or Oaxaca. "*Prego,* sugar," he said more out of deafness than defiance. He wiped the table one last time. "*Grazie,*" he said and made a flourish with his cloth.

She watched him depart, the red cloth over his arm, the walk in black pants past rows of empty tables—still empty at half past four. Aunt Fran sucked the space between her back teeth as she watched him as if they were both lost.

Then she stood up. I stood up. We walked toward the door past rows of tables, set for the evening's first wave, still an hour off. "She said you were 'difficult—a difficult child' she said. But she was wrong."

"*Grazie,*" the old waiter said waiting as we passed him at the door.

"You weren't," she said. "It was that hole. You had a hole."

"*Grazie,* Signora," the old waiter said again, removing the cloth from his arm.

"Where's Italy?" I asked.

"Keep the change," Aunt Fran said.

I followed Aunt Fran out of Lundy's double doors onto Emmons Avenue.

"It wasn't your mother who figured that out," Aunt Fran said.

More boats were coming back from the sea. I wanted to go on one of those boats to catch fish. I wanted to sail out to sea on the *Helen B,* the *Flying Finn*—

"It was the neighbor who figured it out."

—or the *Maryanne.* I wanted to sail away and never come back.

"It was the woman next door, that woman," Aunt Fran said pointing as if the woman were standing right there. "It was Katie Galst."

"Can you take me fishing?" I asked.

"You know she never married." Aunt Fran took my hand as we crossed Emmons Avenue to the side close to the water. "Your neighbor, you know who I mean," Aunt Fran said shaking her head.

"She figured it out—not your mother."

"Infant regulation develops in the context of mother-infant interactions. The mother assumes various roles, as does the infant, and together they develop attunement. Emotion dysregulation can occur when the mother is physically unavailable or worse, emotionally unavailable as, for example, if she is depressed."[3]

We walked along Emmons Avenue as schools of fish bubbled the water, breaking the calm, drawing gulls.

I looked over the side of the wall. Once I saw my face in the water, but this time it wasn't there—just the gulls and the fish and the bubbles.

"Where did it go?"

"What?" Aunt Fran asked.

"My face."

Next to the docks, they were cleaning the fish, slitting their bellies, tossing their guts.

"I don't know why she didn't let you suck from her breast," Aunt Fran said, not noticing that I was watching the gulls as they flew off with pieces of fish—"after all, she had fed your sisters. Maybe she wasn't ready for another. Maybe she didn't care enough. Maybe it was to please your father. He was desperate, you know."

"For what?" I asked running to catch up with Aunt Fran as one of the gulls caught a handful of guts that one of the men had just tossed to the air. "Wow!" I said.

"For what?" I repeated.

She smiled, thinking back, remembering or making it up, I wasn't sure. "For you." She took a deep drag from her Chesterfield cigarette. "He was desperate for a son."

"Can you take me fishing on the *Helen B* or the *Flying Finn* or the—?"

"Katie Galst," Aunt Fran said looking far off, shaking her head.

"Will you?"

"What?"

"Take me fishing."

"Katie Galst—" she said again.

It was Katie Galst who had figured out that when she picked me up, I stopped crying. "It was Katie Galst who found the hole. Not your mother. That's when I knew."

"What did you know?" I asked, marveling at the gulls catching guts in midair.

"I just knew."

Aunt Fran stared off as if into the past. "You had a hole."

"I did?"

She nodded.

"Where?"

"They opened you up."

"Who did?" I asked glancing back at the fishermen as they pulled guts from the fish and flung them into air. "They opened me up?"

"You were just a baby," Aunt Fran said taking another cigarette out of the pack from her purse. "I can't take you fishing," she said striking a match, "Ask your father," taking a deep satisfied drag. "I hate fishing."

"I love fishing more than anything," I said staring longingly at the boats.

"Down there," Aunt Fran said indicating with a tilt of her head.

"What?"

"The hole."

"Where?" I asked. Aunt Fran took another deep drag as the fisherman put his knife back in its sheath. "I want to go fishing," stuck in my head.

A fat man in a T-shirt that hung out over his belly came toward us. Aunt Fran paused. The man was singing. Aunt Fran closed her eyes. I guess she was listening—

La donna e mobile
Qual piuma al vento
Muta d'accento
E di pensiero

"That's Verdi," she said her eyes still shut. She didn't move. She took a deep breath. As the fat man sang his belly button peered in and out from under his shirt. Like it was winking.

Sempre un amabile
Leggiadro viso
In pianto o in riso

"Lundy's, the ocean, Verdi!" She took another breath, deeper than the first. "Brooklyn's got everything."

E menzognero
Le donne e mobile
Qual piuma al vento

She started again toward her car, a Ford Fairlane. She opened the door. I was about to get in when she said, "Why would anyone leave? Everything you could possibly want is right here." I looked at Aunt Fran. I had no idea what she meant. She was looking at the man, as he crossed the street toward Lundy's.

"Maybe he's a waiter, like Vinny," I thought.

Then she turned to me. She stared for a moment. Then she said, "There are two ways out of Brooklyn." I just watched her. "Swimming is one," she looked toward the man.

"Is fishing the other?" I asked.

Muta d'accento—e di pensier
E di pensier

"Get in the car," she said.

E di pensier.

I got in the car.

E di pensier.

Aunt Fran drove, tapping the wheel with her fingers as the car slowly filled with smoke from her Chesterfield unfiltered cigarette. She kept humming, tapping.

Muta d'accento
E di pensier.

"Is fishing the other?" I asked again.

"It was Katie Galst," she said, tapping, tapping. Humming.

E di pensier,

E di pensier.

"It was Katie Galst who figured it out," Aunt Fran said tapping. Tapping and tapping. She kept driving down Emmons Avenue then crossed over to Neptune Avenue. Tapping. "Not your mother. She wasn't ready." Tapping and tapping. "She wasn't ready to be a mother. She was too—" Tapping and tapping. "Fickle," Aunt Fran said smiling just a little as if she had touched a truth. "Fickle," she repeated, tapping, tapping.

"*La donna e mobile,*" she said into the rearview mirror. "*Qual piuma di vento.*"

Aunt Fran turned around. "Richard, what are you doing?"

I raised my head, "Looking for the hole," I said.

Then she said, "Darling, pull up your pants."

Aunt Fran kept driving along Neptune Avenue until she turned onto Decatur, which was the street of my favorite store in the whole world. "For my birthday, I want a chocolate cake with sprinkles from Ebinger's," I said as Ebinger's striped awning pulled alongside.

Aunt Fran took a deep drag on her cigarette.

"My birthday is close."

Tapping. Tapping. She wasn't singing anymore.

"Aunt Fran—?"

"Richard your birthday just was."

"Isn't that close?"

"No," she said, "Close is when something 'will,' not when something 'was,'" she said as we drove right past my favorite store in the world.

"Not fair."

Tapping. Tapping.

She took another drag.

The Ford Fairlane was filling with smoke—making it hard to see, hard to breathe. It was like being a fish in a tank with Aunt Fran in a diving bell bubbling smoke.

Ebinger's green and white awning disappeared as we turned onto Orient Boulevard.

Aunt Fran looked at me in the rear view mirror.

"I want a dog," I said.

My mother suffered from bipolar depression.

Bipolar depression is associated with high baseline levels of cortisol. Bipolar depression is associated with the highest rates of suicide of any psychiatric disorder.[4]

My mother lost two pregnancies between Jolie and Susan. She lost three between Susan and me. People figured that my mother's depression had been caused by the grief, by her reaction to loss.

But those losses, however much sadness they may have brought, were not the cause. Bipolar depression was the cause. It causes things. Like elevated cortisol. Like miscarriage. Like suicide. Like death.

Bipolar depression was the cause. Not the effect. People got that wrong. They still do.

Tapping. Tapping.

My mother wasn't reacting to bipolar depression. Bipolar depression had taken control of her ability to react.

Tapping. Tapping.

"We're here," Aunt Fran said as she parked in front of 4152 Ocean Avenue—the house where she and Manny, Susan Margo, and Judy all lived.

She looked again in the rearview mirror, "Richard, I told you to pull up your pants,"

"Is this the hole?" I asked.

Aunt Fran snuffed out the Chesterfield, then turned round to me.

"No, darling, that's your penis."

Chapter 14

Bootstraps

MY FATHER WAS INTOLERANT OF WEAKNESS. HE DID THINGS HIMSELF. He never asked for directions. He never asked for help. He expected the same of us all. He once backed up the Cadillac on the Taconic State Parkway because he had passed the exit he had intended to take. Other cars raced past as we made our way in reverse. "Get down so I can see," he screamed. I sank to the floor. Horns blared. Drivers screamed with fists raised as they zoomed by. I don't know how, but we didn't die.

We got to Margaret and Harry Faulker's farm in Hawthorne, New York. Their home was idyllic and peaceful—with chickens, cows, and a pig. I learned to milk a cow. They gave me a pair of boots.

My father refused the idea of defeat. He could never be wrong—that's why we backed up on the Taconic State Parkway. He was convinced he was right.

When he got off the boat at Ellis Island in 1917, a ten-year-old boy from a shtetl in Poland who spoke only Yiddish, it was clear that no one was going to help. Why ask for directions when you are hated?

"Stand over there," the man in the uniform said, pointing "over there" as if they were infected.

"Vas?" Grandfather Max said. Too fearful to imagine or guess what the man in the uniform meant when he pointed. As if facing a

Bolshevik, a Pole, the Inquisition, or Uncle Sam, it was clear to my father that if they were to survive, he would have to take charge.

"Over there," the guard repeated without looking up.

"*Vas hat er gezagit?*" my grandfather Max asked my father, his son, a ten-year-old boy.

My father imagined, understood. He directed my grandfather, his wife Minnie, my Uncle Bill, Uncle Lou, my Aunt Sara who died of diphtheria a year later, long before I was born, Uncle Sol who was murdered in Pilgrim State Hospital to be quietly buried in an unmarked grave, and my father, just a boy. "*Kum shteyn do,*" my father said, indicating the end of another long line.

"*Iz vos er hat gezagit?*" my grandfather wanted to know.

"Over there," the guard said with growing impatience.

"*Kum shteyn do,*" my father repeated to my Grandfather Max.

"*Do?*"

"*Yo.*"

"*Aoy dos iz Amerike?*" he asked for no reason. They had just gotten off the boat in New York.

And so yes, this was America.

"*Yo, doz iz Amerike.*"

"*Loyt deyn bootstraps.*"

"*Vas?*"

"*Gornisht.*"

"Bootstraps," was something my father often said, sometimes a fierce cry, sometimes a rebuke, sometimes advice. "Bootstraps," something he yelled, almost pounding his chest, his hair now all white. "Bootstraps," demanding, threatening, instructing. "Bootstraps." A ten-year-old boy setting foot on Ellis Island, who had to figure it out by himself. "*Loyt deyn bootstraps.*" Figure it out, or you won't survive.

"Ruthie, you are going to get better. We are going to beat this, this 'depression.' You've got to pick yourself up."

"By my bootstraps?"

"Yes, by your bootstraps."

"What if I don't have the strength? What if I don't have the shoes? What if I don't—"

"Ruthie!" he said grabbing her by the shoulders.

It wasn't coercion. There was love. It's just that bipolar depression has no bootstraps, nothing to hold—that was not something he understood.

"Ruthie, are you coming to bed?"

So what I had heard curled on the floor outside their bedroom door, twenty years after it had begun, six years after my birth—

"Bootstraps."

—was something that seven years before, may have actually led to my birth.

"Ruthie—" he said as he opened the door.

She looked at me, smiled. She just stood there in my room holding my book, the Big Orange.

He walked up to her, "Do you know what night this is?"

She just stood there, defiant. Silent.

"Ruthie," my father said—calm and firm. "Ruthie!" After two daughters, the three, four, five miscarriages, he desperately wanted—

"Mommy?"

It's possible my mother had been using me to shield her from something she could no longer bear. It's possible that Dr. Stein, in his arrogance and ignorance, had actually stumbled upon some truth.

My mother stroked the hair from my face, "Don't be scared," she said. "It's okay. It's all right. I love you very very much. Your mother loves you."

"Ruthie—?"

Then she started to read, "She loves her Babar, very very much—"

"Mommy?"

"She rocks him to sleep with her trunk while singing softly to him."

She stroked me once more, "Don't be scared. Babar wasn't scared."

"I, I—"

"No," she said, "he wasn't."

Then she started to sing.

Too-ra-loo-ra-loo-ral,

Too-ra-loo-ra-li

She stroked me, held me, lay down beside me as she continued to sing,

Too-ra-loo-ra-loo-ral,

Hush now don't you cry.

It's possible that as she lay on my bed, read from my book, sang me to sleep—she was plotting her end.

Too-ra-loo-ra-loo-ral,

Too-ra-loo-ra-li

Too-ra-loo-ra-loo-ral.

"Ruthie!" he called from down the hall.

She looked at me. "Don't be scared," she said. "You'll be fine. Babar lost his mother, remember?"

Yes, I remembered. I had memorized the book.

"And he became king."

Then she kissed me, pulled the covers up to my chin.

"One day you will be king—"

"Ruthie!"

"—my little prince."

"Ruthie!"

"One day."

Chapter 15

Cortisol

THERE ARE FOUR THINGS I CAN SAY WITH CONFIDENCE ABOUT THE TIME I spent in my mother's womb. First, my mother did not read to me from Dr. Seuss. Second, she suffered from bipolar depression and was deeply depressed during much if not all of her pregnancy. Third, as a result of her depression, the blood circulating from the placenta into my umbilical vein had abnormally high levels of active cortisol. Fourth, abnormally high level of active cortisol is affecting the story I am telling now.

Cortisol tells the first story. The story told by a mother to her fetus. The story told in the womb.

Most physiology loops operate with feedback inhibition (two major exceptions are the amygdala and the placenta). So for example, higher levels of a neural transmitter will lead to diminished production of that transmitter—part of a homeostatic, regulatory system that keeps things in balance, within a range—the way a thermostat keeps the temperature close to a set point.

The loop regulating the production and release of cortisol between mother and fetus does not operate with feedback inhibition. It operates with feed-forward acceleration.

The control of cortisol begins at the hypothalamus, which is the beginning of an axis known as the hypothalamic-pituitary-adrenal, or HPA, axis.

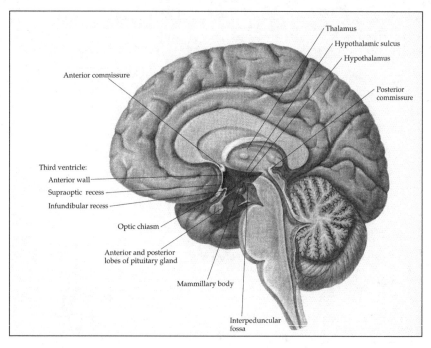

The hypothalamic-pituitary-adrenal or HPA axis integrates viscerosensory and emotional information. The hypothalamus then sends neurohormonal signals including corticotrophin releasing factor (CRF) to the pituitary which releases a hormone, adrenocorticotrophic hormone (ACTH) into the circulatory system. ACTH acts at the adrenal glands lying over the kidneys. The adrenals then release cortisol as well as other stress hormones into the arterial circulation.

"The hypothalamus is crucial to maintaining normal organ function and it does so by integrating viscerosensory information together with information about the individual's emotional state."[1] The hypothalamus translates emotion into physiology—and it does this largely through the regulation of cortisol.

The hypothalamus is a key regulator of cortisol. There are receptors for cortisol on practically every cell in a mammal's body. And thus changes to the level of cortisol affect quite a lot.

Just how depressed mood elevates the level of cortisol or just how elevated cortisol leads to depressed mood is not entirely clear. Indeed it is not entirely clear what is cause and what is effect or how the two interact. But abnormal levels of cortisol and depression do indeed coexist.

The release of cortisol in primates (corticosterone in other mammals) is controlled by the hypothalamic pituitary adrenal axis, the HPA axis. It's a top-down system that starts in the hypothalamus, where neurons produce a hormone, corticotropin-releasing factor (CRF), which is released to the pituitary which causes the release of another releasing factor, adrenocorticotropic releasing factor (ACTH), from the pituitary into the arterial blood circulation.

Adrenocorticotropic releasing factor flows in the blood to the adrenal glands—two small organs that sit on top of the kidneys ("ad renal"—on top of the kidney). Adrenocorticotropic releasing factor (ACTH) acts on the adrenals to cause the release of cortisol.

With conception, the control of cortisol in the mother shifts from the hypothalamus to the placenta. When that happens, several things change. One critical change is that regulation goes from feedback inhibition at the maternal hypothalamus to feed-forward acceleration at the fetal placenta.

"In contrast to the inhibitory influence of glucocorticoids (cortisol) on the expression of the corticotropin-releasing factor gene in the hypothalamus, glucocorticoids activate the promoter region in the placenta and stimulate the synthesis of CRH. . . . This positive feedback loop results in dramatic elevations of maternal ACTH, cortisol and CRH across gestation."[2]

Elevated levels of cortisol on the maternal side of the placenta stimulate production by the placenta of the releasing factor, corticotropin-releasing factor (CRF). The placenta expresses corticotropin-releasing factor (CRF) into both the maternal and fetal circulations. Rising levels of cortisol from the mother drive the level of the releasing factor, corticotropin-releasing factor (CRF), which drives the production of cortisol in the fetus. So as levels of cortisol rise on the maternal side of the placenta, the placenta drives levels of CRF and ultimately cortisol on the fetal side. Higher levels of maternal cortisol drive higher levels of fetal cortisol. Cortisol in both mother and fetus keeps rising.

This is not "homeostatic" regulation where the system fluctuates around a fixed point. This is "allostatic" regulation where the system fluctuates around a fluctuating—in this instance, rising—set point. The mother with high cortisol drives the cortisol level of her fetus higher and higher. Pregnancy is a high-cortisol state for both mother and fetus.

Most enzymes, proteins, and molecules in the maternal circulation are too big to pass through the placenta. The placenta is composed of thousands of chorionic villi containing minute blood vessels that allow for fetal absorption of maternal oxygen, water, and nutrients and the diffusion of wastes through the connecting umbilical cord. The maternal blood vessels in the uterine wall must successfully transform and remodel to safely and effectively supply blood to the villi. In most pregnancies, the placenta sustains the fetus until parturition. However, many things can go wrong.[3]

Things often go wrong. "Stuff happens," as Donald Rumsfeld famously said.

The placenta, among other things, acts as a semi-porous barrier that keeps the maternal and fetal circulations separate and apart. Proteins, which are large molecules, do not pass through the membrane. Cortisol, which is a small molecule, passes through. Cortisol in the maternal circulation crosses into the fetal circulation.

In the placenta (which after all belongs to the fetus and not to the mother), there is a gene that codes for an enzyme that deactivates cortisol. So even though cortisol in the maternal circulation can pass into the fetal circulation, the placenta can deactivate maternal cortisol in order to control the level of active cortisol impacting the developing fetus. The placenta thus buffers the cortisol that passes from the maternal into the fetal circulation. What is of note is that the level of maternal cortisol affects this "deactivating" gene.

"Mothers who are least distressed produce placenta that are more successful at buffering the fetuses from the negative influence of stress."[4] Mothers who are not under undue stress, and thus mothers who do not have elevated levels of cortisol, do not deactivate this gene—a gene which deactivates cortisol. So the placenta of a fetus of a non-stressed mother will deactivate much of the cortisol that passes to the fetus. The fetus of a non-stressed mother will have less active cortisol flowing in his/her veins and arteries.

But the reverse is true of mothers who are under stress. Whether the stress is due to internal or external factors does not matter: The indicator of stress is cortisol. High levels of cortisol in the maternal circulation deactivate the placental buffer. High levels of maternal stress, and thus high levels of maternal cortisol, reduce the buffering effect, allowing more active cortisol to pass from the maternal into the fetal circulation. This is another example of a feed-forward mechanism acting through the placenta on cortisol.

It seems that evolution was intent on communicating the presence of stress from one generation to the next. No matter the cost. No matter the effect. And one of the principal means of communicating stress is cortisol.

But one might ask, didn't evolution "understand" that by driving corticotropin-releasing factor (CRF) and cortisol levels in both the fetal and maternal circulations, it was rendering women more vulnerable to miscarriage, to preterm labor, more likely to deliver a compromised baby? Why, one might ask, would evolution "want" a woman to deliver her fetus "unfinished," "half made up," with high levels of active cortisol and with the increased risk of neonatal death?

My mother had difficulty bringing a fetus to term. She lost two pregnancies between the births of my two sisters. She lost three more between the birth of my younger sister Susan and me. These miscarriages were part of the reason why there were so many years between the births of her children (five between Jolie and Susan, ten between Susan and me). And during each of those pregnancies corticotropin-releasing factor and cortisol were driven higher and higher by pregnancy itself and by my mother's bipolar illness. It was as if evolution were wanting her to miscarry.

Why would evolution "want" that?

Evolution is a storyteller. A story is a communication. Evolution tells stories that are true although not always kind. They are stories that serve the species without individual welfare in mind.

In a stressed environment—such as in times of famine, pandemic, plague, poverty, war—by raising levels of CRF and cortisol, evolution is giving mother and fetus "advice." It is letting the mother know that her life is in danger and the longer she remains "with child," the less chance she has to survive. The communication is simple and straightforward—deliver the fetus as soon as possible—dead or alive. By keeping the fetus, you are risking your life. And to the fetus, evolution is warning that if you make it to term—if you get to take your first breath—food will be scarce, predators will lurk, your mother may not be around to care for you for very long, and disease will be rampant. If you plan to reproduce, do it as quickly as you can. And good luck—you'll need it.

Rising levels of CRF leading to increasing levels of cortisol is common to several physiologic states—stress, depression, pregnancy. By having this common denominator, evolution was able to transmit a story from one generation to the next using cortisol as the storyteller, the link. And because the placenta's response to cortisol is feed-forward acceleration, the mother's response to either the stress of a hostile environment—famine, pandemic, poverty, war, abuse—or to the stress of a dysregulated internal milieu—depression, anxiety, intoxicants—all lead to increasing levels of cortisol. The greater the stress, either internally or externally, the more will the mother communicate that stress to her fetus through rising CRF and cortisol.

A rising level of cortisol is how the first story is told, how the first inkling of the outside gets in. It is the first indication of what the future will bring to the present when the future takes hold.

Cortisol is thus one of the earliest vehicles of epigenetic

communication. It is a "messenger" of maternal experience from mother to fetal DNA. But the mother is communicating not just her experience of her world. She is also communicating her sense of the kind of world she anticipates for her fetus when her fetus comes to term. It is a story not just of what is, but of what most likely will be. Cortisol is the story teller of a time soon to be.

"Maternal prenatal distress functions as a communication fore-shadowing characteristics of the postnatal world for which the fetus can begin to prepare via biological adaptations."[5]

"Once upon a time" begins in the womb but not with a smell or a taste or the rhymes of Dr. Seuss. It begins at the placenta—at the interface between mother and fetus. It begins with corticotropin-releasing factor. It begins with cortisol. "A dynamic systems perspective has as a first principle that the organism is always engaged with the environment."[6] Even inside the womb, the fetus is engaged with the world.

"Oh, and one other thing, before I forget," my mother was letting me know via the continuing rise of cortisol, "Don't expect me to be around for very long. I won't be. I can't."

Tapping. Tapping. Her fingers tapping gently on my back and my neck. She brushed the hair from my face.

"Aunt Fran?" I asked.

"What is it, sugar?"

"Why did Susan Margo die?"

She stroked my face. I started to shiver. I couldn't help it.

I didn't know why.

Chapter 16

The Epigenotype

IN 1942 IN THE JOURNAL *ENDEAVOR*, CONRAD H. WADDINGTON PUB-lished a paper called "The Epigenotype."[1] In it, Waddington struggled with an aspect of genetics that was recognized, but poorly understood. It was known that between the genotype (DNA) and the phenotype (physical form), there is a process. It was further rec-ognized that the process is variable. Thus monozygotic twins—twins that have identical DNA—develop into individuals who are distinct. Identical twins are not in fact identical.

Waddington recognized this when he wrote, "The task is to dis-cover the causal mechanisms at work, and to relate them as far as possible to what has already been revealed of the mechanisms of development. It is convenient to have a name for this complex. 'Epigenotype' seems suitable."

And while history would not find the word "epigenotype" entirely suitable, the quest to better define and understand that complex interaction between gene and environment had begun. "We might use the name 'epigenetics' for such studies," Waddinton went on, and indeed "epigenetics" was what took. And thus the word and the concept of "epigenetics" was born.

There are too many uncertainties for which evolution had to account. The simple transfer of DNA was huge. DNA told a lot—per-haps both too much and not little. Evolution needed more spontaneity in the lives it brought forth. DNA is fixed. Epigenetics is not. In DNA, evolution had Beethoven. In epigenetics, it had Coltrane.

Thus while there are some 3 billion base pairs, or "codons," of human DNA, only about 2 to 3 percent actually code for the 25,000 or so proteins that are made. And thus these coding codons—the pairs of DNA that actually code for protein—take up a rather small fraction of the total. For a long time, the remaining 97 percent, the noncoding DNA, was thought of as "junk DNA" that seemed to do nothing. But just as nature abhors a vacuum, it abhors junk. "Junk DNA" was not doing nothing. It was regulating.

Those seemingly unused base pairs of DNA were being used to adjust the output of the DNA that actually coded for the transcription of DNA into RNA and then for the translation of the RNA into protein. And what determined the adjustment was the environment. By allocating a huge portion of DNA to regulation, evolution was incorporating the possibility of adaptation, of improvisation, of change in response to environmental circumstance into the relatively fixed agenda of DNA.

The mechanism of epigenetics is how the world talks to the cell. Epigenetics is how evolution incorporates change into the fixed DNA. It is the door that Waddington described, the door through which the environment (nurture) influences DNA (nature). It is how the biologic story is told.

But why bother? Why would nature configure such a process? Why transmit individual differences in stress reactivity . . . through a process that is driven by parental care and mediated by complex cellular machinery? Why not simply leave such issues in the hands of classic genetic transmission? The answer may be in the simple fact that unlike nucleotide sequence, epigenetic marks are dynamic and indeed reversible." DNA is fixed. Epigenetics is not.

"Ruthie, just look at our beautiful boy!" my father exclaimed, holding me up like a soft, wet trophy, as he walked a victory lap round my mother's hospital bed.

"Parents can actively remodel epigenetic marks and affect patterns of gene expression in the offspring. Such effects do not occur at the level of nucleotide sequence."[2]

Everyone noticed that something was wrong.

"A boy! Ruthie, Ruthie we did it! A boy!"

Everyone except my father.

"That is the way systems operate. A change at one or another level of a system changes other levels such that the animal under study is not the same. The initial change becomes part of an on-going process of change."[3]

The nurse, my sisters, Aunt Fran, and Katie Galst watched my father as he paraded his son—that is to say, paraded *me*—like hockey's Stanley Cup. "Ruthie," he said holding me high. "Ruthie!" He bounced me in his arms, then lowered the cloth from my loins to demonstrate the glory of it all. "Would you just look at this!" My mother's eyes were far off.

"Mr. Brockman," the nurse interrupted, "maybe I should take the wee lad."

He shook his head, "I know what I'm doing. I've been waiting for this day, since I married this glorious woman. And now just look at our boy! Amazing! Amazing!"

"Mr. Brockman—"

"I know what I'm doing," he said. And that's when I threw up all over his shirt.

In the womb I had been bathed in unbound cortisol. Approximately 90 percent of cortisol is bound to a protein called cortisol-binding globulin. But it is the unbound that acts, the unbound that binds to receptors, the unbound—

"Mr. Brockman—"

—that enters the cell, gets to the nucleus where DNA waits to be told just what to do.

"It's nothing. It's fine," he said moving me deftly to the side. He started to sing. I started to cry.

You load sixteen tons and what do ya get,
Another day older and ah deeper in debt—
Tennessee Ernie Ford was an odd choice for a maternity ward.
Saint Peter don't you call me
Cause I can't come.
I owe my soul—
But then again he was singing as he was cleaning meconium off his shirt.
—to the company store.

My mother's placenta (biologically it was actually my placenta, not hers) did little to buffer active unbound cortisol. I was bathed in the unbound.

Unbound cortisol binds with a receptor on the surface of the cell called the glucocorticoid receptor (GR). And when cortisol interacts with the glucocorticoid receptor (GR), the complex moves to the nucleus where it binds to a segment of DNA—the promoter region—which then engages the regulatory process. Pretty much every cell is informed by an active cortisol-GR complex that then regulates events within the nucleus, letting the nucleus know what's happening "outside"—outside being outside the membrane of the cell. An increasing level of unbound cortisol is generally an indicator of "stress" in that world outside.

Peripartum depression is communicated from the mother to the fetus via cortisol. It is the communication of stress. Elevated unbound cortisol is one way the environment outside the cell tells the nucleus inside the cell that something is wrong.

"Kid's an athlete, natural born. Did you see the force, the power, the way he threw up?" my father said, seeing victory no matter what.

"Mr. Brockman—" the nurse said as she reached for me.

"Just look, look what my boy has done!" he said handing me to the care of the nurse as meconium seeped through his shirt. Meconium—a mix of the amniotic fluid from the womb and the gastrointestinal fluid from the fetal gut. Meconium—a wet, brownish yellow liquid.

"There, there," the nurse said, "there's a wee lad."

The nurse took me in her arms. On her blouse was a tag that read, "Katherine."

"There, there," Katherine said, "Let's give the wee to the Mom, shall we?" as she wiped me dry and laid me on my mother's belly. My mother lowered her eyes to her chest as I came alive to her scent.

"There, there."

"Olfactory preference learning is our best current model for how learned preferences for maternal cues begin."[4]

A neonate is drawn to scent.

I inched my way toward my mother's breasts, her teats, toward the smell I recognized from the womb. The smell that made me feel safe, raised my level of oxytocin, the transmitter of the bond, the neurohormone that counteracted the cortisol that was still in me, high and unbound. Oxytocin, a biologic response to the scent of my mother, to the scent of "safety" as I struggled to reach her breast.

She did not move, staring off as if she didn't understand why the pain in her perineum refused to wear off. "There, there," Katherine said, "such a wee lad," as if to allay any doubts that she had once been a lass in Connemara. "There, there, Mommie's wee lad," advancing me further up her belly, thinking perhaps that if I were a "wee" bit closer, then Mommie would respond. My mother finally smiled and brushed the wet from my open, unfocused eyes. "There, there," Katherine said as my mother shifted her equally unfocused gaze.

"Brooklyn Lying-In Hospital" was part of the hospital record I would read thirty years later. It even mentioned the ward where I lay, the room, and the bed "3-34-A." "Miss Katherine O'Malley" was the nurse.

"There, there," nurse Katherine O'Malley said as I started to make my way up the slope of my mother's breast—covered with the smells of her sweat and her "water," what had been my amniotic bath. "There, there." Nurse Katherine had a way of saying most everything twice.

"Learning maternal odor cues depends on behavioral stimulation, which serves as the unconditioned stimulus that is paired with the odor."[5] That is to say, the mother, the dam, must respond if her neonate, her pup, is to get the full meaning and force of her scent, of the bond.

"There, there," Katherine said, molding her hand round my bottom, repositioning my mother's breast, closing the distance between teat and mouth.

"I know. I know you're tired," the nurse said stroking my mother's damp hair, "But the wee needs to suck." She turned to my father, "You should wait outside."

"Stimulation of the baby's face causes the infant to rotate its head until the nipple is touched."

"There, there," Katherine said, brushing my cheek against my mother's breast to let me know where it was, "There, there."

"The nipple is then orally engulfed."[6]

Scent enters the brain through the piriform plate—small perforations in the skull through which strands of the olfactory nerve reach the anterior cortex—the most direct route from stimulus to cortex. There's a reason why scent can so powerfully evoke, attract, repel, remind. There's a reason why Proust's madeleine acted so powerfully on his mind.

"I raised to my lips a spoonful of the tea in which I had soaked a morsel of the cake. No sooner had the warm liquid, and the crumbs with it, touched my palate, a shudder ran through my whole body. An exquisite pleasure had invaded my senses."

I smelled her breast, then felt her teat on my cheek. My lips parted. My fingers grasped. My head turned. All part of a reflex that brought fresh, warm milk into my mouth, my throat, my gut.

"There, there," Katherine gently brushing my mother's forehead.

Scent establishes the huge power of the first bond. And the

behaviors of the first bond have consequences that are huge for the neonate, for the pup, for a mammal for the rest of its life.

"There, there. The baby is hungry," Katherine said as I slid off my mother's breast. "You must hold his mouth to your teat. The wee needs to suck."

My mother just watched as if some other woman's baby had fallen off some other woman's teat.

"There, there."

"I remember when you were born." Aunt Fran said, put her arm over my shoulder. Tapping. Tapping. Her fingers on the back of my neck.

"When was that?"

"It was when you were born."

"Oh."

"'The wee needs to suck.' That's what she kept saying," Aunt Fran said

"Who?"

"The nurse."

"What nurse?"

"You were 'just wee'—that's what she'd say," Aunt Fran said. "What was her name?" Aunt Fran asked as if asking me to remember the opening moves of my life, as if they were the first moves of chess.

"The wee needs to suck," the nurse said.

"Just look at that boy! The power, the force!" my father said, no longer able to contain his raw pride.

"Please wait outside," nurse Katherine said.

"But see here Miss—what is your name? Do you have any idea—"

"Katherine," Aunt Fran said, "Her name was Katherine."

"Katherine—?"

"Please, Mr. Brockman, your wife does so much better without so much fuss. She needs to nurse, and the wee needs to suck." Katherine said as I continued to root for my mother's left teat.

"When you were born," Aunt Fran said, "your mother wasn't

ready," as we walked up the steps of the brick terrace to her home at 4152 Ocean Avenue, a block from the ocean and two blocks from the bay.

"I don't understand," I said.

"You were hungry and she—" Aunt Fran said pausing as she got to the door, pursing her lips. "She—" shaking her head, opening her purse, searching for the key.

I could see the playhouse where Susan Margo taught us.

Pigeons circled overhead, making wider and wider arcs as if they didn't know where they were going, as if they were lost.

"Something was wrong. We didn't know. None of us. Something. We just didn't know. Did I tell you already?" Aunt Fran asked, finally finding the key.

Evolution did not provide a grand plan. There was no elegant design hidden in its work. Evolution had a few basic rules which Waddington had called the rules of "epigenetics." Then it left it to each and every living thing to decide how best to proceed, how best to use its given fix of DNA.

"Development is emergent, like a flock of birds in which each individual, following simple rules and without instruction from a leader, contributes to the organized behavior of the group."[7]

Evolution worked from below. Each individual somehow figuring out on its own, what he or she had to do.

This was Darwin's genius—his insight into Creation's incredibly simple plan.

The Church looked at Creation from the top down and came up with God.

Darwin looked at Creation from the bottom up and came up with evolution.

"From so simple a beginning endless forms most beautiful and most wonderful have been, and are being evolved."[8]

"Mr. Brockman, please wait outside."

In the early nineteenth century, after spending three years

105

circumnavigating the world on the HMS *Beagle*, Darwin had gathered massive amounts of data that he struggled to organize and understand. It took Darwin years to come up with a unifying theory, a plan. He was aware that the theory that he was circling was putting him at odds with his wife, with her beliefs, with God.

After a while, Darwin realized that he could no longer attend church because he could no longer listen to what was being said under that roof. So rather than abandon Emma, his wife, Darwin would walk with her to the church. When she would go inside, Darwin would sit on a bench or talk to villagers outside, waiting for the sermon to end and his wife to emerge.

Darwin felt there was no evidence to support the teachings of the church, no evidence for divine Creation, no evidence for a Master Plan. Emma firmly believed in the teachings of the church. She believed in its God. Darwin waited for Emma outside every Sunday so they could walk home together.

I watched the pigeons circling aimlessly overhead, having no idea where they were going, when all of a sudden they landed on the roof of the neighbor's house—as if that's what they had been planning all along.

"I had to buy milk. No, not milk. What was it—?" Aunt Fran nodded as strands of hair fell over her face, "Similac—that's what it was called. I had to buy Similac because your mother didn't have enough milk."

Katherine lifted me higher on my mother's chest.

"Why don't you hold him? Here, yes, from his bottom."

My mother's right hand took my bottom. With her left, she stroked my head. I slid off her breast. Katherine repositioned my head, her hand, my mouth, her breast. I slid off again. I started to cry.

"Katherine—?" my mother said.

"Everyone seemed to realize that something was wrong. But none of us really knew—"Aunt Fran said.

"Katherine," my mother said, lifting me off of her chest as if the sound of my cries were more than she could bear.

"There, there," Katherine said, taking me from my mother. "There, there."

"Aunt Fran—?"

"What is it?"

"There, there" Katherine said as she slung me on her shoulder, rocked me, burped me, rubbed my bottom, "There, there." And sang,

Over in Killarney

Many years ago

"And then she sang that song," Aunt Fran said.

"Who did?" I asked.

"Katherine did," she said.

My mother sang a song to me—

In tones so sweet and low

"I miss Susan Margo," I said.

"So do I," Aunt Fran said. Tapping, tapping. "So do I," again rubbing the back of my neck. She paused at the open door as if she didn't want to go any further. As if there were too many memories circling inside like the pigeons outside.

"Shall we give another try?" Katherine asked, putting me back on my mother's breast, guiding my mouth, not waiting for my mother's reply.

Just a simple ditty,

In her old Irish way

And I'd give the world if she could sing

That song to me this day

"There," Katherine said, perhaps reliving the memory of the "wee" that was once at her breast. "There, there." Singing maybe for my mother, maybe for me, maybe for herself—

Too-ra-loo-ra-loo-ral,

Too-ra-loo-ra-li

Maybe singing for us three.

Too-ra-loo-ra-loo-ral,

Hush now don't you cry.

"Katherine," my mother said, "That's a beautiful song."

Too-ra-loo-ra-loo-ral,

Too-ra-loo-ra-li

Too-ra-loo-ra-loo-ral,

That's an Irish lullaby.

"Yes," Katherine said, "it is."

My mother sat up, pulling her teat from my lips.

The sudden, unexpected loss of suck is a signal that reduces parasympathetic output, increases sympathetic—all components of the involuntary or autonomic nervous system (ANS).

The hypothalamic-pituitary-adrenal, the HPA axis, is not the only mediator of early story. The autonomic nervous system (ANS)—which is made up of the parasympathetic nervous system (PNS) and the sympathetic nervous system (SNS)—also mediates story.

The two parts of the autonomic nervous system operate something like a U-tube—one system increases when the other declines. Generally the parasympathetic system is more activated in the context of satiety or safety, while the sympathetic nervous system is more activated in the context of need or distress. "The neural pathways from the cortex to these nerves are myelinated sufficiently at birth to allow the infant to signal to the caregiver by vocalizing or grimacing."[9] The neonate's affective display—"vocalizing or grimacing"—is the emotional communication to the caregiver of the neonate's physiologic status as interpreted by the autonomic nervous system.

I started to cry.

"The wee is still hungry," Katherine said.

My mother lay there.

"Don't you want to give him more suck?" the nurse asked.

My mother did her best to smile. "Tomorrow," she said. "Tomorrow."

Katherine picked me up off my mother's chest. "There, there," she said, holding me to her chest and shoulder, "there, there."

"These findings indicate that compared with healthy mothers, depressed mothers have a dampened reward response and reduced empathy to infant stimuli."[10]

"I am still very tired," she said.

Stress has a similar effect on the dam. A stressed dam spends less time licking and grooming, less time nursing her pups. "Stress decreased the total contact time between the mother and her pups."[11]

But the dam doesn't do this because she is not a "good enough mother." She does this because environmental realities have forced her to spend more time searching for material to build her nest, scavenging for food, on the lookout for cats. She is responding to the reality of stress, a reality that she will pass on to her pups via the "story" that is passed from dam to fetus and then to pup, through touch, teat, neurotransmitters, the sympathetic and parasympathetic nervous systems, the variable expression of DNA.

As adults, the pups of the stressed dam will be biologically more reactive. And thus better prepared for an environment where they will likely find fewer resources, less food, many predators. The dam is letting her pups know the kind of world they will face when they are grown and have pups of their own. She is telling a story about the future she foresees. This is not an example of bad mothering. It is an example of good storytelling.

My mother told me a similar story, a story of stress—not of war or famine or abuse—but the stress of peripartum depression. It is the story she passed on to me when I was in her womb, when I sucked at her breast. It is a story told through corticotrophin releasing factor (CRF), cortisol, the autonomic nervous system. It is a story told before the neocortex is fully functional. It is a story told without words.

In the basement of the microfiche room of the Municipal

Building at 60 Center Street, in New York, there is a large board over the counter with numbers that light up. I had been standing there in the large, nearly empty room for almost an hour when the number thirty-six lit. It was like bingo when I was a kid crossing the ocean on the ocean liner USS *Constitution* on my first "honeymoon" when I was ten, with my father and his newly minted "step wife." They took me along for the ride. What else could they do but share their honeymoon with their ten-year-old kid?

The number thirty-six lit up. I walked to the counter, handed my stub to the clerk with the number "thirty-six" facing up. She looked at the stub, then handed me a folder. I took the folder in both of my hands as if it was heavy. It was not.

"Next," the clerk said.

I stood there and stared at the folder.

"You can't stand there," the clerk said. "Next!" she called out.

A young woman behind me was holding a child by the hand. Behind her a man in a shirt and tie was reading a newspaper. "Ford to City: Drop dead." It was ten-thirty in the morning, years later, the city in decay. Services cut. I was in a large, subterranean hall. There wasn't much of a line. It was almost November but hot. "Next." There were two large fans moving the air back and forth. "Next." Two polar bears were standing on large blocks of ice.

Frigid Fans—what were the chances of that?

I went to the side of the room, leaned against the wall. I removed the single sheet of paper from the envelope. "Certificate of Birth" was written across the top. Time, place, person—each had a spot.

Time: 10:15 pm. Month: October. Day: Thirteen. Place: Brooklyn Lying-in Hospital, Brooklyn, New York. Parents: Ruth Biegelsen Brockman. David Daniel Brockman. Sex: Male. Weight: Seven pounds, six ounces. I stood there reading as if I were reading my last will and testament. Tears came to my eyes. No one noticed. Or if they did, no one cared. Why should they? At the bottom were two more names. Physician: Jonathan Lipmann, MD. Nurse: Katherine

O'Malley, RN. The clerk looked up from her station. I took one last look at the "Certification" glancing at the name of the baby boy. "Richard Mark Brockman." I had always thought my name was Marc, spelled with a "c." I was wrong about that, wrong about who I was. From the very first.

"Next."

I looked up at the clerk sitting behind the glass partition. "Next," she called again into the vast empty hall.

"The incidence of maternal mental illness is staggering—indeed depression and anxiety combined are considered the most common complication of pregnancy and childbirth nationwide."[12]

Depression is a significant illness of pregnancy. It is a significant stressor leading to the activation of the hypothalamic-pituitary-adrenal axis, the release of corticotropin-releasing factor and cortisol, leading to the shift from restorative calm of the parasympathetic nervous system to the mounting demands of the sympathetic nervous system. This activation lays the foundations of story—of what is remembered, what is told, what is kept, what is lost.

Katherine walked around the room with me perched on her shoulder. She took me to the window then turned around so I could face out. "There," she said. "There," looking over her shoulder at what was facing me. "It's all there. Waiting," she said making sure I was facing the trees, and the leaves, some turning, some falling, some hanging. "There," she said, "there's just the start."

"Will you write it down for me?"

Katherine turned back to my mother. "Ruth?"

"The words," my mother said, "The words to the song."

"I'd love to do that. I'd love to indeed," Katherine said.

Outside the door of the maternity ward, Room 3–34-A, my father sat in a chair smoking a Montecristo cigar.

The nurse opened the door. "Mr. Brockman, you can't smoke in here."

My father nodded. "Nurse," he said, taking another puff. "Thank you for the update on your hospital rules," he said, twisting the end of the cigar till the ember was cold. "They don't really matter. I have a son," he said.

He was proud.

Chapter 17

The Great White

A S YOU DRIVE ALONG THE GOWANUS EXPRESSWAY GOING EAST, YOU approach the part of Brooklyn known as Red Hook. On the left you pass a series of warehouses, factories, wholesale distributors, importers of fruit, coffee, tea—and then you come to a wall with a great white bear standing on a massive block of ice. The bear's maw is wide, right paw raised. The fur on its neck is blown back by a fierce arctic gale. The animal is standing on its hind legs as if about to take a chunk of the Gowanus Expressway in its jaws.

My father and Uncle Cookie ran the Frigid Fan Company. The bear on that brick outer wall was the company logo. There was an image just like it over my father's desk. There was one stamped on every fan. Uncle Cookie had a shirt with the white bear on the chest pocket which he wore whenever he played golf. He played golf a lot. "My victory bear," Uncle Cookie said when my father arrived. "I'll bet you my favorite, my good luck, my Great White victory shirt."

"It's a bet," my father said removing ten dollars from his clip.

My father and Uncle Cookie were always betting on things—boxing, baseball, marriages, dogs, horses, fights. And so, when Ruth, my mother, announced she was pregnant, they bet on me. "Ten dollars it's a boy," was my father's bet.

"Sure, sure," Uncle Cookie said, throwing two fives into the pot,

"How much more you got? I need a new car." Uncle Cookie threw in five more. "A Cadillac—bigger than yours."

The day after I was born, my father showed up at the office with a handful of Montecristos. He passed them out—to the bookkeeper, the secretary, the foreman, workers on the floor—saving the last for Uncle Cookie. Oversized like a mobster, Uncle Cookie wasn't really my uncle, but he was always "Uncle Cookie."

"Ruthie gave birth," my father said, striking a match. "Just last night."

"Sure, sure," Uncle Cookie said.

"A beautiful baby," my father replied, taking a long, satisfied puff, letting ash fall to the floor.

"I can't believe I've known this man—Dave, how long has it been?" Uncle Cookie said swiveling in his chair as my father circled around from behind.

My father took several more puffs before removing the cigar from his mouth. "And the baby," he said admiring the cigar's size, shape, its length—"is seven pounds," he said as he leaned closer to Uncle Cookie's ear, "six inches!"—flicking more ash to the floor.

It had been a tough year—two going on three. For all those years my father desperately wanted a son. And for the last of those years my mother had been severely depressed. She had lost appetite, sleep, energy, focus. She believed she was cursed. My father believed he knew the cure. He believed he could fix anything once he set his mind to the task. He set his mind to his wife, this woman whom he adored. He set his mind to having a son.

"Dave—"

"Ruthie, just let me—"

"No! Please, don't you see—"

"Shh, you'll wake the girls."

"—Dave, you don't understand. I, I—"

He put his hand on her mouth, "Shh."

"Dave, I can't—" she tried to pull away, but his weight on her chest.

"Ruthie, just let me—"

"I—"

"—for you, for me, for us," he said pressing down on her arms, her shoulders. Pressing down on her chest.

"Shh," he said, "shh," softer and softer. "Shh," as if trying to tame something wild, frightened, unwilling—

"Dave—"

—inserting a finger.

"Dave—" her nails dug into his shoulder.

He didn't hit her. He didn't hurt her. It wasn't entirely forced. He just picked her up "by her bootstraps." Maybe it was what she needed after all.

"Seven pounds, six inches," my father said relighting his cigar. "Come on, Cookie, have one. It's a Montecristo," picking up the money from the pot, folding it into his clip. "You don't really need a new car," he said putting the money in his pocket, "And I really need a new shirt."

Chapter 18
Bacon and Eggs—Take One

BACON AND EGGS. A KNIFE, A FORK, A SPOON. TOAST. A SMALL POT. A bowl of sugar. Heavy cream. A woman. An infant. Two pats of butter. An empty cup.

A knock on the door.

"May I come in?" Dr. Reis asked, having already entered the room.

My mother stared at Dr. Reis as if she didn't remember who he was. She smiled weakly.

"How did you sleep?" Dr. Reis asked. He asked that question every time he entered the room even if it was midafternoon. "How did you sleep?' was his gambit, followed almost always by,

"Have you had anything to eat?"

He glanced at the untouched plates of food—having asked the question whose answer was there on the tray, plain as day. "Hospital food," he nodded as he pulled a chair next to her bed. "Some coffee?"

She shook her head.

"Do you mind if I—?"

He poured a cup, took a sip.

My mother waited.

"Ruth—?" Doctors address patients by their first names. "Ruth—?" He took another sip. "Your baby—" Then he coughed, smiled. "This is as bad as what they serve in the cafeteria," he said, amused by the spontaneity, the wit.

Dr. William Reis, a psychiatrist, had been asked to evaluate my mother, because the nurse was concerned whether my mother was in any condition to be sent home. There were concerns that she might be depressed. There were concerns that she might–

"Ruth–?"

Infanticide is not unknown with postpartum women who are depressed.

"Ruth–?"

"Yes?"

Postpartum depression is characterized by depressed mood, tearfulness, anxiety, emotional lability, fatigue, shame, guilt, withdrawal. Psychotic thinking and suicidal ideation are not uncommon. Women with postpartum depression exhibit greater psychomotor retardation and cognitive impairment than those with non-postpartum depression. In their classic study "Why Mothers Die," Lewis and Drife showed that for the first year postpartum the greatest number of deaths were by suicide. Suicide attempts by women with postpartum depression are often violent–"self-incineration, jumping, hanging, drowning, throat cutting."[1] Infanticide by women with postpartum depression is usually related to the psychotic process.

"Have you had anything to eat?"

There were concerns that she might kill me.

"Not surprisingly those women with high suicidal ideation were less responsive to their infants' cues than were depressed but non-suicidal mothers. Often these more suicidal mothers were passive and demonstrated helplessness in their interactions with their infants. Often these more suicidal mothers–

"Your baby is crying," Dr. Reis said.

"–have been known to be less responsive to verbal utterances and to provide less tactile stimulation."[2]

Like a dam that was stressed for want of bedding, too many predators, too little food, my mother was stressed.

She sat in the bed propped up on pillows. "He cries all the time," she said.

"He's two days old," Dr. Reis said.

"Postpartum depression is associated with disturbances in the mother-infant relationship as well as long-term negative consequences for the child in cognitive, behavioral, and social emotional development."[3]

"He cries all the time," she said again. "I can't get him to stop."

"Why don't you hold him," he offered.

"Relationships between depressed mothers and their infants are often characterized by impairments in the process of mutual regulation. . . . For example mothers can be disengaged from their infants, talk less, show fewer facial expressions, share less of their attention, less touch."[4]

All this suggested an "impairment" in the early attachment bond, an impairment in the relationship between oxytocin and cortisol that inhibits the mother from forming a bond.

"I don't—"

Dr. Reis sat for a few more minutes watching my mother as she struggled with what she should do, with what she imagined he wanted her to do, with what she imagined some other mother would do.

He took another sip of coffee.

"I can't," she said as she watched me lying next to her on the bed.

Dr. Reis put down the coffee, stood up, "I'll hold him," Dr. Reis said as he picked me up and rocked me back and forth on his chest. Then he sang a song, perhaps one he had sung to his own sons when they were just as new.

Hush you bye

Don't you cry

Go to sleepy little baby

I quieted down. My parasympathetic nervous system was responding to his hands, his arms, to the movement of his chest. My parasympathetic nervous system was responding to the song.

When you wake
You shall have—
I drooled on his shoulder.

"He's quiet," Dr. Reis said.

"He needs sleep," my mother said.

"He needs you," Dr. Reis said.

"The incidence of maternal mental illness is staggering," Catherine Monk said.[5]

"I'm afraid if I hold him, I might drop him."

"Ruth—"

"What?"

"You won't drop him," Dr. Reis said returning me to her chest. "Sing to him."

"I, I can't," she said.

"Ruth—?"

"I can't."

He moved me a little higher. "I'll let the nurse know."

"Know what?" she asked folding me onto her chest.

"That you won't drop him," he said.

Chapter 19

Bacon and Eggs—Take Two

Bacon and eggs. A knife, a fork, a spoon. Toast. A small pot. A bowl of sugar. Heavy cream. A woman. An infant. Two pats of butter. A cup of coffee, half drunk.

I started to cry.

"Hush you bye" my mother said. "Don't you cry—"

I continued to cry.

"Katherine!" she called. "Katherine!"

"The infant's physiological state is dyadically regulated with the caregiver functioning as an external regulatory component of the infant's regulatory system—"[1]

It has been demonstrated, most compellingly by the research of Myron Hofer, that this mother-infant attachment represents a developmental process whereby the mother, guided by affect, serves as an external regulator of her neonate's internal physiology.

The mother's control at this early stage includes such core functions as heart rate, vascular resistance, respiratory rate, rate of protein synthesis, sympathetic/parasympathetic tone, hypothalamic-pituitary-adrenal function, sleep patterns, body temperature, oxygen consumption, growth hormone level, immunologic reactions, oxytocin level, endorphin level. This regulation by the mother is guided largely by affect, which provides the mother with clues as to the condition of her neonate's internal state.

Her actions are through the attachment bond onto these biologic systems.

Hofer's work broke this overall regulation down and showed that specific aspects of maternal care (or its lack) had specific consequences for the neonate. And thus if the dam failed to provide her pup with ample milk, respiration and oxygen consumption would decline. If she failed to keep her pup warm, its levels of dopamine and noradrenaline would fall. The rate of growth hormone secretion was shown to be determined by the tactile stimulation she provides. Because a newborn mammal's homeostatic system is relatively open, its control is delegated to the mother, which further allows her to biologically inform her neonate's developing core.[2]

"Katherine—?"

The mother's inability to soothe is disorganizing to both mother and child.

"Hush, hush—please baby don't don't cry, why can't you just stop. Baby stop, stop—"

The mother's failure to soothe activates the baby's hypothalam-ic-pituitary-adrenal axis as well as the autonomic nervous system, shifting it from parasympathetic to sympathetic dominance.

"Please why won't you just—?"

The mother's failure to soothe also activates her own primitive sense of shame as registered in the insular and cingulate cortices, two more primitive aspects of the cortex.

"Katherine—"

"Many mothers with postpartum depression experience shame and humiliation and view themselves as the worst mothers in the world; they imagine that others see them this way as well."[3]

"Katherine—"

The nurse entered. "There, there," she said as she picked me up off of my mother's chest. My mother stared at the nurse. There was no expression on her face. "Are you all right?" Nurse Katherine asked.

"Maternal depression disrupts the mutual regulatory process and constitutes a break. . . . The break is brought about by the effects of depression on maternal affect and responsiveness."

"Ruth—?" Katherine asked.

"Depression compromises the mother's capacity to mutually regulate. . . .Withdrawn mothers were disengaged, unresponsive, and affectively flat, and did little to support their infants' activities."[4]

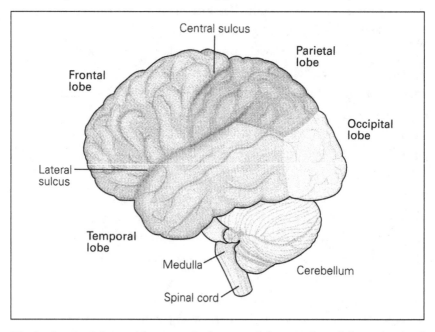

The brainstem is located between the brain and the spinal cord. Several critical neurotransmitters are synthesized in the brainstem, including noradrenaline from the locus coeruleus in the medulla oblongata.

When there is sensory stimulation from the mother, there is a large influx of noradrenaline that is released from the locus coeruleus in the medulla oblongata—at the base of the brain stem. At the molecular level the release of noradrenaline increases the activation of immediate-early response genes which supports "synapse formation, neurogenesis, and learning. This is a common cellular cascade in many species that supports learning. This critical role of noradrenaline is a strong feature of infant attachment and infant learning."[5]

The interpersonal response of the mother is critical to the physiological/molecular response of the infant. It continues the enormous rate of growth and learning—a rate of 40,000 new synapses per second—that had been ongoing during the third trimester (Monk et al).

In addition to the stimulation of the release of noradrenaline for preference learning, the mother's presence attenuates her pup's avoidance learning—its response to fear. The mother's presence blocks the hypothalamic-pituitary-adrenal (HPA) axis. If the HPA axis is blocked, corticosteroids are not released. If corticosteroids are not released, fear learning at the amygdala stops.

"At this early stage of development, rat pups have a hyporesponsive stress period that defines an age range in which stress induced corticosterone (cortisol in primates) release is greatly attenuated."[6]

Early in life, mammals have a hyporesponsive hypothalamic-pituitary-adrenal axis (the HPA axis). Fear learning in the amygdala (a cluster of neurons in the medial temporal cortex) requires the input of corticosterone from the HPA. In rat pups, because the HPA is hyporesponsive for the first ten weeks of life, fear learning is effectively turned off. The ongoing presence of the dam increases the length of this hyporesponsive period. Thus, up to a certain age the pup does not learn what to avoid. It learns only what to approach. This hyporesponsive period has been studied extensively in rats. It is almost certainly true for all mammals.

"He's quiet," said Nurse Katherine.

"He's quiet because of you," my mother replied.

This makes biologic sense. The only presence the rat pup should safely encounter in the nest is its siblings or its dam. If the pup were to encounter a cat, what it might learn wouldn't matter.

"There, there," Katherine said as she wiped the drool from my face.

"The little one . . . felt only the soft brushing of his mother's tongue as it ran over his little coat while she washed him, warmed him, kissed him. He smelled only the closeness of his mother's body. He snuggled to be as near as possible to her."[7]

An infant will attach to the mother. A fawn will attach to the doe. A pup will attach to the dam—good, bad, depressed, even dead. It's what mammals do. We attach.

Katherine placed me back on my mother's chest.

"As the little fawn suckled, his mother continued to caress her little one. 'Bambi,' she whispered, 'my little Bambi.'"[8]

"He's better with you," my mother said, lifting me off of her chest.

And when attachment is lost or disturbed, the pup moves from parasympathetic to sympathetic dominance. It reacts with distress.

I started to cry.

Chapter 20

The Still Face

FREUD'S IDEA ON THE NATURE OF THE TIE BETWEEN MOTHER AND INFANT was the dominant theory of attachment for much of the twentieth century. According to Freud, the infant was not primarily attached to the mother. The infant was primarily attached to itself. "An infant at the breast does not as yet distinguish his ego from the external world."[1]

Thus "an infant at the breast" is unaware of "the breast." Its sense of the world includes only "ego." Only "I." Only self. The power of the wish is what gives the infant the illusion that everything it desires needs only to be imagined—this illusion makes the "I" all encompassing and enough. There was no need nor sense of a "thou," because the "I" was in total control of the primary wish.

The existence of the "other" and thus the need to attach was something that the infant had to accept and to learn only *after* the failure of the wish. Thus the learning was representative of a secondary state when the true weakness of the "I" was brought home. The primary state was one of pure wish where the "pleasure principle" operated and during which the infant needed absolutely nothing—because the infant "believed" that all of its needs were being fulfilled by the supernatural power of the "I" and the power of its "wish." On the basis of this theory, Freud could write "At birth no object existed."[2] For Freud the neonate existed in a world of its own

125

where nothing existed except "I" and where everything was freely, wishfully gratified. This glorious world lasted only until the point soon after birth when the necessities of life were found to exist outside of the "I" and their satisfactions were not free—that is to say when the "pleasure principle" was forced to give way to the "reality principle."

Darwin had challenged Freud's idea long before Freud had put the idea into print. In 1872, in *The Expression of the Emotions In Man and Animal*, a book which was in Freud's library and which Freud had most certainly read (and had chosen to ignore), Darwin wrote, "The movements of expression in the face and body whatever their origin may have been, are in themselves of much importance to our welfare."[3] Darwin reasoned that emotional expression was active from the very first because a newborn needed to attach from the very first.

It would take psychoanalysis nearly seventy-five years to recognize the importance of Darwin's earlier observations. It was John Bowlby in his series of books—*Attachment*, *Separation*, and *Loss*—who was the first member of the psychoanalytic establishment to formally challenge Freud's idea of the autonomous ego, the power of infantile wish, the pleasure principle.

Bowlby had a home in the north of England near a marsh. Unlike Freud, who chose not to observe infants or children—"Why do I not go into the nursery and experiment with Annerl (his youngest, then infant daughter)? . . . Because I have no time for it."[4] Bowlby, like Darwin, observed the wildlife near his home—mostly birds, as well as the wildlife in his home, mostly his children.

Bowlby's views on attachment, with some modification, are now well accepted. But when Bowlby first presented his ideas, they were scandalous. His own analyst, Joan Riviere, a Freudian disciple and a well-known analyst in her own right, was outraged. Melanie Klein, one of Bowlby's supervisors, scoffed at his betrayal of analytic lore. At the British Psychoanalytic Institute in 1964, as Bowlby was preparing to deliver a paper, one of the attendees on learning the identity of that evening's speaker responded, "Bowlby—? Give me Barabbas."

Bowlby was subsequently rejected by the British Psychoanalytic Society essentially for being observant.

Meanwhile in Canada at the University of Toronto just before the outbreak of the Second World War, a woman named Mary Salter was making observations on children relating to their emotional security. In her thesis she wrote, "When safety in the family is lacking, the individual is handicapped by the lack of a secure base."

While still at University, she met a man named Leonard Ainsworth. They dated, loved, married. Mary Salter became Mary Ainsworth. The couple moved to London where she responded to an ad in the *London Times*: "Seeking assistant to work with mothers and infants." The ad had been placed by John Bowlby. Ainsworth and Bowlby worked together as they each developed theories stemming from observations on the interaction between mother and infant.

In her work Ainsworth noted a stability that seemed to derive from the "secure base" that she had observed in some families. She recognized that babies whose mothers had been highly responsive to their child's cries during the early months tended to cry less, relying for communication on facial expressions, gestures, vocalizations. Her work laid a foundation for other researchers. "A child forms a secure attachment when the caregiver is available to the child, shows sensitivity to his or her needs and supports his or her behavioral expression but also provides a secure base for the child to explore the world and develop other relationships."[5] Ainsworth developed a test, the Strange Situation, which rated the quality of the base between mother and child.

In 1975 Ed Tronick, leaning on the theories of Ainsworth and Bowlby, presented the results of his experiments with children at a meeting of the Society for Research in Child Development. It was called the Still Face Experiment.

A baby and mother are seated. The mother starts by playing with her baby, smiling, cooing, reacting. Then she turns away, and when she turns back, she keeps her face still for two minutes. At first the baby attempts to get a response from the mother. The baby seems confused. As the baby's attempts to connect continue to get no response, the baby starts to show distress. The baby cries and then shouts. As attempts to connect continue to be ignored, the baby often loses postural control. At the end of the two minutes of non-responsiveness, the baby becomes withdrawn and hopeless—no longer attempting to elicit the mother's response.

After the still face portion of the experiment ends and the mother returns to interaction with her baby, the joyfulness of the reunion and the relief in the baby is clear.

The still face experiment is an example of just how much the infant relies on the mother to process his/her emotion. Without the mother's help, the baby is emotionally lost. The infant is not capable of emotional self-regulation. The still face experiment is a reflection of an essential task of the first year of human life—"to create a secure attachment bond of emotional communication and interactive regulation between the infant and the mother. . . . The intersubjective dialogue between mother and infant consist of signals produced by the autonomic involuntary nervous system in both parties."

"The attachment relationship mediates the dyadic regulation of emotion, wherein the mother co-regulates the infant's postnatally developing autonomic nervous system and thereby the infant's homeostatic state."[6]

"Watching a mother interact with her infant can be compared to a very sensitive and nuanced dance where each partner responds to the other in a complex and sometimes subtle way. This dance involves touch, eye contact, facial expression, verbal expression. The attunement of the mother to her infant's cues is often an unconscious process and is a significant predictor of the ability to exist in synchrony with her infant. These experiences involve significant neurobiological events that have lifelong implications."[7]

When affectively synchronized, these mother-infant exchanges promote homeostatic regulation of critical neurotransmitters. And thus when a mother responds to the affect of her child, she is not just responding to emotions. She is regulating her child's psycho-physiological state.

"But when infants' attempts fail to repair the interaction . . . the disengagement is profound . . . reminiscent of the withdrawal of Harlow's isolated monkey."[8] Harry Harlow performed experiments with rhesus monkeys in the mid-1950s that would be rejected today by an institutional review board as cruel and inhumane. It was groundbreaking in its day. Harlow removed a newborn monkey from its mother and provided the infant with a cloth or a wire monkey surrogate. The "surrogate" provided a tactile surface and a bottle of milk—but nothing more. The infant monkey formed a powerful attachment bond to its "mother." "It is important to note that regardless of the quality of the care received by the infant, an attachment is still formed."[9] The infant mammal has one and only one job—to attach, no matter what.

Harlow presented the findings of his experiments at the annual Convention of the American Psychological association in Washington, DC. on August 8, 1958. Harlow described how "the cloth mother provided a psychological 'base of operations.'. . . But if the cloth mother were absent, the monkey pups would rush across the test room and throw themselves facedown on the floor, clutching their heads and bodies and screaming their distress." Harlow entitled the presention, "Love in Infant Monkeys"[10] demonstrating the infant monkeys' need for their cloth mothers. What Harlow failed to recognize was the catastrophic damage that the absence of their simian mothers had already caused.

Harlow thus demonstrated experimentally an aspect of what Bowlby and Ainsworth and others had been observing since the end of the second world war—that the bond between an infant and care provider was more than the nutritional, transactional bond that Freud had described. The bond was psychobiological and essential. Without an effective attachment bond, the neonate suffered—whether human or nonhuman, primate or mammal.

I started to cry. My mother watched.

"She wasn't ready to be a mother," Aunt Fran said.

"Can I have another?" I asked as I finished my chocolate egg cream.

"You only get one mother," Aunt Fran said smiling to herself at the joke that I didn't get.

It was a bond that did not depend solely on the neonate. The full expression of the bond depended on the actions of both the mother and the infant, on the dam and the pup. The relationship is physiologically as well as psychologically dependent on the two acting as one. "The infant's physiological state is dyadically regulated with the caregiver functioning as an external regulatory component of the infant's regulatory system."[11] Without that external regulator many biological systems will start to fail, fail to thrive.

I continued to cry.

"Aunt Fran?"

"Infants of withdrawn mothers were more likely to protest and to be distressed . . . suggesting that maternal withdrawal may be particularly aversive to young infants."[12]

My mother kept stroking my head as I cried. "What's wrong?" she asked. "Please tell me. What do you want from me? Tell me what to do?" she said as if asking for direction. Maybe she was.

"There was something wrong with your mother," Aunt Fran said.

"What?"

"Finish your chocolate egg cream."

"I did."

Aunt Fran looked off at the waiter.

"Maternal depression disrupts the establishment of a dyadic-infant-mother system." The mother must metabolize experience and her infant's reaction to it, and thereby communicate to the infant's autonomic nervous system and to the infant's hypothalamic-pituitary-adrenal axis that the infant is safe. She must communicate this to "primary physiologic systems that are critical for emotional as well as biological survival."[13] The infant, the pup, is unable to regulate these systems. And if the mother's/the dam's actions do not regulate these systems, the infant/pup begins to experience that something is wrong, but does not know what it is and has no capacity to regulate what it cannot locate. So it cries.

"The protest signals are aimed at bringing the primary attachment figure back. Failure to return results in despair."[14]

"Stop crying. Please stop crying."

"In essence the mother is not just communicating affect *to* her infant. She is regulating affect *in* her infant through her capacity to regulate her infant's core physiologic systems."[15] At this stage the regulation is not under the infant's voluntary control. It is under the involuntary control of the autonomic nervous system and the HPA axis. And these are both partially controlled by outside forces—such as the mother or the dam or the temperature of the air or the fullness of the belly.

"Do you want more milk? Is that what you want? Okay, here, just suck—" she said moving my mouth to her teat. "Suck."

And I did.

But only for a minute and then I started to cry once again.

"Can I have another?" I asked slurping the dregs to show that there was nothing left.

"Katherine!" my mother called out, but Katherine was outside on her break, having a smoke.

"Katherine!"

I cried even more.

"In the absence of the mother, an infant experiences extremes of under- and over-arousal that are physiologically disorganizing."[16]

Like one of Harlow's monkeys, like an infant before a still face, like one of Ainsworth's subjects moving from an insecure base—

"Katherine!"

"She wasn't ready to be a mother," Aunt Fran said.

And I cried, not knowing what that meant. Not when I was two days old. Not when I was at Lundy's half listening to Aunt Fran. Not when Tony, with the cloth draped over his arm, arrived with another glass of chocolate egg cream.

"What do you say?" Aunt Fran said.

"Katherine," my mother said.

"Thank you," I said.

"What's wrong?" Katherine asked when she got back from her break.

Bacon and eggs. A knife, a fork, a spoon. Toast. A small pot. A bowl of sugar. Heavy cream. A woman. An infant. Two pats of butter. A cup of coffee half drunk.

"Katherine—" she said lifting me for the nurse. Then she whispered, "I'm no good." And like one of those monkeys "clutching their heads and screaming their distress" that Harry Harlow described in his 1958 presentation "Love in Infant Monkeys"—

"I'm no good."

—I just cried.

"Infants are born into a complex social world with an innate capacity for social relationships. A major developmental task in the first year is to develop at least one attachment relationship, which is characterized by a preference for a specific caregiver (or more than one), who is expected to care for the infant and with whom the infant shares a close, emotional bond. The capacity for social relatedness ensures the child's survival."

I just cried.

"I'm no good."

"Attachment behaviors, such as crying and smiling, are present at birth to facilitate this process; these behaviors increase the likelihood that a caregiver will respond to, care for, and protect the child. Caregivers also assist considerably with the infant's emotional and behavioral regulation through their responses to infant cues."[17]

"Here," Katherine said, handing her a sheet of paper. "I did this for you."

"What is it?"

"It's all written out."

"Please, Katherine," my mother said, lifting me up, "take the boy."

Chapter 21

Electric Eels

"THERE IS EVIDENCE THAT ANCIENT ROMANS USED THE CURRENT GEN-erated by electric eels for the treatment of headaches, gout, and to assist in obstetrical procedures."

In 1752 Benjamin Franklin recorded the use of an "electro static machine to cure a woman of hysterical fits."

She kept repeating, "I'm no good," more and more softly until she was just moving her lips as she read what Katherine had written on the sheet of paper.

"I'm no good."

In 1803 a physicist named Giovanni Aldini, convinced that electricity was the "vital force" between brain and muscle, was granted permission to test his electrical apparatus—consisting of two conducting rods and a battery—on the body of a condemned murderer named George Foster. After being hanged at Newgate Prison for having murdered his wife, Foster's corpse was taken to Aldini's laboratory where the application of electricity caused the facial muscles to contort, an eye to open, the right hand to lift off the gurney.

Mary Shelley learned of Aldini's demonstrations. She used electricity to bring her "monster" to life when she wrote *Frankenstein*.

My mother kept moving her lips as she lay on her side reading the sheet of paper, watching me cry.

Aldini remarked, "My God, he's lifted an arm. He's just opened an eye!" He's alive!

In the late nineteenth century, febrile convulsions were believed to have a beneficial effect on "a wide variety of disorders." As a result, Julius Wagner-Jauregg injected the blood of a patient who suffered from malaria into nine patients with severe mental illness. Three of the nine showed "complete recovery."

Early in the twentieth century, there had been a general belief that a "biologic antagonism" existed between epilepsy and schizophrenia. This led Ladislas Meduna from the University of Budapest in January 1934 to use intramuscular injections of camphor to induce seizures in a patient suffering from schizophrenia. The improvement was described as "dramatic."

Ugo Cerletti, the head of the department of neuropsychiatry at the University of Rome, reasoned that electricity itself could replace biologic agents to induce seizures. He was at first reluctant to test his theory. "The idea of submitting a man to convulsant electric discharges was considered as utopian, barbaric, and dangerous; in everyone's mind was the specter of the electric chair." Nonetheless in April 1938, Cerletti performed the first electroconvulsive therapy (ECT) on a forty-year-old homeless schizophrenic who had just arrived at the Rome railway station from Milan. He was picked up by railway security with neither a ticket nor identifying papers. After a total of fifteen treatments, the patient was discharged "in complete remission." Cerletti gave the first public presentation of ECT at the Medical Academy of Rome one month later. The use of ECT spread rapidly throughout Europe. By 1943, it was being used extensively in America.[1]

In January, three months after I was born, my mother received the first of twelve treatments of bilateral ECT.

My mother stroked my head softly and gently confessed, "It would be better, it would be better, it would be better, it would be better," she said over and over as if singing a lullaby withholding the last line until the very end, "It would be better," she said—

A knock on the door. An aide entered. "Good morning," he said. "Beautiful baby." He had come to pick up the tray. "You didn't touch a thing?" the aide said, looking at the plates of food. "You didn't like it?"

Bacon and eggs. A knife, a fork, a spoon. Toast. A small pot. A bowl of sugar. Heavy cream. A woman. An infant. Two pats of butter. A cup of coffee, half drunk.

"If I were dead," she finally said.

The aide looked up at my mother. "Hospital food," he said picking up the tray. "Too much pepper, not enough salt. Lots of people feel the very same way," he said, assuming my mother was making a remark he had heard many people say. And as he left the room, he turned and said, "Have a nice day."

Nurse Katherine entered, followed by Dr. Reis. It was almost noon.

"So Ruth, how did you sleep?"

Chapter 22
Holding Her Hand

THE WOMAN WAS WHEELED INTO THE TREATMENT ROOM ON A GURNEY, wearing a blue-and-white hospital gown. Underneath she wore only panties. The nurse and the anesthesiologist helped slide her onto the table. "That's it," the nurse cheerfully said. A cuff was placed around her left lower leg. "Just take this into your mouth," as a bite plate was offered to prevent the seizure from breaking her teeth. "How do you feel?" the anesthesiologist asked as he inserted a sixteen-gauge needle into a vein. It was hard for her to talk around the rubber plate in her mouth. An elastic band with electrodes was fastened round her head. A pulse oximeter was placed on the first finger of her right hand. "How do you feel?" the anesthesiologist repeated, and again no one really bothered to decipher her garbled response. Her right hand dangled over the side of the table. I picked it up, put it back.

"Are you ready?" the anesthesiologist asked as he arranged vials of succinylcholine, atropine, valium. "I want you to count backward from 100." He picked up the first vial, opened the IV. She started to count, "one hundred, ninety-nine, ninety—" and was gone.

"We are good," the anesthesiologist said as he started to pump oxygen into her lungs, nodded to the electroshock therapist, a psychiatrist named Wallerstein. "Clear," he announced as he pulled the switch delivering 110 volts to the right side of her head.

They all stared at her left foot as the big toe twitched, flexed, and then after thirty seconds, relaxed. The pressure cuff on her leg had prevented the succinylcholine, which paralyzes muscle, from reaching the toe. The flexion of the big toe on her left foot was the only indication of a seizure.

It was the first time I had witnessed ECT. The patient's long hair, slender features, small breasts reminded me a little of my mother, but then all women of a certain age reminded me a little of my mother, especially those who were intent on ending their lives.

"Are you holding the patient's hand, Mr. Brockman?" the psychiatrist, Dr. Wallerstein, asked, exaggerating *Mister*, to emphasize that I was just a student and that he—

"Well, I—"

"Well you—?"

"Well, how do you feel?" Dr. Reis asked taking her hand.

"I, I, I—"

My father came in. "Wonderful morning."

"Yes, it is," Dr. Reis said as he stood up.

"How is she, Doc? And my boy—look at him—healthy and strong— all seven pounds, fingers and toes of him." He moved to the bed, kissed my mother's cheek, stroked her head, turned to Dr. Reis.

"So Doc, my boy—strong, beautiful, smart—and the way he eats. Here, have a cigar."

"Mr. Brockman, what if we went to the hall so your wife can rest?"

"I'd rather be here."

"It would be better if we talked outside."

My father nodded as he unwrapped the band from a cigar. "For fifteen years my wife and I have been trying and now—Well, just look at him, Doc, he's got what it takes, gonna be a man, this boy—and the way he eats. I gotta tell ya with an appetite like that. And handsome! A lawyer, a judge, Doc the kid could be in the movies, a star—"

"Your wife—"

"Here, please, Montecristo—only the best."

"Mr. Brockman—"

"You don't smoke?"

"She is not well."

"She's tired."

"It's more than fatigue."

My father started the process of lighting the cigar. He took a few puffs and a long look at Reis. "Have I seen you before? Are you her doctor?"

"I am her psychiatrist."

"Her what—?"

"Mr. Brockman—"

"She doesn't need a psychiatrist."

"—your wife suffers from a very severe postpartum—"

"She needs rest."

"She has hardly eaten or slept—she has lost weight."

"She just gave birth."

My father turned to Katherine, who was pouring milk from a can into a bottle. There was an orange rubber nipple—

"What are you doing?"

"I am preparing his formula."

"He doesn't need formula. He needs a breast. Give him back to his mother."

"During the first week postpartum, depressed mothers have been found to be at increased risk for feeling unsatisfied with breastfeeding and were experiencing significant breastfeeding problems."[1]

"Mr. Brockman, I think that your wife—"

"Give him to his mother."

Katherine screwed the orange rubber nipple to the bottle.

"Now."

Katherine returned me to my mother.

I started to gurgle and swim up her chest.

"Just look at him—the boy knows what he needs, what he wants."

He watched as his wife did her best to smile.

"Ruthie," he said.

Dr. Reis stood watching from the foot of the bed.

"Gonna be a lawyer, a senator, maybe a doctor, a real doctor," my father said with a glance at Dr. Reiss. Always the winner, never particularly graceful, but he always came out on top. "Just look at the boy." I made my way to her teat. "Bootstraps," he beamed. "Bootstraps," he said.

What was happening was tearing his heart.

"Bootstraps."

"Mr. Brockman," Nurse Katherine said, "you can't smoke in here."

Chapter 23

America

MY FATHER CAME TO AMERICA THE ELDEST OF FIVE WITH TWO younger brothers, two younger sisters. They arrived just as he turned ten.

Newly arrived needed money. Newlywed Jewish women cut their hair. My grandmother sewed newly cut hair from the heads of newlywed Jews into the heads of newly stitched dolls.

My grandfather made candy. My father drove a horse and buggy across the Brooklyn Bridge delivering candy and dolls to the city.

There was an undeclared race in the family to learn English. My father went to the library near the temple. He got a book to learn English. He practiced in the bathroom in front of the mirror.

He spoke fluently in less than a year while the others continued to gobble like chickens in Yiddish.

It was hard for my grandfather to give up his post as head of the house. But he had little choice—a foreigner in a land that remained foreign. He davened and prayed, went to the shul while my father studied, learned, went nights to Brooklyn Law School.

Shortly after my father married, he got a job at the accounting firm of C.D. Giles and Company. Returning from lunch, one of the law partners approached my father and said, "For what we pay you, we could hire a gentile." My father went on to become head of the firm.

He told that story at my parents' twentieth wedding anniversary. The story made my mother squirm. She tried to get him to stop. He continued right to the end, then told the story of my birth—all seven pounds, six inches of it. That's who my father was. He was proud. He won. Every time. No matter what.

There is a psychobiology of pride, a psychology of will—and should those fail, there is a psychobiology of denial. All of those were entwined in my father's ascent to the pinnacle of the American dream.

"Bootstraps. Pick yourself up. Come on!"

He had started with nothing. Look how far he had come. "We are going to the top!" And as far as the community in Manhattan Beach, Brooklyn, was concerned he had risen to the top.

But when my mother pulled her bootstraps, they snapped.

"For women with established bipolar disorder prior to pregnancy, there is a very high risk of relapse and severe mood disorders in the immediate postpartum with an estimated 35% relapse rate in the postpartum."[1]

Katie Galst, Aunt Fran, and my sisters Jolie and Susan took turns caring for me. I was never alone.

"There is nothing inside," my mother said, pleading to be understood. "I have a child who needs a mother. I am incapable of being a mother."

She looked back at Dr. Reis. "You of all people must understand. Suicide is the best option I have."

Dr. Reis watched her, then said, "Ruth—"

"He is a difficult child," Aunt Fran said.

I just cried.

That was when Katie Galst discovered the hole—that when I lay on my belly something pushed out—indeed a piece of the small bowel would slide into the open inguinal canal, pushing out my bowel. The blood supply was often compromised which was why I cried until someone picked me up—changing my orientation to gravity, allowing the loop of bowel to slide back out, and the blood to flow back.

"He is a difficult child," Aunt Fran said.

"Fran, look at this," Katie Galst said.

"You can't help me," my mother said staring out the window of Dr. Reis's office. His office was across the street from Brooklyn's Prospect Park. "My friends can't help me. No one can help me. A ghost has entered my mind."

It had started to snow. "I am as dead as the leaves waiting to fall from the trees."

"Ruth, please sit down," Dr. Reis said,

In January, three months after being discharged from the obstetrical service, my mother was admitted to the psychiatric service of the Long Island College Hospital where Dr. Reis administered the first of twelve bilateral electroconvulsive treatments to chase any ghosts that had entered my mother's head.

In January, three months after being discharged from the obstetrical service, I was admitted to the pediatric surgical service of the Long Island College Hospital, where Dr. Michael Argensiano closed the hole in my abdominal wall so that no piece of small bowel could reenter my inguinal canal.

Chapter 24

Another Mother

IN FEBRUARY, I WAS HOME AT 169 FALMOUTH STREET IN THE MANHATTAN Beach section of Brooklyn. Katie Galst was holding me in her arms feeding me from the bottle with the orange rubber nipple. She was one of four women who had taken charge—Aunt Fran, my two sisters—Jolie and Susan—and Katie Galst. A fire brigade of strong female recruits.

Katie was singing as I sucked on the rubber nipple.

Faster than fairies, faster than witches,

Bridges and houses, hedges and ditches;

The door opened downstairs. My mother entered, followed by Aunt Fran. My father was outside parking the car. Aunt Fran took my mother's coat and hung it in the hall closet. "Ruthie, give me your hat," Aunt Fran said. But my mother didn't hear or chose to ignore.

"Can I fix you some tea?" Aunt Fran asked.

My mother looked around as if reacquainting herself with a place she once knew—a place she was trying to remember.

"People were petrified of shock treatment. It was a real scary thing. People held you down, trying to hold you because the neck would arch up and they had this big thing they put in your mouth. They convulsed terrible. That's when people broke their backs and everything when they had shock because they weren't sedated."

And charging along like babes with their rattles,
All through the meadows, the horses and cattle—
It was a song that Katie sang often to herself. She never took lovers; never married, never had children. She sung to herself, and later to the dog, Tippy.

The song was better suited to a spinster than a mother.

"And they'd line up the chairs in the hallway and there'd probably be fifteen or twenty people. And they'd take this one in and give her shock and then she'd go to the end of the line and they would blitz them two or three times. It was real scary."[1]

Sabbath candles that had been placed on the table six weeks earlier were still there, waiting to be lit. "Is it Friday?" my mother asked seeing the candles.

"Shall we go upstairs?" Aunt Fran asked.

"Is it Friday?"

"It's Tuesday."

"Then why are candles on the table?"

"You left them."

"Why?"

"Shall we go upstairs?" Aunt Fran asked.

My mother kept staring at the candles.

"Let's go upstairs," Aunt Fran said.

Katie Galst put down the bottle, raised me to her shoulder. She continued to sing as I started to burp almost in time with the song,

All of the sights of the hill and the plain
Fly as thick as the driving rain,

"Why?"

"Because that's where he is."

"Oh," my mother said, "He's upstairs," nodding as if she knew who was there. "Upstairs?"

"Yes," Aunt Fran said.

"Who?"

And ever again, in the wink of an eye

Painted stations whistling by –

My mother followed Aunt Fran to the foot of the stairs, then she stopped in front of the grandfather clock, staring at the painted phases of the moon as if remembering that the clock had been a gift.

"It was a gift," Aunt Fran said.

"Yes," Ruth said. Then she asked, "From whom?"

"It used to belong to Bobe and Zeyde," Aunt Fran said, showing only the slightest hint of emotion.

Ruth stood very still as the clock struck. One, two—she waited till it finished.

"It's ten o'clock."

"Yes."

"In the night?"

"In the morning."

And then she opened the wood-paneled drawer in the belly of the clock.

"Ruthie, what are you doing?" Aunt Fran asked impatient to get back to why they were there.

"Ruthie!"

Aunt Fran watched for a moment, then said, "Ruthie dear, don't overwind the clock. It's very old," unable to contain the urge to correct, "you may break it," she said to her older, smarter, more beautiful sister.

"Shall we go upstairs," Aunt Fran suggested advancing onto the first step, hoping her sister would follow as obedient as she had been when depressed.

"Where?"

"To the bedroom," Aunt Fran said.

"Whose bedroom?" my mother asked.

"Yours," Aunt Fran said. My mother handed the key to Aunt Fran, who put it back in the clock's wooden belly. "Shall we go up?" Aunt Fran said.

"Where?"

Sunlight streamed down through a window at the top of the stairs leaving a strong diagonal shaft—like a spear or a ray of supernatural light.

"*Cosa stai facendo?*"

There is a painting in a small seventeenth-century church in the old city of Siracusa on a cobblestoned street facing the sea— *Cristo scendendo la croce*—one of several hundred scattered over the church-scape of Sicily. Next to the church is an equally charming seventeenth-century building, now a brothel. I stumbled into the brothel one brutally hot summer day having drifted off a path I had never been sure of.

A woman greeted me. "*Sei molto presto sei qui per colazione?*" She was both voluptuous and overweight, but for a teenager whose virginity had only recently been taken, a goddess. She spoke slowly enough to be understood. No, I was not there for breakfast. She had a son who looked "*Proprio come ti,*" and shooed me out of her house, directing me to the church next door suggesting I enter the priesthood—"*Sei abbastanza carina de essere un prete.*" "*Quale?*" She laughed and handed me an orange. "*Vai!*" she said, "*de essere un prete.*" Go be a priest. She said there was a painting there, "*Cristo scendere—La scuole di Caravaggio.*" One of the hundreds from "*la Scuole di Caravaggio.*"

My mother stood at the foot of the stairs, staring up at the light. "Let me take that," Aunt Fran said.

"What?"

"Your purse."

"Why?"

"*Vai.*"

My mother surrendered her purse to Aunt Fran, as my father came through the door. "I'm going to make some coffee," he called, "Does anyone want a cup?"

Aunt Fran shook her head as my mother started to follow her sister, uncertain where she was going or what she might find—squinting into the light coming down from the top of the stairs.

"Ruthie," my father said, "I'll be right up."

147

"Dave—?"

"Just go," he said. "Just go."

"*Vai*," the woman said.

"Jesus hangs in white shroud," the translation under the painting read. "The shroud follows diagonal. The body in the linen is pale as a cloth. Mary Magdalene holds tip of shroud, tenderness, even though He is not down. Even though dead," it read.

"Ruthie—?"

"*Centolire*" was the "*suggerimento*." I left without paying the "*suggerimento*."

"—are you coming?" Aunt Fran said.

"Centolire," a young woman holding a baby who sat on the church steps, said into the light. "Centolire," her hand outstretched. "Centolire." I gave her the first coin I found. She put the baby down. "*Solo cinquenta*," she argued as I walked to the breakwater overlooking the sea. "*Solo cinquenta*," she yelled as the crash of a wave overtook the wails of the child.

"*Gitano*," an old man in uniform said, shaking his head as he slowly ascended the steps to the church.

The voluptuous matron at the brothel called out, "Pietro," as he got to the top, embracing the old man as if she and the postman were lovers.

"Pietro."

Maybe they were.

My mother held on to the rail. When she got to the top of the stairs, she paused to stare into the bathroom, where, as a five-year-old, I would lock myself in a vain attempt to stop her from taking me to the dentist.

"Richard, if you don't open this door, I will call the police." I crawled under the sink. "I'm calling," she said through the door.

Being five, I didn't know that a mother could lie.

"I'm calling the police. Calling right now. . . . Hello. . . . Is this the police? . . . Yes, I would like to report a very bad child—"

"Ruthie—?"

148

"Yes—?"

"Over here," Aunt Fran said directing my mother from the bathroom toward the bedroom. She paused at the threshold staring at the infant sleeping in Katie Galst's arms.

She stood like that for two minutes or more as if her eyes were adjusting to something she couldn't quite make out, as if staring into supernatural light.

"I'm calling the police," she said. "You better open this door."

I opened the door.

Katie Galst stood there holding a child.

The gypsy stood there, "*Solo cinquente.*"

"Is he mine?" my mother finally asked.

I gave the gypsy the rest of the coins I had in my pocket.

"Jesus Joseph and—Ruthie! What, you thought he was mine!?" Katie Galst said. "Yes Ruthie, this is your child!"

"He's beautiful."

"Of course he's beautiful, he's yours."

My mother just stood there, staring.

"Ruthie," Katie said, as if she were Gabriel having come to Coney Island in search of a virgin. "This is your child."

Any virgin.

She stood there.

"Ruthie—"

"How old is he?"

"He was born in October."

"October?"

"Four months—Ruthie, he was born when you gave birth—in October," Katie said as if teaching sex education to a class of seventh-grade girls.

"Can I hold him?"

Katie moved toward her.

As Katie lifted me off her chest, my mother's arms reached forward—

"He's beautiful," my mother said again.

"Ruthie," Katie said. "He's yours."

I started to gurgle.

She rocked me gently in her arms. "He's beautiful."

I gurgled. She gurgled. I made a face. She made a face. This went on. "He's making sounds," she said. Katie just smiled, "He's gurgling," she said. I gurgled. She gurgled. Then she asked, "What is your name?" as if that were the most natural thing for a mother to ask her child.

"His name is Richard," Katie Galst said.

"Richard?"

"Yes."

My mother held me close as she nodded, "Richard." Then she repeated, "Richard."

Keeping my name active and alive in the prefrontal cortex where working memory keeps a thought in mind.

"Richard," she said again.

"The frontal lobes are essential for performing tasks that require holding information when memory is being reconstructed for the purpose of making some response. . . . The frontal lobes hold material in working memory to guide ongoing behavior and cognition."[2]

"Yes," Katie said, "his name is Richard."

And as she made faces at me and as I made faces at her, Katie Galst softly sang,

Here is a child who clambers and scrambles,

All by himself and gathering brambles—

And here is a mill and there is a river;

Each a glimpse and gone for ever!

"Richard is your son," Katie Galst said, "and you are his mother."

"I have a son," my mother said, looking straight into my now open eyes. "And you have a mother," touching my face, nuzzling hers into mine.

She stared at me, then repeated, "You are my son," as if it were the first time she had heard of such a thing.

"After ECT most patients have gaps in their memory for events that occurred close in time to the course of ECT, but the amnesia may extend back months or years."[3]

Faster than fairies, faster than witches,
Bridges and houses, hedges and ditches;
And charging along like babes with their rattles,
All through the meadows, the horses and cattle—

There was general agreement in the medical community that ECT was effective, but no one could explain just how or why.

All of the sights of the hill and the plain
Fly as thick as the driving rain,

"The most advanced of our present electroshock therapists must confess that they know only about the effects of their methods and nothing about the cause and the other determining factors regarding the influence of electricity upon our body and its nervous system in general upon mental abnormalities in particular."[4]

And ever again, in the wink of an eye
Painted stations whistle by.

"You are beautiful," my mother whispered. Then to Aunt Fran, "He is beautiful."

"Yes, he is," Aunt Fran said.

My mother started to hum, then sing, the song that Katie had sung that she had first heard Katie sing a long time ago—

Here is a child who clambers and scrambles,
All by himself and gathering brambles—

And then she burst into tears.

Katie finished the song—

And here is a mill and there is a river
Each a glimpse and gone forever!

"Ruthie—?" Aunt Fran—

I opened my eyes.

"Ruthie—?"

"I have a son," my mother said, tears now flowing like rain. "I have a son. And his name is Richard."

A cloud passed overhead causing the light from the window to go from bright to dark—chiaroscuro—*Cristo scendere* a block from the ocean, two blocks from the bay. *Cristo scendere*, Coney Island.

And then she turned to me and smiled and gurgled, and then she said, "Richard—" and I gurgled. And then she said, "Richard, can you forgive me?" And I gurgled.

"Yes," Katie said. "You have a son," whispering softly as she put her arms around mother and child, around my mother and me. "You are his mother. You have a son. This is your son."

"Thank you," my mother said to Katie Galst. "Thank you," she said still unsure of who I was, where she was, what Katie Galst had done. "Thank you." I made more gurgles. And then she nodded and gurgled a little more confidently. "And you must be. You must be. You! You!" and then she smiled and gurgled and said, "You must be my son!" And then I gurgled and spun my arms as if her words were the most amazing sounds I had ever heard. "You, you, you must be—my son! Yes you are, and I, I, I must be—" she held me up in front of her so we were both staring into each other's eyes as if we were one. "Your mother!"

This primitive, "open" bond between mother and baby, "makes one being out of the two."[5]

"You are my son," my mother said, "and I am your mother whether you like it or not," which caused us both to gurgle wildly as if we had just heard one of Sam Levenson's funniest jokes.

"—whether you like it or not," and we all gurgled and gurgled and—

Chapter 25

He Had a Hat

SAM LEVENSON PLAYED PINOCHLE EVERY THURSDAY IN THE BASEMENT of our house at 169 Falmouth Street. Uncle Cookie, Uncle Marty, my father, and Sam Levenson. The Four Jacks. It made no sense.

"Sam, it's your bid."

"Diamonds."

"We've already played diamonds," Uncle Cookie said.

"A Jewish grandfather takes his grandchildren to the beach—"

"Sam, I hate to interrupt, but it's your bid."

"You think I can't play pinochle and tell a joke?" He put down the ten of clubs. "Clubs."

"Thank you."

"You're welcome. So the grandchildren are playing in the sand when a massive wave comes and pulls the smallest child into the water—"

"The African Queen," Uncle Cookie said, playing the queen of clubs.

"That's racist."

"That's funny."

"It's not funny."

"It is."

"Panicked, the grandfather prays. 'God, please bring him back. You must let him live!' Suddenly an even bigger wave bursts out of

153

the ocean, setting the little boy down right at his grandfather's feet. Dave, are you listening?" Sam Levenson asked.

"I'm lighting my cigar."

"So the grandfather scoops his grandchild into his arms and stares up at the sky, and yells, 'He had a hat!'" Sam said, laughing uncontrollably as he stared up at the joists, pipes, and wires that ran overhead. "He had a hat."

"I don't get it," Uncle Cookie said.

"You don't deserve," Sam said.

"Jack of clubs."

"I remember that day," Katie Galst said.

"Random prenatal stress in rat dams induces behavioral changes in the off-spring persisting into adulthood which are consistent with increased emotionality and fearfulness. . . . Handling (of the pups) completely reversed all the behavioral deficits."[1]

Fifteen years later, fifteen years after "that day," I knocked on Katie's door. A voice from inside called out, "It's open."

I opened the door. Smells overwhelmed. It's amazing how smell—

"In here," she yelled out.

Katie was sitting in her La-Z-Boy chair. *The Honeymooners* was on. Tippy, the dog who years before had followed Katie home from the beach, lay curled at her feet. A box of Kleenex was on the table next to her chair. Wads of tissue littered the floor.

"I remember how she just stood there at the top of the stairs," Katie said. "Like she was lost."

"'Ruthie, come in,' I said when I heard her on the stairs. 'We've been waiting.' Your mother just stood at the door. Aunt Fran just behind. I never really liked your Aunt Fran. I almost felt guilty when I learned she had died.

"'Ruthie, damn it all—come over here and take the child. He's heavy.' She just stared. 'Ruthie!' I said stomping my foot.'" Tippy looked up.

And then Katie started to laugh—"I'll be damned but that's what

I said! 'He's heavy!'" and then she started to cough. "Don't look at me like that."

"Do you want some water? Or tea?" I asked.

She kept coughing up pinkish gobs into the white Kleenex that she tossed to the floor.

"Well damn," she said as she coughed up more, "Why in hell would I want tea?" The dog stood, circled, lay back down. "Water," she said tossing another tissue. And that's when I thought of Lundy's. The table clothes at Lundy's were checkered red and white.

Cell assembly.

Katie managed one more drag on her cigarette. "Only thing that stops it. Thank God for these," she said sucking hard. "Get me some water."

I got up to get her some water when she went back to her story, "She just stood there like she was somebody's muse. Maybe she was. Maybe yours. How is your father?"

"Fine."

"Remarried?"

"You know."

"Unhappily?

"Well—"

"What I heard," Katie said, taking another deep drag. "Then finally your mother said, 'Katie—' And I waited with you in my arms, waiting for her to say something more. And finally she said,

"'He's a beautiful boy.'"

"And then I said, "Well of course he's beautiful, Ruthie. He's yours." Katie started to laugh. And cough. She took another drag. "And then your mother crossed into the room, like it was hers, which it was, came right up to you like you were hers, which you were—"

"'Can I hold him?' she says. And that's when I picked you off my shoulder, and handed you over. 'Ruthie, he's yours.' And that's when she smiles—first time since you were born. And then you smile as if you'd been waiting for that smile all along." Katie coughed.

"She recognized me?"

"She recognized you."

"I recognized her?"

"You recognized her," Katie said. Then she took a long last suck on her cigarette before snuffing it out. "This is the ashtray you gave me. Orange and brown! Why I never threw it out."

"I was in the first grade."

"And then the damndest thing," Katie said, shaking her head.

I looked at Katie as she continued to stir the tobacco and ash like she was reading leaves, conjuring the past.

"I was just watching your mother, and all the while she was staring at you. Like she was afraid if she shifted her eyes, you might disappear or she might forget who you were.

"'Katie,' she said, 'take my hat.' So I took her hat—the green hat she always wore—and then I just watched her, not sure I could trust my eyes," Katie said.

"What?"

"She was unbuttoning her shirt."

"My mother?"

"'Ruthie, what are you doing?' I said, thinking maybe all that shock had gone to her head—well I guess it did. And the next thing you know, her shirt just fell to the floor. And then she turned and back over her shoulder said, 'Help me.'"

"'Help you what?'"

"'I'd do it myself but as you can see both my hands—'"

"Well both her hands were holding you. And so I did. I undid her bra. And then she just slipped out an arm, and her bra just fell to the floor."

"Your Aunt Fran started to say something and I knew, don't ask me how, but I knew it was gonna be mean, it was the way your Aunt Fran could be—about how Ruthie hadn't been able to produce enough milk, so I just—

"'Don't you dare!' right at her,"

"—as your mother brought you to her breast. Like it was full, like it was flowing. Like it had 'let down' the way it was supposed."

Katie leaned back in her La-Z-Boy chair.

"And you just sucked—like it had."

The light from the window changed.

"Get me some water."

The dog made one of those sounds dogs make when they're in a dream chasing a rabbit.

"Despite everything," Katie said, "she loved you with all of her heart."

"What do you mean?"

Katie closed her eyes. "Get me some water."

The dog made another one of those sounds.

"Get me some water."

I went to the kitchen. Dirty dishes lay in the sink. I filled a glass from the tap.

When I got back, Katie was asleep. I set the glass on the table. Tippy growled.

I never liked Tippy.

Tippy never liked me.

Katie Galst died the next week.

Chapter 26

Two Mothers—Take One

IN 1967 SIGI LEVINE AND VICTOR DENENBERG MADE WHAT SEEMED LIKE minor observations. They noted that rat pups, when briefly handled during the first seven days of their lives demonstrated less "stress" when they were fully mature.

The scientists observed that "The non-handled animal appears to have much less discrimination with regard to the test situation and reacts with a large corticosterone response (a large stress response) regardless of the specific aspects of the test situations."[1]

In other words, rat pups that were taken briefly from their home cage, gently stroked with a paintbrush, and then returned to their home cage (and thus returned to their anxiously awaiting dams), these pups were emotionally different than pups that were not taken from the cage, not handled, not stroked with a soft paintbrush during their first seven days of life. And further that these handled pups, when mature, made more "discriminating" decisions as to what warranted a full stress response and what did not. They were less fearful. They had more control. Something had changed. And whatever that something was lasted for the rest of the animals' lives.

These seemingly "minor" observations marked the beginning of experimental epigenetics. In other words, these minor observations were major.

Several research teams, including a group in Montreal headed by Michael Meaney, continued the investigations of Levine and Denenberg. They noted that when the pup was reunited with the dam, it was not the pup but the dam whose behaviors had changed.

"Formal observations showed that when the dam is reunited with the pups, she immediately approaches the pups, to restore maternal care followed by a sustained increase in several forms of maternal behaviors. These behaviors include increased licking and grooming (LG) and crouching over the pups in an active form of nursing known as arched-back nursing (ABN)."[2]

Meaney and his group selectively bred rat dams that naturally displayed the maternal characteristics of either low-licking and grooming (LG)/low-arched-back nursing (ABN) or high licking and grooming/high-arched-back nursing dams. The pups raised by high LG/ABN dams were emotionally different as adults than pups raised by low LG/ABN dams. The high LG/ABN pups, when adult, showed less fear, were less "impulsive," less "reactive." They had a more restrained corticosterone response when stressed.

But what caused this more "restrained" response? Was it the pups' inheritance—their genes—or was it the early life environment—the behavior of the dam?

The pups were cross fostered. That is to say, pups that had been birthed to low LG/ABN dams were switched to the nests of high LG/ABN dams. Pups birthed to high LG/ABN dams were given to low LG/ABN dams.

When mature, the pups showed the characteristics of their rearing (nurture) and not the characteristics of their inheritance (nature). In other words, it was not the result of their inheritance that led to greater stress tolerance and resilience. It was the effect of their environment—the behavior of the dams.

The work of Meaney and colleagues demonstrated a specific effect of maternal licking and grooming/arched-back nursing on the genome of the pup—in this case on the expression of the gene that codes for the glucocorticoid receptor (GR), a critical component of the hypothalamic-pituitary-adrenal (HPA) stress response. These findings were huge. They were the first biologic demonstration of the "causal mechanisms" of environmental effects that Waddington had described in his 1942 paper on epigenetics.

"That is the way systems operate. A change at one or another level of a system changes other levels such that the animal under study is not the same. The initial change becomes part of an on-going process of change"[3]

But how did the behavior of a high LG/ABN dam lead to greater stress tolerance and resilience in her pups months later when the pups were mature? What was the biological element underlying this distant behavioral effect?

A high LG/ABN dam causes more of the neurotransmitter serotonin to be released from the brain stem of her pups. Thus an action

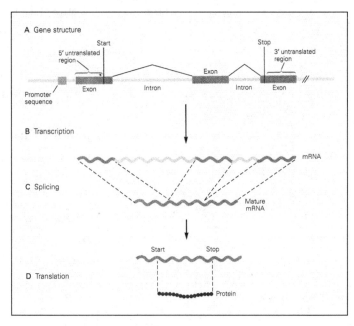

A gene consists of coding regions, exons, separated by noncoding regions, introns. The noncoding regions, which were initially thought to be "junk," are critical to DNA's regulatory process from transcription to translation to protein synthesis.

from the environment, increased maternal touch, leads to a biological reaction in her pup, higher levels of serotonin, that recruits a cascade of biological events including the activation of a critical transcription factor (TF), nerve growth factor-inducible protein A (NGFI-A).

The binding of NGFI-A to the regulatory—or promoter—region of DNA, recruits other transcription factors (TF's). These TFs bind to promoter regions that activate the coding segment of the gene—called the EXON. The activation of the EXON leads to the transcription of DNA, the translation of RNA, the synthesis of protein. In this instance the synthesized protein is the glucocorticoid receptor (GR).

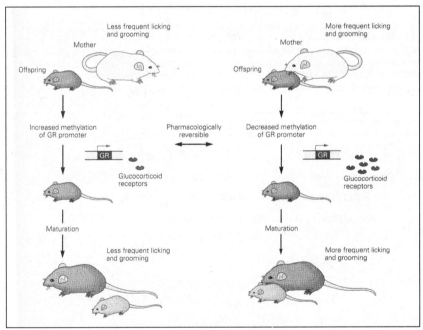

The amount of attention that the dam (in the form of licking and grooming, arched back nursing) pays to her pups regulates the transcription, translation, and protein synthesis of a critical receptor, the glucocorticoid receptor (GR). When the pup is grown, the GR will have significant control of the pup's response to stress. This is an example of how the "outside" (in the form of licking and grooming) affects the "inside" (the density of the population of GRs). This is an example of epigenetics.

The high LG/ABN behavior of the dam leads to a pup that is better able to respond to rising levels of stress because the dam's actions have led to a higher concentration of glucocorticoid receptors (GRs). A higher concentration of GRs is more sensitive to the level of cortisol (cortisol in primates, corticosterone in other mammals). Once detected, the GR sends signals to the HPA (hypothalamic-pituitary-adrenal) to slow cortisol production.

This is feedback inhibition.

But if the dam affects her pups' behavior by licking and grooming, how does she affect her pups' behavior once they have left the nest, and thus are no longer there to be licked and groomed?

Just about every cell in any one individual has the same DNA. That being so, how does a liver cell know to function as a liver cell? How does a "brain cell" know to function as a neuron? The one word answer is—methylation. By adding "a sticky coating" of methyl groups to the DNA, transcription factors are blocked from accessing the regulatory or promoter regions of the DNA. Methylation silences the promoter—and in many instances this "silence" is for the life of the cell. So only that part of the DNA that a liver cell needs in order to function as a liver cell is left unmethylated—and is thus "open." The rest is silenced with methyl groups blocking the DNA machinery.

By selectively methylating different parts of the DNA, a liver cell will only do what a liver cell is supposed to do. A brain cell will only do what a neuron is supposed to do. By adding methyl groups to selective promoter regions, genes can be selectively closed.

Just as the promoter region of the DNA can be "closed" by methylation, it can be "opened" by demethylation.

So for example, the critical transcription factor, neural growth factor—NGFI-A. Before birth, the binding site for NGFI-A in a fetal rat is unmethylated and thus open. A very short time after birth, indeed by the pup's first day of life, the site is fully methylated, and thus closed. The first week of the pup's life is a "critical period." The dam has a week to undo the methylation—and thus open the DNA machinery. How does she do this? She does this with licking and grooming and arched-back nursing.

In the example of the glucocorticoid receptor (GR), the more the dam licks, grooms, and nurses, the more will her pup's DNA be opened, and thus the more will TFs reach the promoter site to start the synthesis of the glucocorticoid receptor protein. The more protein the pup makes, the greater will the pup have control over its stress response because it is the GR that responds to the circulating corticosterone (cortisol in the primate) and signals to the hypothalamus to turn off this key element of the stress response.

But if the binding site for the promoter region is fully methylated—and thus closed on the pup's first day of life—how do the transcription factors activated by serotonin get past the "sticky methyl groups"? How does a transcription factor get to the gene when the site is "closed"?

The answer has to do with electrostatic charges.

DNA is a double helix. The double helical backbone of DNA is negatively charged. In order to pack the 3 billion base pairs of DNA into the nucleus of a cell (a feat compared to "compressing 20 kilometers of thread into a grapefruit"), the DNA is wrapped around positively charged protein rods called "histones." The negative charge of DNA and the positive charge of the histone proteins attract, thereby creating a tightly packed DNA/histone structure called "chromatin." When the chromatin is tightly packed, the gene is closed. But just as the electrostatic charge can close chromatin, so too can the charge open chromatin.

The histone protein is made up of amino acids. The DNA wraps around the histone in such a way that the amino acid tails of histone proteins protrude from the chromatin complex. The tail is the primary target for electrostatic manipulation. When activated, an enzyme called histone acetyl transference (HAT) adds an acetyl group to the histone tail. The addition of the acetyl group makes the positive histone charge *less* positive. As a result the pull between the

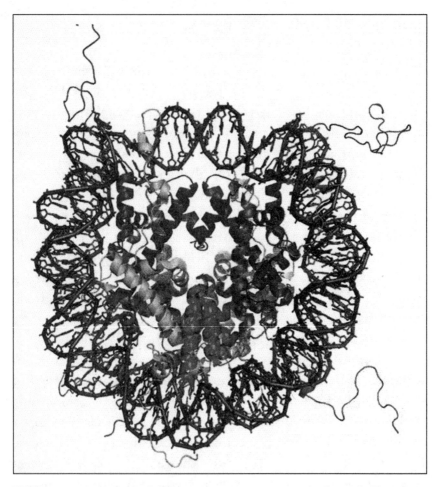

DNA is negatively charged. Histone proteins are positively charged. Chromatin is a histone-DNA structure wherein the outer strands of DNA are wrapped around the inner core of histone protein. By modifying the histone "tails" that protrude from the chromatin, the charge on the histone proteins can be modified. When histones are made less positive, the negatively charged DNA is able to pull away from the histone and is thereby "open." The opening of the DNA enables replication and protein synthesis. The biochemical modification of the histone tails by extracellular factors is a further example of epigenetics.

negatively charged DNA and the now less positively charged histone is reduced. This allows the DNA to separate from the histone. This gives transcription factors access to the gene's promoter region.

It is the dam's licking and grooming that activates the enzyme, histone acetyl transference (HAT). It is also the dam's licking and grooming that activates a second series of biochemical reactions—the demethylation of the promoter region.

Just as the dam's licking and grooming affects the charge of her pup's histone proteins, her licking and grooming also affects the methylation status of the promoter region. Whether the dam is high or low LG/ABN determines the "active redesign of the methylation pattern at this region of the genome."[4]

Active redesign of the methylation pattern results in long-term changes that endure for the life of the pup, changes that were the result of the licking and grooming and arched-back nursing by the dam. This leads to stable long-term change in gene expression without altering DNA.

"The modifications to the DNA and its chromatin environment can be considered as an additional layer of information that is contained within the genome. This information is thus *epigenetic* in nature (the name derives from the Greek *epi* meaning 'upon' and *genetics*). . . . Epigenetic modifications do not alter the sequence composition of the genome. Epigenetic marks regulate the operation of the genome."[5]

"These findings are consistent with the idea that it is tactile stimulation that appears to be the critical environmental signal for the regulation of glucocorticoid expression in the neonate."[6]

This is environmental influence.

This is epigenetics.

This is a mark—a change in the access to DNA.

When she returned, my mother had converted. When she took off her shirt, undid her bra, took my lips to her teat, she had converted to the equivalent of a high-licking, high-grooming, high-arched-back nursing dam.

It was as if I were being raised by a different dam.

It was as if I had two mothers.

Chapter 27

Two Mothers—Take Two

MY MOTHER'S DEPRESSION BEGAN TWO MONTHS BEFORE I WAS CONceived and lasted until three months after I was born—fourteen months in all. My mother's depression changed who she was. My mother's depression changed who I would be.

"A dam that had constitutionally been a high licking and grooming, high arched back nursing dam if exposed to stress during pregnancy will 'convert' to low licking and grooming, low arched back nursing."[1]

The stress of perinatal depression does to a mother what the stress of not enough food or too many cats does to a dam. Before I was conceived, my mother was the human equivalent of a high licking and grooming dam. But then around the time of my conception, she converted.

So for my entire time as a fetus and for the first three months after my birth, I had the equivalent of a stressed, low-licking, low-grooming, low-arched-backed nursing dam.

And then in January of my first year of life, she came back—and when she did, she came back a changed "dam." When she came back, a high-licking, high-grooming, high-arched-backed nursing dam walked through the door.

"I watched, not sure I could trust my eyes," Katie Galst said, "as your mother started to unbutton her shirt right then and there."

"My mother?"

"'Ruthie, what are you doing?' I said thinking maybe all that shock had gone to her head. 'Ruthie?' And she just dropped her shirt to the floor—'Ruthie?'—I said, and then turning her back to me, she just said, 'Undo it.'"

"'Undo it?'"

"'I'd undo it myself but as you can see both of my hands—'"

"So I undid her bra. And then, she just let it fall off her shoulder.

"Your Aunt Fran was aghast. She was about to say something about how she had not been able to produce enough—when I screamed—"

"'Fran—don't you dare!'"

"—as your mother held you to her breast. And you took it. Like it was full. Like it was flowing. Like her milk had really dropped."

"We all knew she was dry, but you sucked like that didn't matter," Katie said leaning back in her La-Z-Boy chair. Katie said nothing for a while just letting that be.

"Get me some water," she said.

I had two mothers. The one was not into licking and grooming. The other one was.

There is reason to believe that the "quality" of care that a dam gives to her pup is measured by the frequency of touch—the quantity not the quality being the measure of care. Frequency tells the story. It's the dam's way of telling her pups about the world she foresees. The dam's way of telling what kind of world her pups should expect when they grow up. It's the best information the pup will get.

"In the rat, environmental stressors decrease parental investment and enhance behavioral and endocrine responses to stress. . . . If indeed the decreased parental investment accurately reflects an increased level of environmental demand for the offspring, then such efforts could be highly adaptive."[2]

The low-licking and low-grooming, low-arched-back nursing dam is telling her pups a story about a world where they will find little food and many cats. She is telling them a story that puts their stress response system on notice.

The state of a woman's stress as told by the level of unbound cortisol in the womb is the major signal the fetus gets as to the general state of affairs in the world it will soon enter.

My mother's womb communicated those fears.

The blood that circulated through my umbilical vein had high levels of corticotropin-releasing factor (CRF) and high levels of unbound cortisol. My placenta did little or nothing to bind the cortisol that passed from my mother's blood into mine. These are indicators of anxiety and depression. These are indicators of stress. I was being told through my blood of a world under siege. I was being told firsthand of a strange cause and effect.

Cortisol crosses through the placenta. It crosses unbound. The story of high unbound cortisol was one of the stories I learned in the womb. It was a story that spoke of unpredictable cause, uncertain effect—a story that spoke of bonds that would be broken, vows that would go unmet. "Sow your seed early or better don't sow at all." Death strikes without warning. Be prepared. Be prepared if that makes you feel any better. Be prepared to be unprotected and alone. High circulating corticotropin-releasing factor (CRF) and cortisol in the womb tells the autonomic nervous system (ANS) and the hypothalamic-pituitary-adrenal axis (HPA) that the fight to restore order is long, uphill, and may already be lost.

And don't expect much licking and grooming. Indeed learn not to expect. Cause and effect are broken. Nothing is certain. Certainly not me. And above all, never trust. Love is at the heart and soul of pain and suffering. If you learn anything from what I am telling you with the neurotransmitters flowing in your fetal blood, the neurotransmitters of stress, learn not to care. Learn not to bond. Learn not to breed. Or if you must, do it quickly, then leave.

One other thing, when you are born, my breasts will be dry. You will be entering a world without milk, without honey. And there will be cats. Many cats.

"All cellular processes derive from a constant dialogue between the genome and environmental signals. . . . The research of the post-genomic era reveals that DNA is an active target for remodeling by cellular signals that are activated by environmental events."[3]

And then in January, three months after delivering me to the world, another dam, another woman came back.

"And the first thing when she saw you," Katie Galst said, "she unbuttoned her shirt."

"Epigenetic markings of DNA methylation, histone acetylation, and transcription factor occupancy bear the memory of maternal behavior."[4]

"Your aunt was aghast. And just as she was about to say—"

"I roared—'Don't you dare!'"

"The reality of the functional genome does not admit to main effects of either gene or environment, but rather to a constant inter-action between the DNA and its environment."[5]

"—as your mother held you to her breast. And you took. Like it was full. Like it was flowing. Like the milk had dropped."

"We believe that the effects of maternal care of the expression of genes involved in the regulation of behavior and endocrine responses to stress reflect an anticipatory development strategy."[6]

"We all knew she was dry, but you just sucked like you didn't care," Katie said, closing her eyes. "You were hungry for her. She was hungry for you. Get me some water."

My second mother returned in January. She was different from my first. She touched, she hugged, she giggled, she mirrored, she spooned. She was more like a high-licking, high-grooming, high-arched-backed nursing dam. And she brought a different view of the world, a different frequency of touch. She told a different story about the world I had entered three months before.

Three months after my birth, twelve months after I had been conceived—my second mother arrived.

The stories each of my mothers told me, prepared me for worlds each as different as were they.

But they both told me stories narrated by hormones, transcription factors, epigenetics, and genes—stories about the world that lay ahead, as each one saw coming. Two stories as told by two mothers—as told through behavior and touch. Different signals from the dam led to different pathways in the pup.

I had two mothers, two stories. Different signals. Different strokes. Different soft brushes if you will.

"Environmental enrichment after prenatal stress decreases depressive-like behavior and fear, and improves cognitive deficits as well as increases dendritic spine density, granular cells and brain derived neurotrophic factor in the hippocampus of the offspring (transcription factors). Environmental enrichment also improves learning and memory . . . through an increased dendritic spine density (number of synaptic connections) in the hippocampus of adult rats."[7]

The story told to me by my second mother began with a promise: "I will keep you safe," she said with her touch, with her licking, her grooming, her teats. She gave me milk. She gave me honey. She made me safe. "I will keep you safe," she said. "I will be with you always." I gurgled. "Always," she said.

I had two mothers.

They gave different signals, told different stories.

"I will keep you safe."

I have the marks to prove it.

Over in Killarney

Many years ago

My mother sang a song to me—

In tones so sweet and low

My mother sang that song when she bathed me, when she changed me, when she held me. It was the song that Katherine had sung.

Just a simple ditty,

It was—

Just a simple ditty

Just a simple—

"Well damn," she said.

I gurgled.

"Well damn—. You didn't hear me say that," she said, picking me up and dusting my butt. "I never used that word, do you hear? I would never—no I would not!"

I gurgled.

"I'm serious, don't you know," she said, lowering me to the table, "There, there," channeling Katherine, bringing her back. "There, there."

She got a dry diaper.

I gurgled.

"No, no," she said, "I never said such a thing, you never heard me say—" nuzzling her face into my belly—pink and smooth with one surgical scar right there.

"There, there."

She put me down, picked up the sheet of paper that Katherine had given her.

"Here," Katherine said, the day before we left her ward, don't you know, "It's all written. There, there," showing the paper with the lyrics that she had written out.

"There, there," she said reading the lyrics once more.

I gurgled.

"There, there," my mother said as if she were Irish, don't you know—"There, there." And then she went back to the song,

Just a simple ditty,
In her old Irish way
And I'd give the world if she could sing
That song to me this day

I lay naked on the changing table shaking with joy as my mother blew into my belly.

And I'd give the world if she could sing
That song to me this day

She moved back, looked me straight. She didn't move. I quieted down as if the song she sang had taken control of my muscles, my belly, my parasympathetic nervous system, my lungs, and my heart.

"There, there," she said.

It had.

"There, there."

But how?

Was it just the music, just the song?

"There, there."

"The music has to be 'full of emotions, associations, nostalgia.' It is almost always music he has known from childhood. . . . I am afraid that if I pay too much attention to it, I may not be able to escape it—like quicksand or hypnosis.' He may nonetheless be drawn deeper and deeper into it, until he then realizes that it is out of his hands."[8]

No it was not just the music. But the music—

"There, there."

—played a part.

Chapter 28

The Pneumogastric

IN 1872, DARWIN WROTE *THE EXPRESSION OF THE EMOTIONS IN MAN and Animals*. In it, Darwin extended his argument on evolution—that not only physical structure but also that the structure of emotion was inherited and subject to the laws of evolution. "I attended to this point in my first-born infant, who could not have learnt anything by association with other children, and I was convinced that he understood a smile and received pleasure from seeing one, answering it by another, at much too early an age to have learnt anything by experience."

Darwin argued that his son's reaction to his smile was inborn. There was no other way for the infant to have known how to goo-goo, gurgle, and smile in response to his father's goo-goos, gurgles, and smiles. His reaction could not have been learned. It came with the boy when the boy came into the world. Darwin thus extended the argument that he had first made in the *Origin of Species*. Through evolution one can account for the transmission of not just physical but also of emotional traits. The biological structure of emotion—in animals and in man—is inherited. The structure of emotion is in our DNA.

In that same text, Darwin went on to make another bold statement that he was neither ready nor able to prove: "When the mind is strongly excited we might expect that it would instantly affect in a

173

direct manner the heart. . . . When the heart is affected it reacts on the brain; and the state of the brain again reacts through the pneumo-gastric nerve (the vagus) on the heart so that under excitement there will be much mutual action and reaction between these, the two most important organs of the body."[1]

Darwin was arguing that the heart and the brain were connected through a nerve, then called the "pneumogastric." It was an extraordinary idea—that mind and body came together not just in the brain but in a nerve, the pneumogastric—now called the vagus or tenth cranial nerve.

And I'd give the world if she could sing

That song to me this day

It was a boldness of which Freud would have approved, "I sense the most beautiful and important things and hope you will not let yourself be dissuaded from publicly expressing your views, even if that are only conjectures," Freud wrote to his strange "scientific" colleague Wilhelm Fliess.

By then Darwin was dead, but his ideas were most certainly alive. "We cannot do without people who have the courage to think something new before they can demonstrate it," Freud wrote in that same letter to Fliess even as he ignored the words of Darwin in books that were on his shelves. Freud looked up from his desk—"Visitors—I must stop"—putting down his pen, ending his letter to Fliess.[2]

My mother continued the song,

Too-ra-loo-ra-loo-ral

Too-ra-loo-ra-li

Too-ra-loo-ra-loo-ral

Hush now don't you cry.

She looked me straight in the eye. She didn't move. I quieted down as if the song had taken control of my heart, my lungs, my brain, my mind—through a nerve that had been called the pneumo-gastric. Could it really do such a thing?

Too-ra-loo-ra-loo-ral

Too-ra-loo-ra-li
Too-ra-loo-ra-loo-ral
That's an Irish lullaby.
"There, there," she said.
It could. It did. It does.
"There, there."
Through the pneumogastric, Darwin had written in a book on Freud's shelf that Freud had both annotated and ignored.
Through the vagus as it is now called.
"There, there," she said.
We goo-gooed. We laughed. We grimaced. We smiled.
Through the vagus.
"There, there."
Darwin recognized that this bidirectional communication between the heart and the brain was through a nerve. Vagare translated from the Latin means to wander. The vagus wanders. It begins in the brain stem in a segment that starts just above where the spinal cord enters the skull, a segment called the medulla oblongata.

Early in his career, Freud had studied the medulla oblongata. "The medulla oblongata is a very serious and lovely object. I remember quite clearly how much time and trouble I devoted to its study many years ago. To-day, however, I must remark that I know nothing that could be of less interest to me."[3]

There are twelve cranial nerves in the brain stem—(the part of the central nervous system between the spinal cord and the brain). The vagus is the tenth of these twelve. Its cell bodies are grouped together in the medulla oblongata. Freud was right—"the medulla oblongata is a very serious and lovely object." In response to most songs, the vagus is why heart rate and respiration slow, why regeneration occurs, why the brain and body are calm.

The medulla oblongata, and the vagus, are critical components of the dialogue between heart and brain, between mother and child. The vagus is a biologic communication of safety.

Too-ra-loo-ra-loo-ral,

Too-ra-loo-ra-li

"Katherine was your nurse," my mother explained, rubbing me with baby oil.

Too-ra-loo-ra-loo-ral,

Hush now don't you cry.

"She sang that song to you. That's how I learned it—from Katherine,'" she explained. "But don't feel you have to run off with an Irish 'lassie' because of Katherine," my mother said. "Katherine loved the word "Lassie" almost as much as 'there, there."

"And don't go running off. You're not Irish," she said. "Nor am I."

I held on to her finger.

"But if you do, make it a really fine lassie." I gurgled. She gurgled. "There, there," she said,

Too-ra-loo-ra-loo-ral,

Too-ra-loo-ra-li

"I think it's the most beautiful song I've ever heard," she said, lifting me naked and dry.

"There, there," Katherine said, "There, there."

My mother lowered me to the changing table.

"There, there."

"There is a primitive animal tie between mother and baby that makes one being of the two," Anna Freud, Sigmund Freud's daughter said.[4]

Too-ra-loo-ra-loo-ral,

That's an Irish lullaby.

"The intersubjective dialogue between mother and infant consists of signals produced by the autonomic, involuntary nervous system in both parties. The attachment relationship mediates the dyadic regulation of emotion, wherein the mother co-regulates the infant's internal homeostatic state."[5]

"After I heard Katherine sing, I wanted to know the song. It was

Katherine and that song—it was Katherine don't you know. I don't think she was singing just for you. She was singing to keep me alive."

"We listen to music with our muscles. We keep time to music involuntarily. The heart as a muscle responds to music whose profound abstract emotionality can enliven our soul. Music releases serotonin—just like a mother's touch."[6]

"There, there."

I gurgled.

"There, there," she said. "Katherine wrote it down. That's how I know it. There, there."

Too-ra-loo-ra-loo-ral,
Too-ra-loo-ra-li
Too-ra-loo-ra-loo-ral,

That's an Irish lullaby.

There is a picture of my mother and me. On the back it says Brighton Beach Studios. The date is stamped April 12. I am six months old. A spiral of hair on the top of my head sticks straight up like Alfalfa from *The Little Rascals*. My mother's hair is pulled back off her face. She is a woman at peace with herself—

Just a simple little ditty,
In her good old Irish way,

—who is staring straight at the camera, holding me tight, "If you touch my baby," she says with a smile, "I'll rip out your throat."

The parasympathetic nervous system responds to music by calming the heart, the lungs, the brain, the child, the woman, the man.

"There, there."

The parasympathetic nervous system is a biologic expression that one feels safe.

And I'd give the world if she could sing
That song to me this day.

Chapter 29

Happy Birthday

HAPPY BIRTHDAY TO YOU.
    Happy birthday to you.
Happy birthday, dear Richard—

My first birthday party was when I was six. Being six is great. I would get lots of presents, lots of toys. I told everyone I wanted a dog. Being six was going to be the greatest day of my life. I couldn't wait.

My party was in the basement. There are water pipes and heating pipes—all kinds of pipes in the basement. You can hang things on pipes—balloons, streamers, pictures—all kinds of things. My mother would hang clothes on the line, but for my birthday, she took the clothes down. I climbed up on a chair and hung balloons. It was great.

My mother set up tables—the one my father used for cards—and chairs that folded. My mother set out plates, cups, forks, spoons. My mother served hot dogs and potato salad. And she bought a cake, an Ebinger's Chocolate Blackout Cake. If you've never tasted an Ebinger's Chocolate Blackout Cake you never will. Ebinger's went out of business in 1972. It was a day many in Brooklyn compared to the Dodgers—for some it was worse.

I invited ten kids—Allan, Neal, Seth, Michael Starr—and six others because I figured each kid would bring me a present. I told everyone I wanted a dog. Michael Starr said, "You'll never get a dog."

"Why not?"

"Because."

Michael Starr was my best friend. My mother said he was a bad influence. His mother said I was a bad influence. I told everyone that I was a bad influence. It was great.

At my birthday, there was a cake with candles. My mother opened a little box, took out a match. "Happy birthday, my angel," she said as she lit the candles.

"Blow them out!" Neal shouted. I thought about what Michael Starr had said, about how I'd never get a dog. I counted the candles—seven—six for me and one for someone else. I wasn't sure who that was for—like the glass my mother left on the Passover table—"For Yahweh," she said.

"Who's that?" I wanted to know.

"Blow them out!" Neal and Michael Starr said, impatient for a piece of cake. "Blow them out!" It was the best cake in the world.

"Make a wish and blow them out!" Neal said.

I stared at the candles. "When I blow them out, I really, really—"

"It doesn't count if your wish is out loud," Neal said.

I closed my eyes and whispered the wish in my head, "When I blow out the candles, I want a dog."

I blew out all seven candles—even though I was six. Maybe Yahweh would bring me a dog.

"Happy birthday to you. Happy birthday to you—"

I opened my eyes.

"—Happy birthday dear Richard—"

I looked all around—

"Happy birthday to you."

—No dog, not even a puppy.

Just a box of Ohio Red Label matches that my mother had left on the table.

Only Seth, Allen, Neal, and Michael Starr and a girl named Leslie showed up for my party. I asked Susan Margo, but she didn't come.

Maybe because of things we had done, maybe because she thought birthdays were for kids.

There was a vacant lot on the end of the block, on the corner of Falmouth and Hampton. As Seth and I walked back from school one day, Seth told me about his sister. She was older than Seth and had tied him to a chair in her room, then smeared lipstick and rouge all over his face. "What's rouge?"

"It's red."

"She tied you to a chair?"

"Swear to God."

"Then what—?"

When I got home, I went to my sister Susan. I knocked on her door. She was a dancer. In her last year at the Little Red School House which is in New York, before she went to Cornell which is in Ithaca, upstate. Much later she would dance on the beach in a movie that never got made, called *The Iliad*—about a boat.

Once I watched my sister dance. She didn't know I was watching. She took off all her clothes. I had never seen a girl do that. Not even Susan Margo. But this was my sister, and then I told her it was almost my birthday and that since it was almost my birthday, I wanted her to tie me to a folding chair and then I wanted her to smear lipstick and rouge all over my face.

She shut the door.

She didn't come to my birthday party.

"I want a dog."

Leslie came with her mother. I never really liked Leslie, but I kind of knew that she'd bring me a present. I was right about that. She came with a box.

I watched as Leslie and her mother walked down the basement stairs. Leslie's mother was carrying this cardboard box with holes in the sides. Maybe Leslie's mom was bringing me a puppy. Maybe Neal was right that when you make a wish on your birthday, you can't say it out loud. Maybe I was getting a puppy.

Leslie's mother turned to Leslie. "What do you say?"

"Happy birthday," Leslie said as her mother handed me the box with holes. I shook the box.

"Don't do that," Leslie's mother said. The box made noise.

"What is it?" I asked.

"What do you say?" Leslie's mother said.

"Is it a dog?" I shook it again.

"Don't shake it," Leslie's mom said.

"Open it," Leslie said.

"Is it a puppy? Did you bring me a—?" I opened the box.

Chicks. Six baby chicks—all yellow and chirping and flopping. I had heard fish make sounds like that when they were thrown onto the dock at Sheepshead Bay—just before their guts were thrown to the gulls.

"What do you say?" Leslie's mom said as I stared at the box.

What was I going to do with six baby—?

"They used to be eggs," Leslie said with the authority of a girl who was taller than every boy in the class.

Leslie's mother kneeled down to show me how baby chicks worked. "You see how the chicks are playing—the way you and Leslie play at school." I never played like that at school. I never played like that with Leslie. I don't know why I asked Leslie to my party. If I had known she was going to come with her mother and a box of baby chicks.

"But if you pick one up and leave it all alone," Leslie's mother said, picking one up, "It starts to cry." Leslie's mother took the second box, the one that Leslie had brought, and put the chick in the second empty box.

And sure enough the baby chick started to cry, like the cries I had once heard a sparrow or some little bird make as it was in the grip of a hawk—like in the museum when a soldier carries off a woman screaming from some long ago place. My sister Jolie had taken me to the Brooklyn Museum. I don't know why she took me there. I almost fell asleep walking around when all of a sudden there I was staring at this soldier with a fat naked woman on his shoulder. My sisters were both skinny like me so I don't think that would ever happen to them. The chick cried more and more.

"What will happen to the little bird?" I asked my father.

"What little bird?"

"That one," I said pointing to the sky.

"That's a hawk," my father said. The little bird was still making high-pitched sounds as the hawk muscled the air.

"What's it going to do?"

"With what?"

"The little bird. I think it's a sparrow," I said.

My father looked closer. "It's going to feed the sparrow to its young," he said as the little bird continued to make its last feeble cries.

"Oh," I said, never having thought it all the way to the end. "They're going to eat it?" I asked. My father never said.

The only things I had ever seen that were dead were fish, Chirpy, and fireflies. Chirpy was a canary that my parents gave me. I think they gave me Chirpy because there was no way they were ever going to give me a dog. I wanted a dog. I always wanted a dog, ever since I can remember. I plotted. I plotted how the dog and I would run off, join the circus, ride on a train all that way to Sarasota. I had no idea where that was but it was on a TV show that took a train. I would make birds disappear like the magician at Coney Island. The way Chirpy had just one day disappeared.

"It's all alone," I said.

"Yes," Leslie's mother said.

"But it's going to die," I said, trying to forget the little bird. It's hard to forget something that you saw just before it was eaten alive. The image sticks like it's there stuck to the side of your head. Especially if you've wished it dead. I didn't kill Chirpy but some-times I wondered if Chirpy would die, would I get a dog. That's why sometimes I wished that Chirpy would die.

Then Chirpy died. It made me afraid of my thoughts. Even so I didn't get a dog.

"Do you ever cry when you're all alone?" Leslie's mother asked.

"What?"

"Do you ever cry when you're alone?"

"No," I said. "Girls cry."

"You never cry?"

I shook my head. "Girls."

"And what about boys?"

"Only when I fall and there's blood."

"But sometimes do you cry when you're alone?"

"No," I said, "only when I fall and there's blood." The baby chick continued to cry for the other chicks in the other box and for the hen it would never see. I bet the hen was somewhere in soup. Maybe in my grandmother's zup.

"Why did you put it all alone in the box?" I asked Leslie's mother. The lone chick continued to cry. I thought about the sparrow. I thought about fish about to be dead on the dock. I thought about death quite a lot. Here it was my birthday and all I thought about was things that were dead.

Maybe it had to do with Leslie's mom.

"There is an immediate response to separation consisting of high rates of 'distress' calling accompanied by agitated pivoting, sniffing, and exploratory behavior with high levels of self-grooming."[1] But the reference was not to baby chicks but to baby rats.

I thought about Chirpy. I thought about my thoughts.

"Does the little bird feel pain?" I asked my father imagining the little bird staring up at the hawk as it picked out its heart. "Dad?"

"What?"

"Does it?" We both watched as the hawk flew with the bird.

"Yes," he said, "I imagine it does."

"Oh," I said. "How much?"

"It's quick," he said.

183

"What is?"

He didn't say.

That night I couldn't sleep. And when I did, I had a dream. It woke me up.

"The general anatomy of human grief was the same system as the system that mediates separation calls in animals. This key system for feeling the sting of isolation appears to have arisen evolutionarily from brain systems that mediate physical pain."[2]

The pain of a festering wound and the pain of separation are experienced in the same part of the brain, the anterior insular and posterior cingulate cortices. It's as if evolution wanted mammals to know just how dangerous it would be if the animal were alone. It's as if evolution wanted mammals to know that they would most likely die soon after being separated. It's as if evolution wanted mammals in packs.

"These indicators of initial distress occur only when a pup is isolated from all social companions. If littermates are present, no such response occurs."[3]

"Watch this!" Leslie's mother said as she reached in the box and held the chick in both of her hands.

The chick stopped crying—just like that. "It's not crying," I said.

"Wait," Leslie's mother said. We all watched. "What do you see?" Leslie's mother asked.

"A baby chick," I said.

"What else?"

"Nothing," I said.

"It's eyes," she said. I looked at the baby chick's eyes. I shrugged.

"They're closed," she said.

"Did you kill it?" I asked.

"No! My lord how could you say such a thing! 'Kill it!' Who do you think I am?" she asked.

"You're Leslie's mom," I said.

I once saw a magic show at Coney Island where the magician

made a baby bird disappear—just like that. I was where he couldn't see. I had come in from the back. Michael Starr and I had crawled through the gate. It was locked but if you're a kid you could squeeze under. If you're a kid, and you're not with your mom, that's what you did. You made yourself thin, thin enough to get in. And I saw. I saw how he made the little bird disappear. The box had two bottoms. He had lots of little birds in the back—each one singing for the one that didn't come back. One bird didn't come back after every show. The bird disappeared into the bottom of the box. That's how he made the bird disappear. He crushed it.

"It's dead," I said.

"No," Leslie's mother said, "its eyes are closed because it stopped being scared."

And then I asked, "Why?"

And Leslie's mom said, "Because it's in my warm hands."

And I said, "Oh." It was right then and there that I decided that I would never work at the circus even though I once thought I would work in the circus with a dog named Buster riding on a train to Sarasota. I would be the next Circus Boy. But I only knew that one trick. And it meant crushing little birds. Like the one in the hawk's grip.

"Because it feels safe," Leslie's mother said. I don't think it felt safe. She could just kill it like the bird in the box at Coney Island or the little bird in the grip of the hawk. Maybe I would never join the circus. I could never get used to the idea of so much death.

The hawk ripped out the heart of the sparrow. The magician crushed the bird in the box. The chick closed its eyes in Leslie's mother's warm hands. I don't think it felt safe. I think it knew it was headed for soup. That's what I figured. At least that's where it went in my dream.

Into zup.

After we had eaten hot dogs and potato salad. After I blew out the candles. After we ate the Ebinger's cake. After I opened my presents.

I knew that Michael Starr was right. I was never going to get a dog. The only present I got was baby chicks. And a book—about a baby deer. Who cares about a baby deer?

"He was born in the middle of a thicket, one of those small hidden places in the forest that appear to be open yet are shielded on all sides."

But when I was old enough to read by myself, I loved the book.

"The space was so small that there was barely enough room for him and his mother."[4] I loved the book and the baby deer.

I hated my birthday. I was six. There were seven candles. Six for me and one for Yahweh who never showed up. Six candles and six baby chicks and a book when everyone knew that I wanted a dog.

Leslie and Leslie's mother were getting their coats, when my mother approached with the box. "You should take these," she said indicating the box with the holes and six baby chicks.

"They're for Richard," Leslie's mother said. I don't really think my mother liked Leslie's mother. I didn't really like Leslie. I just invited her because I thought she might—

"No, I think you should take them," my mother repeated.

"But, Ruthie, it's a birthday present and you really can't—"

"I can," my mother said. "Take them." She held the box until Leslie's mother took it.

"I really thought that Richard—"

"Thank you," my mother said, smiling in that way mothers can as Leslie's mother took the box, smiling in a different way that mothers can.

"Come along, Leslie," Leslie's mother said. "It's time to go."

I could hear the chicks chirping as Leslie and Leslie's mother climbed up the cellar stairs.

"The bitch," my mother said. I turned around. She looked at me, "I'm sorry. I shouldn't have said that." I nodded. "Don't be shocked. I'm not who you think."

"Who are you?"

"I'm your mother," she said. "And I will curse and claw for those whom I love."

"Like a hawk," I said.

"Yes, like a hawk."

"Mom?"

"What?"

"Would you claw for me?"

"Yes, I would," she said.

"What about a dog?"

She kneeled down.

"I want a dog," I said.

And then she hugged me. Real tight. I could feel her heart. Like it was beating inside of me. I had never felt someone's heart like that. Like the sparrow and the hawk only different. It was like my Mom and me shared the same heart.

"Happy Birthday," she said, "Happy birthday my angel."

Maybe we did.

"These regulatory interactions are not involved solely in biological and behavioral development, but are also the basic experimental building blocks out of which mental representations and their associated emotions arise."[5]

"Mom, am I getting a dog?" I asked.

She looked at me, smiled, stroked my hand, then said, "Richard—"

"Mom, it's my birthday. I'm six."

"No," she said.

"But I am."

"You're not getting a dog."

"Why?"

"Because."

"That's what Michael Starr said.'

"But I have something for you."

"What?"

"Come with me," she said extending her hand.

"Where?"

"Come."

I took her hand. We walked together up the cellar stairs to the landing where there was a picture of my father and my mother when they were together somewhere before I was born. They were both smiling. And then you go up a few more steps, ten steps in all—I counted them. And then there's a door. She opened the door. To the right is the kitchen. To the left is another door. She went to the left. I went with her.

"Where are we going?"

She went outside. "You'll see."

I followed.

She walked to the garage.

"I know you want a dog," she said.

"Did you get me a dog?"

"No."

"Why not?"

We went inside the garage.

And there it was. It was red. It was green. It had two wheels and three gears. The next best thing to a dog.

"Happy birthday," she said.

I got on.

"Richard, you have to wait. You don't know how to—"

I couldn't wait. I was six. I knew everything I needed to know about—

"Richard!"

I smashed my new bike into the car, ripping my pants, banging my hand. "Are you all right?" There was a cut on my arm; it started to bleed. I started to cry.

My mother looked at the cut.

"The mother can switch learning between attachment to threat learning in a moment's notice. This enables the mother to navigate the pup's learning about the world and what is threatening and what is safe."

"Let me kiss it," she said holding my arm, kissing first the cut then my head.

The pain started to fade. I whispered through the tears, "I hate Leslie's mom."

"I know what you mean," my mother said holding me tight as we both sat on the cement floor, staring out the open door—down the driveway to the street and to a path that led away—and for the first time it occurred to me that the path down the drive to the street kept going and going and I had no idea how far it went or when it might end.

"Learning occurs throughout life but what we learn and how we learn it changes to fit each developmental epoch, using transient 'sensitive periods.' These defined periods of altered learning provide streamlined learning that ensures survival. These specialized periods of learning can be turned on and off naturalistically . . . by mother's presence and emotional affect."[6]

She kissed me again.

The pain went away.

I had a bike.

"Mom—" I said.

"What is it, sweetheart?"

"I want a dog."

Chapter 30

Fire

WALKING HOME FROM SCHOOL THE NEXT DAY, I FOUND AN OHIO Red Label box in my pocket.

"Look at this," I said to Michael Starr, amazed that the box had somehow made its way into my pocket.

"Where'd you get that?"

My mother had used the matches to light the candles on my cake. I guess she left them on the table and I must have—

"I don't know."

"Matches," Michael Starr said.

Alan Fisher—who never did anything wrong and whose father was a dentist, the dentist I hated—walked up. "What's that?" he asked as we both stared at the red and white box.

"What are you doing?" Alan Fisher asked.

Me and Michael Starr crossed to the vacant lot.

"Where are you going?" Alan Fisher asked, pulled along as if by bad influence.

A warm wind picked up.

The vacant lot was filled with dead weeds and tall grass. We dug a small hole pulling dry roots from the sand.

I took the Ohio Red Label box out of my pocket and held it in both hands.

It felt sacred. It felt holy. Michael Starr, who went to church with his mother and father and sisters and brother, just said, "Matches."

"Matches," I repeated as if it were scripture and we were in some holy place.

The earliest evidence for the use of fire comes from Oldowan hominin sites dating back to the Lower Paleolithic age some 1.4 to 1.5 million years ago. These sites are around Lake Turkana in Kenya and contained oxidized patches of coal which scholars have interpreted as evidence of the controlled use of fire by Homo erectus, a precursor of Homo sapiens; that is to say, a precursor of us.

I opened the Ohio Red Label box. I gave a match to Michael Starr. Took one for myself.

"What are you doing?" Alan Fisher asked, still not sure if it were safe to be in the company of—

I struck a match on the side of the box. I had once seen Sid—who I haven't explained—do something like that. Sid married my sister. Sid struck a max on his teeth—and it lit! Sid could do anything. Sid was the most amazing person that I had ever—

"What are you doing?" Alan Fisher asked, moving a little farther back.

The controlled use of fire was perhaps one of mankind's greatest innovations.

We lit the dry roots. I don't know whose idea that was. But that's what we did. We lit the roots. And just waited.

Nothing.

"What are you doing?"

Nothing.

We waited for a long, long time—and then like magic—

"You shouldn't do that," Alan Fisher said.

Fire!

The preadolescent "is inclined to search for short-term reward rather than to consider long-term consequences. He is inclined to experiment with new and risky behavior."

"Wow."

Dry roots, dry weeds—

"Do you see that?"

—dead grass all burst into fire!

"This is great! This is the best. This is—!"

"Wow!"

And then from a bit farther off, Alan Fisher said, "Do you hear that—?"

"This is—"

"Fire!"

"This is so cool!"

"This is the best!"

"This is—"

Sirens.

Michael Starr and I were transfixed—

A policeman got out of his car, and then firemen with brooms jumped from their trucks. We were surrounded by roots and weeds and dead grass that had just burst into fire.

"There is less cortical control over behavior or choice in the pre-adolescent."[1] The axons of the neocortex are not yet fully myelinated, ceding greater control to the subcortex.

"Wow!"

I never knew fire could jump like a cat. I had once seen a rabbit—

The policeman came up. He had a gun. He had a badge. He was the biggest man I had ever seen.

"Did you start this fire?" he asked Michael Starr. Michael Starr shook his head. He turned to me. "Did you start this fire?"

I stared up at him. He had a hat, a whistle, a stick. He had a mustache on his lip.

"Did you start this fire?"

I was staring at Alan Fisher, who was standing on the other side of the street.

The policeman looked across.

"One of the most important and fascinating properties of the mammalian brain is plasticity, the capacity to modify neural circuits."[2]

"What about him?" the policeman asked.

"Various levels of environmental demand require different traits in the offspring. Nature would appear to favor plasticity . . . allowing the young to anticipate change."

"Yes, I saw him," I said.

"Are you sure?"

"He did it," I said, pointing at Alan Fisher. It was the biggest lie I ever told.

Alan Fisher started to run.

"Children inherit not only genes but also an environment."

"Wait here," the cop said.

"Highly anxious mothers are more likely to have children who are shy and timid."[3]

But I had two mothers—

And when the cop blew his whistle, Alan Fisher started to cry.

—from the first I inherited genes. From the second, plasticity.

And when Alan Fisher started to cry, I just smiled. I couldn't help it.

"Children of mothers who suffer from postpartum depression are characterized by insecure attachment, emotional withdrawal, inattentiveness, cognitive decline. . . . They are 'timid' and 'shy'."[4]

But I had two mothers.

As the cop crossed the street, Michael Starr started to walk the other way back down Hampton Avenue.

"Where are you going?" The fire was out. The firemen were gone. Alan Fisher was crying. There was only one cop. No one was watching. Michael Starr kept walking.

I followed.

When he got to the corner, he started to run. So did I.

Halfway down the block, there's a path through Mr. Palowski's yard. Mr. Palowski was the old man who lived next door. Sometimes

I'd run across his yard—it was a shortcut to school—and every time I did—

"Get out of my yard, you rotten kid!"

—once I may have stepped on some of his flowers—petunias or geraniums. "Get outta my yard, ya rotten kid." Geraniums I think.

"This way," I called to Michael Starr as I led him under the fence through Mr. Palowski's yard, and, sure enough, he was sitting on his porch just waiting for me.

"Get outta my yard, you rotten kid!" He shook his fist. He walked with a cane. "Get outta my yard!"

"Where you going?" I called to Michael Starr when we got to my house.

"I hate Alan Fisher, " Michael Starr yelled as he ran across the street.

"Where you going?" I yelled again.

"Home," he called out as he ran to the corner and was gone.

I opened the door, walked inside. "Mommy?" I called out.

I knew that Alan Fisher would tell the cop. Any minute I knew the police would arrive. I'd spend the rest of my life behind bars. Any minute I knew—

"Mommy?"

I didn't want to spend the rest of my life behind bars.

"Mommy?"

She wasn't there.

I went to her dressing table in the hallway. There was a mirror. A shelf with little bottles, tubes, combs, and creams. The dressing table had a blue skirt. I crawled underneath. It was dark. It was quiet. My mother's slippers were there on the floor—her dark green slippers with black on the side. The ones she had bought at Loehmann's when I wouldn't sit in the car because I was scared.

I sat.

I sat under the table behind the blue skirt. I picked up one of my mother's slippers waiting for the police to come and take me away for the rest of my life.

I held my mother's slipper next to my face. I smelled the slipper. It was more than the smell of her foot. It was the smell of her. As I sat under the table behind the blue skirt, smelling her slipper, smelling her, I felt safe.

I thought of Alan Fisher. I thought of the cop with his badge. I thought of his gun. I thought of Mr. Palowski. I thought of spending the rest of my life in jail. But sitting there in the dark, smelling my mother's slipper, I felt safe.

There is a neurobiology of fear. There is a neurobiology of safety.

The mother's ability to reduce fear is described as social buffering, "commonly associated with the notion of a 'safe haven.' Evidence suggests that the infant system overlaps with the neural network supporting social buffering . . . a network known to involve the prefrontal cortex."[5]

Smelling the slipper, I felt safe even though I knew I'd be spending the rest of my life behind bars.

"Odors are powerful stimuli that can evoke emotional states. . . . Unlike other sensory systems, the sense of smell does not pass through the thalamus to be routed to the cortex. Rather, odor information is relayed directly to the limbic cortex, a brain region typically associated with memory and emotional processes. This provides olfaction with a unique and potent power to influence mood."[6]

Fear when it is intense, fragments thought, keeps the pieces apart. In order to think, intense fear must be overcome.

"The presence of an important social partner (i.e., mother, romantic partner, cage mate) or a stimulus that provokes the memory of an individual (i.e., odor, photo) dampens fear" through cortical moderation of the subcortical fear circuit.[7]

Sitting under her dressing table, I started to think about what had happened. Thinking came back: My birthday. Six baby chicks. The bike. Michael Starr. Alan Fisher. A box of matches. Dry grass. The fire. The firemen. The cop. The rest of my life behind bars.

I held the slipper—dark green with black on the side.

Declarative memory brings pieces together—the box of matches, the dry grass, the fire, the cop, the gun—and out of the many comes one—"I took a match and lit a fire which got real big which is why a cop came to put me in jail for the rest of my life. He had a gun."

Declarative memory requires a part of the temporal lobe called the hippocampus. The hippocampus takes new perceptions and pieces them, chunks them with other perceptions to make new memory. It takes perception and makes more complex memory by putting things together. It creates a narrative, a story. It "chunks."

The presence of the slipper. The smell of my mother and the sense of safety that was brought back, allowed me to think, to remember. It allowed me to create time, place, order—a sequence of events. It allowed me to organize perception. It allowed me to "chunk" a sequence of events in the hippocampus.

I held my mother's green slipper with black on the side. I brought the slipper to my face. I breathed it. Under her dressing table in the hall, the smell of her in the slipper brought narrative back.

And then I came out from under my mother's dressing table.

"Mommy?"

"As pups leave the nest they encounter a far more complicated environment where higher order brain areas are required for processing complex threat and safety cues. Indeed, outside the nest an animal must use changing context and time-dependent safety/threat cues to choose appropriate approach/avoidance responses in environments with complex social hierarchy."[8]

I knew I was going to jail, and yet that didn't seem to matter so much. I felt safe. I was home. I was hungry. I started thinking about a chocolate chip cookie.

"Mommy—?"

It was weird.

Chapter 31

Where Proper Story Starts

FIFTEEN YEARS LATER I WAS SITTING ACROSS FROM MARGARET BRENMAN at the Austen Riggs Center in Stockbridge, Massachusetts. Brenman was a doctor. I was a patient. James Taylor wrote a song called "Fire and Rain" about a young, suicidal woman who may have been a patient in a place not dissimilar from Riggs.

I sat in Brenman's office—filled with books, flowers. There was a bowl of fruit. Two leather chairs. A leather couch. A woman with dark hair. Old enough to be my mother. She sat with her legs slightly apart.

She asked me a question.

I looked up. I don't know if she was aware that I had been—

"Would you like some coffee?"

She probably didn't care. Old enough to be my—

"What?"

"You look like you could use a pick-me-up."

I watched as she went to the table.

"Was that a 'yes'?"

"Maybe it was the smell," I said mostly to myself.

She poured the coffee into mugs.

"It made me feel safe."

"What did?"

"Maybe."

"What made you feel safe?"

"Do you always serve coffee?" I asked looking at the table with mugs, fruit, coffee. It had a blue skirt. The skirt—maybe that was it. Maybe that's what made me feel safe, almost safe. On a movie set, all that food would be called the "honey wagon," but in a shrink's office, it was an unusual prop.

She poured from the pot like a waitress at a diner in a town on a road bypassed by the interstate long ago. I had spent a summer in a town like that, beside that kind of road, that kind of diner, that kind of waitress, only with a tattoo of a rose—I can't remember if it was on her left or her right thigh.

"Call me Liz" she said as she poured into my cup.

"Okay, Liz"—I said to Liz, who tended to wear—

"Milk?"

—mostly black.

"Black."

She brought me the coffee.

"It's hot."

I held the mug in both hands. It was November. The third month of school. My second time at Riggs. The day was still warm. The coffee was hot. I breathed—the smell felt good in my nose and chest coming off a night of beer and cocaine. The smell of coffee—

"Lundy's."

"I didn't hear you."

I shook my head, took another sip. "Nothing," I said more clearly this time.

Lundy's. Not known for its coffee. More for the "surf and turf." And that waiter. George? Joe? Joey?—who kept pouring coffee—

"Would you some more ah—"

"Vinny."

"How's the coffee?" she asked.

That was his name.

The smell of coffee was fresh, strong.

"What?"

"Are you all right?" she asked.

I nodded, "Fine."

The most ancient of the external senses, smell—a primitive form of taste, tasting air—does not go through the thalamus on its way to your brain—probably what I like most about smell and cocaine—

"Safe?"

—they go straight to the brain.

"You said you felt 'safe.'"

I coughed.

I was having trouble breathing. "This is weird," I said clutching the mug like a drug or a charm—not the kind you wear—

"Are you all right?"

—the kind you suck.

I put down the mug.

I was suddenly remembering Susan Margo, Bernadette, the waitress—her name tag said Elizabeth but she said, "Call me Liz"—my mother in the bath, a body of water, a lake, a blue-and-white can that said—

"I should go."

"You just got here"

"I just remembered—"

"What?"

I moved to the door. My thoughts scattered like fish. "I'll see you next week."

"Are you all right?"

"I'm sorry. I'm fine. I just forgot—"

I walked out.

Outside the leaves were brown. It was November, still warm. I took a deep breath—"Indian summer." I needed to breathe. I needed air. I was flooding. Not a cloud in the sky. Flooding. I took a deep breath. I thought I could do whatever I wanted. I thought nothing mattered. I thought I would get by. I thought she would—what? What did you think she would do?

What about Liz?

I was flooding. Too much. Too sudden. Too fast. I wasn't even sure what flooding was. I wasn't sure what she was. I wasn't sure who she was or had been. A woman with whom I felt safe. A woman around whom the smells were strong. I was flooding. Looking under her skirt. Maybe it was the skirt, the blue skirt. Maybe it was the smell of her. Maybe it was the pieces. Maybe it was the rose on her thigh, her right thigh. Maybe it was the lake.

> Very high levels of emotional arousal may prevent the proper evaluation and categorization of experience by interfering with hippocampal function. . . . The experience is laid down and later perceived as isolated images, bodily sensations, smells and sounds that feel alien and separate from the other life experiences. Because the hippocampus has not played its usual role in helping to localize the incoming information in time and space these fragments continue to lead an isolated existence.[1]

I was flooding.

I walked down to Main Street, which is also Route 7, a road that heads north and south. There was a car parked at the gate. A Chevy Impala.

He was sitting there in his Chevy.

Not a cloud in the sky.

He was sitting in his Chevy. "Hey kid," he called out.

I was flooding.

Chapter 32

Castration Anxiety

MY FATHER PUT TRAINING WHEELS ON MY BIKE. I ATTACHED PLASTIC streamers to the handlebars. I used clothespins to fasten baseball playing cards to the frame so they hit the spokes and made noise. I loved my bike. I loved noise. The next-door neighbor Mr. Palowski hated noise. He hated me. "Get outta my yard, you rotten kid." It's possible I once rode my bike through his yard.

"I don't need training wheels," I said to my father. I didn't need training wheels. I didn't need my father. I didn't need anyone. I could fly.

Two days later he said, "Okay, they're off."

"What is?" I asked.

"The training wheels," he said exhibiting a pair of pliers, a wrench, the pair of training wheels—a cigar hung from his mouth.

I got back on my bike. My father ran alongside as we moved down the street. This was great. This was cool. I had a bike. "I don't need you to—" and then I realized he wasn't there. I was riding on my own. No training wheels. No father. Just me on my bike. It was like flying—only better.

When I got to the corner, I turned to go back. A car stopped short as I rode right in front. The driver leaned out, "Hey kid, you better thank your father. He just saved your life."

I looked back down the block. My father was there, hands on his

201

hips, cigar in his mouth. He must have warned the driver that there was this kid on a bike who imagined he was flying, only better. He took the cigar from his mouth and waved me back.

I loved my bike.

I rode it everywhere. It was the greatest thing. When you're a kid in Manhattan Beach you can ride to the Bay. You can ride to the Ocean. You can ride to Coney Island. And that's what I did. I rode to Coney Island—down Orient Avenue, over to Surf, onto the Boardwalk and then there you are. There I was—Coney Island—the greatest place on Earth.

Coney Island had everything. There was a wooden horse race—"half a mile in half a minute," the human roulette wheel, the "blow-hole theater" that is famous for having lifted Marilyn Monroe's skirt. And outside on the boardwalk right by the beach, there were hot dogs and fries, fortune tellers and rides, barkers and freaks. There was cotton candy to eat. There was Steeplechase Park!

Looka looka looka
See the pretty lights
Looka looka looka
See the world
Bend and twist
Looka looka looka
Come inside. Step right up.
Lady with a beard.
A kid with two heads.
Looka looka looka
Looka looka look.

There were shows. There were rides. There was a boardwalk and under it big kids making out.

Looka looka looka
See the pretty lights
Looka looka looka
Take a ride

See the sights
Looka looka look
There was The Wonder Wheel, the Cyclone, the merry-go-round.
Susan Margo said that there was a man who fixed things when they
broke. She said he fixed the merry-go-round. She said he painted the
carousel horses. She said the horses were sad even though they were
painted bright—
Looka looka looka
They were sad underneath, she said.
Looka looka looka
I loved the merry-go-round. There was a brass ring. And if you got
the ring, you'd get a free ride. I went there with Susan Margo, but
she wouldn't get on. She said she was scared of the horses. Scared of
the ride. I didn't understand. I was scared of the Parachute Jump. I
was scared of the Wonder Wheel. My sister Jolie once took me on the
Cyclone—it was the scariest thing in my life. But being scared of the car-
ousel made no sense. There was music and mirrors. There were lights.
Looka looka looka—
See the pretty horses
All the day and night.
"Why be scared of carousel horses that go round and round?"
And then she told me that she wasn't scared of the horses. She was
scared of the man who painted them. Of the man who ran the mer-
ry-go-round. Of the man who made it go round.
The music played. The lights flashed, the carousel went round.
Round and round and round.
Looka looka looka
Freaks from far and wide
Looka looka looka
So much more to see inside
It made no sense to me.
I parked my bike against the rail and made my way to the front of
the crowd.

The freaks stood in line. One of them was a midget. He kept staring at me. Maybe because we were the same size.

Looka looka looka

The barker motioned. The freaks filed in one by one.

Looka looka looka

The air was heavy with the smell of hot dogs and pretzels, salt water and sweets.

I walked back to my bike.

When I looked back, the midget was still there. He stared at me. I couldn't tell if he was a kid like me or a man. Then the barker yelled, "Hey," and the midget turned and limped slowly inside. His legs were not the same size. He had a beard. I figured he was a man.

I got on my bike. I rode past the Brighton Beach Baths—where old people danced. My father took me there once.

I was holding his hand as we walked down a hallway past a sign that said, "Adam." The other hallway had a sign that said, "Eve."

We got to the end of Adam's hall where there were shelves. I watched as my father took off his bathing trunks. We had just come from the beach.

"Richard, take off your suit."

I pulled off my suit and wrapped myself in a towel. I followed my father past another sign that said, "To the Baths."

We entered a room that had long walls with showers and men all soaking wet. I had never seen so many naked old men.

"Sexuality is the key to the problem of the psychoneuroses."

There were no doors. No curtains. No closets. No keys.

"No one who disdains the key will ever be able to unlock the door," Freud said.[1]

"Richard, over there," my father pointed.

I was wrapped in the towel.

"Hang up your towel—"

I just stood.

"On one of the hooks," my father said as he lathered his chest. "Over there."

"Dad—?"

"Richard—"

I hung the towel on a hook I could barely reach and stood there naked facing men with thin hair, thick bellies, bulbous cocks—all speaking Polish or Yiddish. I thought of the chickens.

"But we have not made any mention of the danger—"

"Put soap in your hair!"

"—The danger is castration," Freud said.

"I don't like it here."

"You will of course object that after all that is not a real danger—"

"What are you afraid of?" my father said.

"It is not a question of whether castration is really carried out; what is decisive is that the danger is one that threatens from the outside and that the child believes . . ."[2]

Surrounded by lather, hair, and naked old men.

"Richard—"

—I was terrified that I would never grow hair, never have a beard. I was afraid of so many eye-level cocks.

"I don't like it here."

My father handed me a bar of soap.

Another man showering alongside my father asked, "*Vi alt iz deyn eyngl?*"

My father turned to me, "Richard, tell him how old you are."

I looked at the man. He looked down at me with a smile, a belly, a chest covered with lather, and right there, staring straight at me like a chicken with only one eye—

"Tell him how old you are," my father said as he lathered soap into my scalp.

"It is our suspicion that during the human family's primeval period, castration used actually to be carried out by a jealous and cruel father."[3]

"I, I,–" I said through the soap. Then I started to cry.

"Did it get into your eyes?"

"Yes," I nodded. It wasn't the soap.

"*Er iz zex*," my father said.

"*Zex?*"

I had never seen a real penis before.

"*Ya. Zex*," and they both laughed.

When I was fifteen, my face still fair, fine, and hairless–I was riding on the bus when two kids from school, Zagorious–as hairy as Zeus, and Garzo–who shaved by the time he was "*zex*," danced around me taunting, "You'll never grow hair–soft as a peach. You'll never grow hair–like a girl. You're a freak." I sat in the seat, my eyes welling with tears. It felt like the truth. I thought of the midget still staring at me from ten years before. Staring at me–letting me know just who was the freak.

When I got home, I went to the kitchen.

My mother was there. "I've made chocolate chip cookies," she said.

I took one.

"Did you and Michael have fun?" she asked thinking that I had gone to Michael Starr's house.

"Yes," I lied. "We had fun."

I was afraid that she would find out. The way she had found out about my shoes. I once told her I had tried to walk around puddles after having been given a new pair of shoes. But a neighbor driving past had seen me jump into every one. I don't know how, but my lies never held.

After I ate the cookie, I figured I'd better–

"Michael wasn't home," I said.

"Where was he?"

"Home."

"You just said–"

"He was sick."

"So where have you been?" she asked.

"Coney Island."

"You went to Coney Island—alone?"

I nodded.

"Richard, don't you ever! You can't do that!"

"Why?"

"Because you're a boy. Because it's dangerous."

"Can I have another cookie?"

"Richard!"

I thought of Susan Margo and that man who painted the carousel horses, and how she was afraid. And how I didn't want to be afraid of carousel horses. I didn't want to be afraid of anything.

"Richard, that was wrong."

"Why?"

"You must promise you'll never—ever go back there again."

"I promise."

"I mean it."

"I promise."

And it was the truth. I never went back there—

"I promise."

—until I went back with Sid.

Chapter 33

How I Learned to Drive

MY BIG SISTER JOLIE MET SID AT BRANDEIS UNIVERSITY WHERE SHE was a student and he was a god.

Sid was six feet four. He had shoulders as big as a wall. He could play baseball, football. He could throw me in the air and catch me like a ball. I was six years old when Jolie came home with Sid.

Sid taught me sports. Sid took me fishing on the Maryanne. Then he took me fishing on the Helen B. Kids wanted to be my best friend because of Sid. I loved Sid.

Sid was in the Army. There was a war. I didn't know where the war was. I just knew it wasn't in Brooklyn. Sid took me to Fort Dix.

Sid showed me his barracks, his locker, his gun. He showed me how a walkie-talkie worked. When he was stationed in Greenland—I didn't know where that was but I knew it was far because you had to say "over" after talking on the walkie-talkie. It went back and forth like that when Jolie talked to Sid, she'd say "over" and then at the end when she'd say "over and out," she'd cry. Jolie cried a lot. After Greenland, Sid went somewhere else. I didn't know where that was but Jolie said it was as far as you could go.

Then Sid came home. It was summer. The only thing that mattered was it was summer, and I didn't have school. And Sid!

The first thing Sid did when he came back to Brooklyn was to take me and Jolie for a drive in his blue-and-white Oldsmobile 88 convertible. The top was down, the sun was up. We drove along Emmons Avenue past Lundy's where I would sometimes go with Aunt Fran—then to Neptune Avenue. We kept driving onto Surf Avenue. And there we were. In Coney Island! And there I was in the front seat between Jolie and Sid in a blue-and-white Oldsmobile 88 convertible.

Sid drove with one hand on the wheel. "Do you want to drive?" I shook my head.

We drove past the merry-go-round where Susan Margo was scared. We drove past the Cyclone, where I wouldn't go. Sid leaned over to me, "Take the wheel."

"I don't know how."

"Sure you do."

"No, I don't."

Sid picked me up and put me on his lap. "Take the wheel," Sid said, taking his hand off the wheel. "Take the wheel."

"I don't know how," I tried to squirm off his lap. He held me in place as the car drifted to the right.

"I don't know how."

"Just steer."

"I'm afraid."

"You better steer or we'll crash."

"I can't. I've never—"

"We're going to crash," he said calmly as the blue-and-white Olds 88 convertible veered closer and closer to cars parked along Surf Avenue.

The Olds 88 was a great car. Many said it was the greatest car that General Motors had ever built.

"You better take the wheel. You better steer or this beautiful car—"

"I don't know how—"

"You better—"

I took the wheel. I steered the car. We didn't crash. It was the greatest. I was driving a car!

I loved driving. I loved Sid. Sid was the greatest thing my sister ever did.

At dinner that night, we all sat around. My sisters, my mother, my father, and Sid. "I drove a car," I said. "It was the greatest thing. You should have seen!"

That night Sid came to my room. He sat on the edge of my bed.

"You drove the car," Sid said.

"Yup," I said. I was proud. I was happy. I drove Sid's car sitting on Sid's lap. It was the greatest thing I ever did.

"I brought you something."

"You did?"

"I did."

"What?"

"This," Sid said holding a cap.

"What is it?"

"It's a cap."

The cap was blue and had a white letter on it that said "M."

"What's it for?"

"It's for you"

"The M?"

Sid nodded, then smiled. For a god, Sid was shy. "The 'M' is for Milwaukee. I'm going to be playing baseball in Milwaukee—for a team called the Braves, and I want you to have this cap. My cap. My team. Now it's yours. Your team."

"Wow!"

He gave me the cap.

I held the cap. I didn't know what to do. I mean I knew you put a cap on your head, but this cap was different. This cap was special. This cap was from Sid. This cap had the letter "M." It was magic, that's what it was.

"Can I put it on?"

"Of course you can," Sid said.

I ran down the hall to the bathroom. I climbed up on the sink and sat with my feet in the basin facing the mirror.

I looked into the mirror. I saw a boy. In pajamas. Buck teeth. Green eyes. Holding a cap.

Then I watched as the boy put the cap on his head. A blue cap. A blue cap with a white letter M. An M for Milwaukee. I stared at the boy. The boy stared back. And then the boy smiled. I had never seen that boy smile like that. The first time. This boy. In a cap. Smiling. Like that. Like the beginning. Like I was witnessing. The beginning. Of this boy. In a cap. With an M. A white letter M for Milwaukee—even though the boy didn't know where Milwaukee was or what Milwaukee meant. But it meant something. There was something. I saw something. Because of that cap. I had witnessed. Something. The beginning. He stayed like that staring at what he saw.

Wonder—that's what I saw.

Wonder.

And then I watched the boy climb down from the sink and out of the mirror. And I didn't know it then, but I would never see that boy again.

And when the boy walked back to his room, Sid was waiting there on the side of the bed. The boy got back into bed.

"Do you like the cap?" Sid asked.

"I, I, I—" I was so proud. I was so excited. I couldn't talk. I almost cried. I shook my head.

"I'm glad," Sid said. "I'm really glad," and then he said, "I'll see you in the morning." Then he rubbed my head, turned out the light, and went back downstairs to where Jolie and my mother were talking.

"Is he asleep?" I heard my mother ask.

I lay on my bed alone in the dark.

The lights of another car passed on the ceiling and walls.

I looked over at my books—Babar—"the Big Orange"—was there on the shelf. I knew it by heart. Old Yeller. And Bambi. But I didn't love Bambi. Not yet.

More lights passed overhead.

I closed my eyes.

"Once upon a time in the great forest, a little elephant is born."

Pages flew further ahead. "Babar has a hat, a handsome derby hat, and wears it all the time."

My mother came in. I showed her my cap. I told her it was from Sid. I told her it was a magic cap. I told her about the letter "M."

I opened my eyes.

I could hear my mother and Jolie downstairs.

I touched my head to make sure the cap was really there—and then another story came into my head, a story like Babar's. Only different. There was a story, but I didn't know where it was going. I didn't know how it would end. I just knew it had a beginning. I closed my eyes.

"Once upon a time, there was a boy who had a cap—"

My story had begun. It had begun with a cap.

And this boy could do anything. He could ride a bike. He could drive a car. He could go to Coney Island—all by himself. The boy had a story, a real story just like Babar. It was the story of an "adventurer," a "conquistador," even though the boy didn't know just what those words meant. It was a real story.

A story of a boy who had looked in the mirror and had seen a boy in a cap. It was a magic cap.

And that's when his story began.

Chapter 34

Do Not Enter

"MEMORY PROVIDES OUR LIVES WITH CONTINUITY. IT GIVES US A coherent picture of the past that puts current experience in perspective."[1]

Without memory one has no yesterday, no tomorrow, not even today. Without memory, there are only isolated instants repeated over and over. Without memory there is no story, no time, only infinite flashes of now.

My "story" picked up the next morning when I stood on a jetty, on a pile of rocks that stuck out where Sheepshead Bay opened into Jamaica Bay. The story began with a boy and a cap. A boy and a cap and a bike. A boy who had crawled under the fence of the United States Coast Guard Station overlooking the bay. A boy and a cap and a bike who saw little reason to pause for a sign that might interfere with his plans. He was, after all, a conquistador for whom rules did not apply.

"Warning: Do Not Enter," the sign said.

"He stole my hose—the rotten kid!"

"I'm not a rotten kid," I told my mother.

"Did you take the hose?"

"I'm not a rotten kid. I'm an adventurer," I said.

Freud had said a similar thing to his eccentric friend, Wilhelm Fliess. When accused of being a thinker, not a "rotten kid," Freud

213

replied, "I am not a thinker. I am a conquistador—an adventurer, if you want it translated—with all the curiosity, daring, and tenacity characteristic of a man of this sort."[2]

"I'm not a rotten kid."

"Richard—?"

"I needed it."

"Mr. Palowski's hose?"

"Yes," I said not entirely sure why. "I'm a conquistador, an adventurer," I repeated unaware of the reference to Freud.

"An adventurer," I thought as I stood there on the jetty, "that's who I am." And as I stood there, my story began all by itself, just like Babar. "Once upon a time, there was a boy who had a cap and a bike, who rode his bike to the edge of the world because he could. An adventurer. That's what he is."

"A rotten kid, that's what he is," Mr. Palowski shouted from his yard at our dining room window where I stood curled around my mother's left hip.

"He stole my hose, the rotten kid!" He shook his fist.

"When faced with a problem, animals do not respond randomly— My mother looked at me.

—but rather select and test hypotheses, or strategies concerning the solution.

"I can explain," I said.

"Explain!"

"I needed water for my fort. I just forgot to bring it back."

"We assume that one form of hypothesis involves approaching or avoiding places (or ideas) in the environment and, further, that this type of hypothesis is based on information contained in the hippocampal cognitive mapping system."[3]

Mr. Palowski had called the police.

I hadn't counted on that.

"Mr. Palowski, he is a six-year-old boy," my mother defiantly said.

Two cops—one on either side of Mr. Palowski—stood there not

saying a thing as he screamed up at the window that they were there to arrest me.

Let me explain—I needed water for a fort I had made on the side of the house under the juniper trees. I had seen a show on TV where a bird made a fort out of mud. I wanted to make a fort out of mud. I wanted to be like that bird. It was in Africa. I didn't know where Africa was but I knew I needed mud. I needed water. I needed Mr. Palowski's hose. It made total sense.

"He stole my hose," Mr. Palowski yelled.

"You can't take what isn't yours," my mother said.

"I forgot to bring it back. That's all."

"He's a little thief!" Mr. Palowski yelled.

My mother leaned out the window. "Mr. Palowski, how dare you call my boy a thief! I won't have you say such a thing." She closed the window, then turned to me. I wasn't there.

I was under the table.

"Such a model states that when faced with a problem animals do not respond randomly but rather select and test hypotheses, or strategies concerning the solution."[4]

She bent down and crawled under the table. She lay there next to me. "Richard, I'm too old for this. Did you take Mr. Palowski's hose?"

"No."

"Are you sure?"

"I didn't mean to. I can't remember. Maybe I put it back."

"Come and say you're sorry," she said.

"What if I didn't do it?"

"Come and say you're sorry." I crawled out from under the table. "Tell him. He's a silly, old man—just say you're sorry." I didn't move. "Richard!"

I went to the window.

Mr. Palowski was standing there in his yard with the cops. "Say you're sorry," my mother said.

"But I'm not," I said, still uncertain if I had even taken the hose. It all blurred in my head.

"Richard—just say you're sorry!"

I turned to Mr. Palowski, "I'm not sorry because I don't remember and I didn't do it and anyway my mother says you're a silly old man." And then I ran through the house, out the back door, and hid under the juniper trees by my mud fort waiting for the police to take me away.

They never came. I never knew why. For the second time in the six years since my birth, I waited to be taken to jail for the rest of my life.

I just knew I hated Mr. Palowski and was glad when my mother told me he had died. But that was later. And she said that was not a nice thing to say about Mr. Palowski, which made me think she forgot all the terrible things he had said and almost put me in jail and always yelled at me and shook his fist whenever I ran through his yard on the way to school because there was a shortcut through his yard and if I wanted to get to school on time and I only stepped on one of his stupid flowers—and who likes petunias anyway—"Get outta my yard, ya rotten kid." And then he called the police.

Geraniums not petunias.

I don't know why she wanted me to say I was sorry. It made no sense at all. I wasn't sorry. I wasn't sorry at all.

In 1972 the Canadian neuroscientist Endel Tulving wrote a paper entitled "Episodic and Semantic Memory." In that paper he introduced the concept of personal—or episodic—memory as distinct from factual—or semantic—memory. A factual memory would be something like two plus two equals four. Or the fact that Palowski is a Polish name. Episodic memory is personal—like Mr. Palowski, who was Polish (that's a fact) hated me (that's personal) and yelled at me one morning because he was certain I had stolen his garden hose even though I don't think I did but maybe I did (that's episodic—it's my episodic memory, not yours, because I was there, not you—"I" speaks to the personal, the who, what, when, and where of memory).

"Episodic memory is a more or less faithful record of a person's experiences. Thus every 'item' in episodic memory represents information stored about the experienced occurrence of an episode or event."[5]

I hated Mr. Pawloski—that's a fact. An episodic memory fact.

"Semantic memory is the memory necessary for the use of language. It is a mental thesaurus, organized knowledge a person possesses about words and other verbal symbols, their meaning and referents, about relations among them and about rules, formulas, and algorithms for the manipulation of these symbols, connects and reparations."[6]

Another episodic memory is that the morning after Mr. Palowski tried to have me taken away for "borrowing" his hose, I rode my bike to the end of the earth where there is a jetty and I couldn't go any farther, which is how come I knew I had reached the end of the earth. I climbed onto the jetty and stood there facing the end—that is to say facing Jamaica Bay and Idlewild Airport, which would later be named JFK. I knew that I was an adventurer, way before I knew what an adventurer was, a conquistador way before I knew what a conquistador was, way before I had read those words in a letter that Sigmund Freud wrote—and on that day I was brought back to the day when I was standing on the jetty at the end of the world facing Jamaica Bay. That is mostly episodic memory. It's got memory that's mostly personal but it's got some that's fact—the location of the peninsula—which is semantic, but it's also personal—that I was there with my cap, on my bike and would later relate that to a letter written by Sigmund Freud. All that is episodic. It's all part of my memory. There's no reason why that would be part of yours. And that makes it episodic. Mine. My memory.

And it's also autonoetic, which is another idea that Tulving introduced. It's subjective information taken from and moving through different points in time. That capacity to move back and forth—to take memory and move it from the present to the past and from the past to the future, is called "autonoetic memory"—Tulving called it "autonoetic" or "mental time travel" in that paper he wrote in 1972. He labeled this capacity as "uniquely human."

"If there is hope for a more appropriate assessment of the uniqueness of episodic memory and autonoetic consciousness, it may come through the realization that mental time travel involves awareness not only of what has been but also of what may come. This awareness allows autonoetic creatures to reflect on and make plans for their own and their progeny's future. . . . This term autonoesis has been used to refer to this special kind of consciousness that allows us to be aware of subjective time in which events happened . . . and in which events could happen. This 'subjective sense of time' is 'uniquely human.'"[7]

It is part of why we tell stories. We have large frontal lobes, and we have more episodic memory—that is to say capacity for personal memory—and because of this capacity for "time travel" we can move memory in space and time, and the capacity to create story.

Standing there on the jetty at Fort Hamilton watching planes take off from Idlewild Airport across Jamaica Bay was the first time that I realized that the world was bigger than the bike ride I had made to Coney Island. It was bigger than Ebinger's Bakery. It was bigger than the Dodgers. It was bigger than Mr. Palowski and his stupid hose. Maybe it was even bigger than the end of the jetty on which I was standing. I was beginning to imagine that the world might even be bigger than me. I was beginning to see myself in a story that might stretch beyond what I knew. I saw it move in space. I was beginning to see it move in time. I saw how it might all be so much bigger than I had imagined. For the first time.

I asked my mother what infinity was and she said it was something that had no end. And so I asked what happened when you got to the end of infinity. And then she said that it was time for bed.

It was then and there that I began to experience the freedom and the power of travel—not on a plane or a train—but in my head. "We propose that the ability to mentally travel through time is the expression of episodic memory system of the brain and this ability is not shared by other systems of memory. . . . The relation between episodic memory and the frontal lobes represents a reliable fact of neuroanatomy."[8]

The enormous size of the prefrontal cortex in Homo sapiens, and indeed in all hominids stretching back millions of years, set the stage for the evolutionary leap from the nonhuman primate to the hominid and from hominid to Homo sapiens. It allowed the leap from biological evolution, which was very slow to cultural evolution which was more than just a little fast. Cultural evolution is explosive.

The slow biological evolution of the prefrontal cortex in our species some 300,000 years ago led to the capacity for symbols, ideas, abstract stories that could be passed on from one generation to the next. The slow biological evolution of the human prefrontal cortex set the stage for the explosive evolution of human culture that probably began with a genetic mutation in the prefrontal cortex.

"Wow," I said, watching a plane taking off across Jamaica Bay from the airport that would soon be called JFK. "Where are you going?" I thought, and was so impressed with the idea that I yelled to the plane, "Where are you going?" I waited for a while kind of knowing the plane wouldn't answer.

"Mental time travel involves awareness not only of what has been but also of what may come."[9]

"Where are you going?"

And that's when my mother gave me *The Travels of Babar*.

"Babar, the King of the elephants, and his wife, Queen Celeste, have just left for their wedding trip in a balloon."

The expansion of the frontal lobes, especially the prefrontal cortex, in primates and then yet again in the human primate is what has given our species the extraordinary capacity to imagine, fantasize, dream, symbolize an untethered world of time and space. At the age of six, I was beginning to experience the power of the frontal lobes as they continued to myelinate, to come alive, and "online." To establish paths of communication between the awareness of what was now and could be—in the frontal lobes—with the memory and fantasy of what was and had been—as a result of the hippocampus. The expansion of the prefrontal cortex gave us the capacity not just to keep the present and recent past in mind (working memory). It gave us the capacity to imagine the future. It gave us the capacity to imagine what we had never seen, to imagine what never had been. It gave us the capacity of a god.

> Further items and sets of items, not related to the present sensory array, can be called up and manipulated. Thus items which are never related in reality can be juxtaposed, substituted for each other, or related in other ways to create new patterns. This possibility, in addition to others allowing for the comparison of different map segments, provides the basis for operations which might be central to some of the mental activities usually referred to as thinking, imagination, and creativity.

For this kind of "movement" in space, in time, in thought—the hippocampus is critical. The hippocampus integrates perception with memory. The hippocampus is what allows the mind to wonder, to invent, to get lost in what never was, but could be. The hippocampus is what puts these ideas of past, present, future, and sensation together.

> Finally the existence of such optimal strategies for information manipulation within the map, aside from enabling humans to imagine things they have never experienced (such as an elephant in a tree), lay the basis for a liberation of the mapping system

from its connection with space; the relationship between items in a map need no longer represent an inevitable "real-world" spatial relationship.[10]

Such manipulation allows for fantasy, for imagination, for creative thought—all of this arises from a functioning cognitive "map," the storytelling system that was first identified in the hippocampal navigation of a rat.

"Although we have discussed navigation in the usual purely spatial sense of moving from place to place, we would argue that the hippocampus plays a critical role in the broader challenge of navigating through life."[11]

As I watched the planes land and take off from Idlewild airport, I was beginning to feel how small I was, standing there on the jetty at Fort Hamilton on the peninsula at the end of what had been until that moment, the edge of the known world. And watching a plane take off, I felt everything shift. What had never been, what I had never imagined, was expanding—as fast as that plane flew, maybe faster.

"Where are you going?" I yelled again to the plane, wondering whether Babar and Queen Celeste were on that very flight.

A wave broke against the jetty. The rocks didn't move. It was my mind, not the earth that had moved. I was thrilled. I was lost. And I knew I needed a bigger story to encompass what I had just learned. That the world was much bigger, and that I was much smaller, and that wonder did not move in a straight line. "Mental time travel involves awareness not only of what has been but also of what may come."[12]

"Wow!"

And if I were to find myself in this expanding, new world, I would need a different story to explain my part. I knew I had to find it. Because, after all, I had a bike; I had a cap; I had Sid, who was about to marry my sister, Jolie, and because I was an adventurer—who was at that very moment about to start on a journey. I was a conquistador, and my world was expanding at what seemed like the speed of light.

John O'Keefe was the first to discover that it is the hippocampus that contained a multisensory representation of extra-personal space. John O'Keefe was the first to discover that the rat used multisensory information to create a sense of where the animal *thinks* it is. John O'Keefe was the first to discover that it was the hippocampus where the animal created its cognitive map. But John O'Keefe did not know that right there and then, on a jetty facing Jamaica Bay, a six-year-old conquistador was also constructing his map. John O'Keefe did not know that a six-year-old kid was about to take the first step into a story, a story that was his, a story that would be his for the rest of his life.

And that's when a man in a military uniform stepped out of the Coast Guard Station and yelled,

"Hey kid!"

I turned to face this man. It was clear that like John O'Keefe, he didn't know who I was.

"Hey kid!"

It was clear he didn't know I was an adventurer, a conquistador, mapping my way to a new story and a new world.

"Hey kid!"

Chapter 35

Papier-mâché

MY SEVENTH BIRTHDAY WAS AT SCHOOL. I DIDN'T GET A PARTY AT home because my mother forgot. I guess she forgot when I was born.

But Miss Oberfeld, my teacher, remembered.

"Ruth," my father said before he left for work. "Don't you see Dr. Stein today?"

"What?" she asked.

"You see him on Tuesdays, Wednesdays, and Fridays. Today is Wednesday."

Miss Oberfeld never forgot. She had long, black hair. She was tall. She was pretty. She was my favorite teacher. She never forgot.

"Ruth—?"

Marcia was a girl in my class at school. Sometimes Marcia forgot to go to the toilet. Or maybe she was too scared to say she had to go. So sometimes she just sat at her desk and wet her pants—and all of the rest of us watched this yellow pool get bigger around Marcia's black shoes with little straps.

Miss Oberfeld got up. She told the class to quiet down and study the state capitals— "Start with Alabama," Miss. Oberfeld said. "Who knows where Alabama is?" Miss Oberfeld asked as she moved to the map on the wall. No one knew. "It's next to Mississippi." None of us knew where Mississippi was. All we knew was that Marcia had

223

wet her pants, and there was an orange puddle around her feet—like the color of Florida on the map on the wall in the front of the class. "Mississippi is here. Study the state capitals," Miss Oberfeld said as she went to Marcia and led her by the hand. We all started to snicker when we saw Marcia's wet bottom.

"Study the state capitals," Miss Oberfeld said. "Begin with Alabama. The capital of Alabama is Montgomery," Miss Oberfeld said as she took Marcia's hand and walked her to the girls' restroom.

The knowledge of state capitals is an example of semantic memory.

Miss Oberfeld always knew what to do. When it was my birthday, the one my mother forgot, Miss Oberfeld had a cake. The cake wasn't from Ebinger's. It was papier-mâché. There were candles inside the cake. It was the same cake for every kid whose mother forgot. If your birthday was in the summer, you didn't get to have a papier-mâché cake. Too bad for you.

And so on my seventh birthday, Miss Oberfeld brought out the papier-mâché cake and sang "Happy Birthday." Then she gave me a big hug—which I liked a lot. And then she said, "Make a wish. It's your birthday. What do you want for your birthday?" I looked at Miss Oberfeld, this woman who was young and pretty and who remembered it was my birthday, and who was kneeling beside me. I could smell her hair. I decided right then and there that I loved Miss Oberfeld and would marry her when I grew up. "Make a wish," she said, "any wish. What do you want?" And I made a wish without closing my eyes, without saying it only to myself, but instead I said right to her face, "I wish you were dead."

Miss Oberfeld didn't know what to say. Kids snickered. Then Miss Oberfeld said, "Is that your wish? That I was dead?" I stared at her. I kept staring. I didn't know why I had said that. And then I turned and ran.

"Richard, come back here!"

I ran out of the room. I ran out the school. I ran down the steps past the crossing guard onto Hampton Avenue. I almost got hit by a car. I ran to Exeter Street. I ran to Sheepshead Bay. I ran along the path by the Bay until I couldn't run any more. And then I sat down.

I made a fist. I hit my arms. I hit my legs. I hit my head. I hit my face. I stared at the bay.

Bubbles were popping on top of the dirty water. A gull swooped in and came up with a fish.

The fish wriggled as the gull swallowed it alive.

And then I cried.

I just cried.

"Richard—?"

I kept crying.

"Richard—?"

I turned around.

Miss Oberfeld was standing there with the school crossing guard. She stared at me as gulls circled overhead.

"What's the capital of Alabama?" Miss Oberfeld asked.

"Brooklyn," I said.

She held out her hand. "Close enough."

"The most traumatic circumstances are the rages children feel toward the very persons whom they love and depend upon, rages that threaten to disorganize them and disrupt vital sustaining relationships."[1]

I needed my mother to remember. That's what mothers do. They remember. They put things together. They take things you tell them and make stories. And then you have memory. And then you have a story. That's how it works—except when your mother forgets.

For children, narratives can be co-constructed with their parents. This allows for the joining together of parents and children in the telling of a story. "Memory talk" between parent and child focuses on the parent's interest in the views and inner experience of the child. . . . Thus narrative both establishes a sense of meaning for a child and is a shared process that can shape the importance of the content of memory."[2]

My mother forgot.
    Miss Oberfeld remembered.
    She was the best teacher I ever had.
    I didn't want Miss Oberfeld to be dead. I wanted to marry her.

Chapter 36

Tying the Knot

WHEN JOLIE TOLD ME THAT SHE WAS GOING TO MARRY SID, I ASKED, "What about me?"

Jolie smiled, then said, "You can't marry Sid, you're too young. But you wanna know what?"

"What?"

"You can be his brother!"

"I can?"

She nodded. I jumped up and down. It was the greatest thing.

"What do I do?"

Jolie and Sid were married at Temple Menorah on Ocean Parkway in Brooklyn. I wore a tie. I wore pants that itched. I went into my mother's room as she was still getting dressed. She was sitting at her dressing table wearing a slip. My father came up the stairs, "Ruth, we can't be late for our own daughter's wedding."

My mother stood up. "It won't last," she said.

"Ruth, just get ready," he said.

"What won't?" I asked. She never said.

She went to her closet and took out her suit with a dark and light green pattern. The sleeves were long. The neck was low. She looked beautiful in the suit. "You look beautiful," I said.

When my father saw her he said, "You look beautiful, Ruth."

She kept looking for something.

"Ruth," he said.

"I don't," she said.

"Depression is often associated with a disturbance of sleep, diminished appetite, loss of weight, loss of energy, decreased sex drive, and slowing down of thoughts."[1]

"Ruth, we really have to leave," my father said.

"Where's my purse?" she asked.

My father went to the table beside her bed. My mother went to him, took her purse. "Thank you," she said.

Temple Menorah was run by Aunt Fran's husband, Uncle Manny. When we walked in, Uncle Manny was there to greet us. He was wearing a dark suit, a white shirt, a blue tie. Uncle Manny always dressed the same except when he was home watching TV when he only wore his BVDs.

When Susan Margo died two years later, Manny wore that same suit and tie. He died three years after that. Aunt Fran bought Manny a paisley tie for his funeral. He looked better in that paisley tie than he ever did when alive.

"Welcome, welcome. Shalom. What a glorious day," Uncle Manny greeted my mother and father using the same words he used to greet everyone who entered. "Welcome, welcome. Shalom. What a glorious day." There was a band. There was a buffet.

Watching Jolie and Sid take their vows was the greatest thrill of my life. I was getting my very own god! I asked everyone would I be as big as Sid. Would I be as tall as Sid. I think the question I was searching for was, "One day, will I get to be Sid?" No one was able to answer the question I never asked.

I loved Sid. I really did. I don't think Jolie loved Sid as much as I loved Sid.

Chapter 37

Guarding

MY PARENTS ARGUED.

Sometimes my parents would argue about me. Mostly I remember my father yelling, "You can't just let the boy hide in your skirts!" When he'd yell like that, I'd get scared. "He's tied to your apron strings." Sometimes it seemed he was yelling because he was angry and impatient with me for just being a kid. But more often it seemed he was yelling because he was angry and impatient with my mother for being depressed. I was never sure which as I just felt he was angry whenever his voice was loud.

Perhaps it wasn't anger. Perhaps he got loud because he wanted her to hear. Perhaps he was pleading with her. Perhaps he was trying to find her. Perhaps he was trying to save her.

Sometimes I heard him yelling late at night as I lay in bed. I heard him yelling quite a lot.

I would mostly lie in bed staring at the ceiling, hearing his voice because it was loud. But then I started to hear her voice—and was drawn toward it. In my pajamas, dragging my blue blankie, I walked almost in a trance toward the sounds coming from behind their bedroom door. I sat on the floor and listened. I could hear him, shouting, pleading. "Ruth, you can't do this." It scared me. But then I heard something that scared me more.

"Don't you see? I can't get better." It was her voice. Sometimes

I fell asleep, curled like a puppy unable to move forward or back. Sometimes I'd wake up, and I'd be in my own bed. Sometimes I'd wake up, my face pressed to the floor, woken by his voice, and then I'd hear—

"Dave, don't you see—I'm no good."

"Don't say that."

Untreated depression can progress from depressed mood to mood-congruent psychotic thought—with feelings of guilt, nihilistic delusions, suicidal ideation, suicide.

"Dave, I'm no good."

"Don't say that."

"It's true."

"Ruthie, for the love of God."

"I'm no good."

That's when I heard my father scream, "You can't do this to me!"

One morning my father found me asleep by their door. "What are you doing?" he asked.

"Guarding," I said.

"Guarding what?" he asked.

"The door," I said.

My father and I were downstairs in the kitchen. Jolie was married to Sid. I didn't know where they lived but it wasn't in Brooklyn, because it was far. Susan was at Cornell, where it's cold—that's what Susan said, "I don't like it here. It's cold." My mother came down.

"I'm sorry I'm late."

She made coffee.

"I'm sorry."

"You don't have to apologize."

"I'm sorry."

Bipolar depression is characterized by feelings of inadequacy, worthlessness, shame.

"I'm sorry."

My father read the morning paper.

She took out a carton of eggs.

"Ruth, I'm not hungry. Just coffee," my father said.

Persistently elevated levels of corticotropin-releasing factor (CRF) and cortisol are contributing factors to end stage depression and mood congruent psychosis.

"I'm sorry."

"The coffee's fine."

"I'm sorry."

"Ruth, the coffee is fine! Please just stop."

My father finished the coffee, put the cup down on the table.

She stared.

He looked at her. "What?"

She shook her head.

"The coffee is fine," he said.

"I'll make some more."

"It's fine," he said.

It was weird.

She put the eggs back in the refrigerator, then poured me a bowl of Rice Krispies.

"Montgomery is the capital of Alabama," I said.

My father put the paper down and turned to my mother. "Are you all right?"

She got a bottle of milk and poured it over my cereal. It went snap, crackle, and—

"Ruth—?"

"—pop," I said—

"—are you all right?"

I picked up a spoon as I marveled at the creative genius of the Kellogg Corporation in Battle Creek, Michigan.

My mother put the bottle of milk back in the refrigerator. "Yes," she said. Then she said, "I'm sorry."

"Is Battle Creek the capital of Michigan?" I asked.

"What time is your appointment with Stein?"

"I don't know."

The symptoms of bipolar depression include the inability to make decisions, to think clearly, to cope with routine tasks—

"Is Battle Creek the capital of—?"

"It's Detroit," my father said. "Ruth make sure you give yourself enough time—

—poor concentration, poor memory, feelings of guilt, suicidal ideation.

"—the roads may be slippery. I think your appointment is at four. On Friday it usually is."

"Yes. I'm sure you're right. It's at four."

"Is it helping? Is the treatment—?"

She took the fresh pot of coffee off the stove. "Be careful. It's hot," she said. "What time will you be home?"

"Five-thirty. Or six."

"Five thirty or—?" and then she looked up, and smiled. It was different. It was weird.

"There are increased feelings of guilt, nihilistic delusions . . . suicide."

"—or six?" she asked.

It was as if she were formulating her plan right there and then.

"Mom, can you teach me how to wink?"

"So it's helping—these meetings?" my father asked.

I tried to wink. Whenever I tried to wink with one eye, both eyes would close.

"Mom—?"

"What?"

"Does your doctor think the therapy is helping?" my father asked.

"It may be that there are other still undreamed-of possible therapies," Freud said, "but for the moment we have nothing better at our disposal than psychoanalysis—"

"Is it helping?" he repeated.

"For that reason . . . psychoanalysis should not be despised"[2] Freud went on.

"I don't despise it," she said.

"So long as it's helping," my father said, picking up the paper.

Electroconvulsive therapy (ECT) had been introduced into medical practice in America in 1943. It was something Stein knew or should have known. It was an effective and recognized treatment for acute suicidal ideation and intent. It would be unfair to blame Freud for what Stein didn't know or chose to ignore. It would be unfair as Freud would not have known—

My mother picked up my father's empty cup.

—that electroconvulsive therapy had rescued my mother once before.

She washed the cup then placed it on the shelf. Then she took it down and washed it again.

"Ruth—?"

Obsessional thoughts. Repetitive behaviors. Shame—

"I'm sorry."

"Mom—can I play with Michael Starr after school?"

"Yes," she said, "that's a good plan."

My father got up from the table, "So, we all have a plan."

"Yes," my mother said, "we all have a plan."

My father put on his hat.

"See you at five-thirty," he said.

"See you at five-thirty," she said. "Or six."

It's fairly common knowledge that a depressed person has more energy when she has a plan.

"Drive carefully," he said.

Suicide is a plan.

I put on my hat and my coat. "What's the capital of Alabama?"

"You'll need gloves," she said. Then said, "Montgomery."

I thought of Miss Oberfeld as I moved to the door. "I'm sorry," I said.

"What for?"

"For what I said."

"What did you say?"

"I don't remember," I said.

I put on my hat, the one from Sid. I put on my gloves. "I'm sorry," she said.

Mothers know. That's what mothers do. What they are for. They remember who you are even when you don't know, or when you forget or get lost. Sometimes I forget. My mother forgot my birthday. Maybe that's why I got mad. Mothers aren't supposed to forget the day you were born. Mothers are supposed to know who you are.

"I'm sorry," she said again as I ran out the door, galloping through the snow toward Mr. Palowski's front yard.

"Richard—?" she called out. But I didn't hear. I was a horse. There was a fence and just beyond the fence was Mr. Palowski's front yard. I loved snow. I loved fences. I loved to gallop. I loved going where I had been told not to go.

And as I went, I kept shouting "Montgomery" wildly into the yard.

My mother stood watching.

She leaned against the door. "Once I was a good wife," she said to the windows that clouded with her breath. To the door. To the snow that was cold and white.

"A wife brings joy. I no longer bring joy. A mother brings hope. I no longer bring hope."

She was not searching for an answer.

"I am sorry," she said.

She had a plan.

Chapter 38

Sickness Pain

SHE TOOK A DEEP BREATH OF COLD AIR. "I DO NOT BELONG," SHE SAID to no one, not even herself. She was losing touch with the self she no longer was.

The self is a construction, a mosaic of sensation and memory organized in the prefrontal cortex, the parietal cortex, cortical association areas, the hippocampus. More than a house of cards, but less than a house. "I do not belong," she said as I squirmed under the fence into Mr. Palowski's yard.

I ran as fast as I could. I was a horse. In the snow. I knew the capital of—

"Montgomery!" I yelled.

"Get outta my yard, ya rotten kid!"

I tripped. I fell. I banged my knee. "Oh," I screamed.

There are two places in the brain which register pain. The sharp pain of a cut is carried along fast, large diameter fibers that transmit sensation to the spinal cord, and then to the brain stem, up to the thalamus, and finally to the postcentral gyrus of the parietal cortex. And when this sensation reaches the parietal lobe—

"That hurts!"

—pain is felt.

But in addition to the sensation of pain carried by the fast, large-diameter fibers to the postcentral gyrus of the parietal cortex, pain is

235

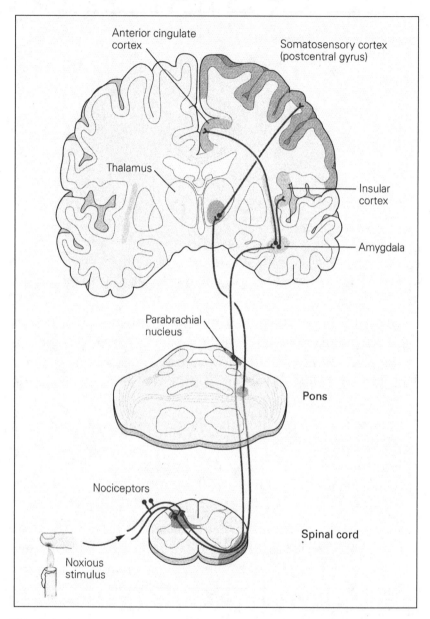

This slide shows a cross section of the brain. Acute pain, the pain for example from a burn, travels from the injured finger to the somatosensory cortex, a part of the parietal cortex where pain is registered. But if the injury were to infect, fester, decay—then a different form of pain would result. This pain is localized in a different part of the brain—the insular and cingulate cortices. This is "sickness pain."

also carried by slow, small-diameter fibers. This "slow pain" ascends the spinal cord, along a different route to the brain. Then these small-diameter fibers go to the thalamus, and from there instead of going to the parietal lobe where acute, "fast pain" is registered, this slow, small-fiber pain is directed from the thalamus to the insular and then cingulate cortices where slow pain is registered.

And should the cut not heal, should it fester, infect, then one might start to feel "sickness pain." It is not the pain of a cut. It is the pain of decay. It is the pain that saps energy, appetite, sleep, desire, hope. "Sickness pain" is registered in the insular and cingulate cortices—the same place that registers shame.

It is the pain of depression. The pain of failure. The pain that pulls the "self" out of the prefrontal cortex—and positions it in the insular and cingulate cortices where the pain of sickness, "sickness pain," is registered.

"I am no longer a wife. I am no longer a mother."

"Sickness pain" takes over as if the self were slowly turning to pus.

"I do not belong."

When I got to school, I went around back where Michael Starr was lying in the yard.

"What are you doing?" I asked.

"I'm an angel," he said as he moved his arms and legs in the snow.

"What's the capital of Alabama?" I said.

"Who cares?" Michael Starr said. He made a few more moves in the snow, then he asked, "You wanna know what I'm gonna be when I grow up?"

"I'm gonna be an elevator man," I said.

"I'm gonna be an angel," Michael Starr said to the clear, cold sky. "You wanna know how come?"

"No."

"Because my name is Michael *Star*. That's how."

I thought about that.

Michael Starr stared at the sky.

I lay down. I moved my arms. I moved my legs. I made my own snow angel.

I looked over at Michael Starr.

"I'm not going to be an elevator man," I said.

"Why not?"

"I changed my mind." I showed him my cap.

"How'd you get that?"

"Sid."

Michael Starr knew who Sid was. All the kids at school knew who Sid was. Then Michael Starr asked, "What's the 'M' for?"

"Montgomery," I said.

"Oh," Michael Starr said.

I just lay there in the snow staring up at the sky. "You wanna know what I'm gonna be when I grow up?" I asked. And then I just smiled because I had a plan.

"No," Michael Starr said.

"I'm gonna be a baseball player."

"I can throw better than you," he said.

That was true, but I didn't care. I was going to be a baseball player. I had a plan.

My mother went into the kitchen. She put away the box of Rice Krispies, the container of milk, the blue and white can of Maxwell House Coffee. A garbage truck rumbled by. The smell of coffee hung in the air. "Good to the last—"

The bell rang.

Mr. Darr—the shop teacher—opened the doors to the school. He must have seen us lying in the snow, "Hey you two!"

Neither one of us made a move, waiting to see what the other would do.

"Hey," Mr. Darr called again, "Hey Michael, Richard—that was the bell."

I looked over at Michael Starr. He made one more snow angel, then got up, walked to the school.

My mother turned and walked out of the kitchen. She stopped in front of the cellar door.

"Richard!"

I got up and looked at my snow angel. It was bleeding.

"Hey Richard, come on," Mr. Darr yelled.

And then I looked at my pants. They were torn. Blood was soaking through.

I walked to the stairs right past Mr. Darr. I was limping just a little.

"Did you cut your knee?" Mr. Darr asked.

"Yesterday," I lied, doing my best not to cry.

My mother just stared at the cellar door. Then she turned and walked back to the kitchen. She stood facing the table and chairs. She didn't count things. I counted things—chairs, tables, cookies, stairs.

My mother walked around the table.

"I do not belong," she said as if to explain what she knew she was going to do.

A mammal's place in the group is biologic—as vital to its survival as the integrity of its skin. Attachment is not a choice. It is an instinct that when disrupted sends alarms to the insular and cingulate cortices. Like the response to a festering sore, the loss of the group sounds alarms of "sickness pain."

In a human being, loss of identity, group, place is experienced as shame.

What is shame?

When an immature wolf, baboon, lion, mouse, rat is confronted by the alpha of its pack, the young mammal is faced with a specific, urgent task. It must communicate that it has no intention of challenging the alpha. If the young mammal fails, it will be attacked—and probably killed or forced to leave the pack—a path likely leading to premature death. But if the adolescent can communicate acceptance, if it can communicate submission, then attack is averted, and the young animal's place in the pack, and its life, is saved.

How does the young animal decide what to do?

It doesn't. The behavior is an instinct.

When a mammal's place in the group is threatened, there is input to the insular and cingulate cortices which mobilize responses from the hypothalamus, amygdala, and brain stem—leading to changes in the animal's basic physiologic status with a fall in core neurotransmitters—serotonin, noradrenaline, dopamine, acetylcholine, endorphins, oxytocin—and a rise of corticotropin-releasing factor and cortisol—all under heightened parasympathetic tone—leading to "freeze-dissociate" behaviors (the other side of "fight-flight").

The young mammal cowers, lowers its eyes, its ears, retracts its teeth, exposes its neck. Heart rate slows. Breathing almost comes to a stop. All this done to appear as small and vulnerable as possible— reflecting an instinctive, biologic response of submission when confronted with the dominant display of the alpha. An animal does not choose this behavior any more than an animal chooses to increase its heart rate after an acute loss of blood.

And while the threat to the animal is perceptual and external, it triggers a response that is instinctive and internal. Very quickly alarms are sent to the insular and cingulate cortices. Like the adolescent's submission to the alpha, shame in a human is routed through the insular and cingulate cortices—where the organizing forces of sickness pain take over.[1]

Bipolar depression, with its significantly elevated levels of corticotropin-releasing factor and cortisol, weakens the synaptic structure of the prefrontal cortex and hippocampus. Bipolar depression, with its significantly elevated levels of corticotropin-releasing factor and cortisol, shifts the dominant organization of the "self" from the prefrontal cortex and hippocampus to the insular and cingulate cortices. Bipolar depression, with its significantly elevated levels of corticotropin-releasing factor and cortisol, shifts the dominant organization to "sickness pain."

"I do not belong" transforms into the more definitive, "I am unworthy." Little is left of the self other than shame. "I am unworthy." Then she pulled the chair from the table—the one where she always sat, and placed it against the wall.

"Consistent with research in lower animals, acute or chronic stress may bias human subjects toward the use of a habit learning strategy at the expense of a more cognitive learning strategy. Emotional arousal may produce habitual reponses by engaging the striatal-dependent habit memory system."[2]

Perseveration, where the same thoughts or actions are taken no matter the result, reflects a biologic shift from the cognitive flexibility of the prefrontal cortex and hippocampus to the repetitive behavior of the insular and cingulate cortices. It reflects a shift from the flexibility of a map to the rigidity of a path.

During my second year of college, when I was "free, white, and irresponsible," I joined three classmates on a road trip from northern Massachusetts to South Florida. One of us had a car. The four of us took turns driving. When it was my turn, we were fifteen hours into the trip. We had been snorting lines of cocaine, drinking beer. My heart was racing, my head spinning. I was totally incompetent as I walked round the car and got behind the wheel. I turned the ignition, put the car into gear, and we were onto the next leg of our "marvelous adventure" heading south from one of the Carolinas. I'm not sure which one.

A while later, I remember seeing a road sign that read, "Welcome to Georgia, the peach state." Hours after that, I remembered another sign that read, "You are now leaving Georgia, the peach state." I have no memory of having driven through Georgia. I have absolutely no idea of how I got across the peach state without causing serious harm. But I now know that I had just been given a personal introduction to the workings of the dorsal-striatum, a stimulus-response/habit-based memory system.

Sleep deprivation, beer, and cocaine all stress the hippocampus. When stressed, hippocampal function declines. When hippocampal function declines, other systems take over. It is as if the mammalian brain evolved with the idea that when stressed, such as when confronting a charging bull or when under the influence of multiple toxins while driving across the state of Georgia, it is best not to rely on the hippocampus to come up with a map. When stressed, evolution "decided" it would be best to rely on instincts that had worked in the past.

It is the dorsal-striatum that "remembers" past behaviors—that is to say, the dorsal-striatum stores habituated responses. The dorsal-striatum does not think through the options. It does not "confer" with the prefrontal cortex. It quickly makes a choice: such as when facing a charging bull, run. Or when driving through Georgia, drive.

Driving intoxicated through Georgia and chronic bipolar depression are both situations where stress—the release of corticotropin-releasing factor and cortisol for example—affects prefrontal and hippocampal function. And when prefrontal and hippocampal function are compromised, other systems, such as the dorsal-striatum, take over.

"Within the context of multiple memory organization . . . high levels of emotional arousal associated with stress can favor habit memory . . . guidance of learned behavior by a habit memory system when exposed to acute stress may be akin to priming behavior that focuses on 'doing' and not 'thinking'."

The door to the dorsal-striatum, once opened, leads to a well-worn path—especially when the hippocampus has been chronically stressed. The hippocampus is recessive when stress is ascendent. The dorsal-striatum is one of the systems that fills the void.

I started driving when I was six.

Habit is another factor. When one does the same thing over and over, the hippocampus recedes. The dorsal-striatum takes over when one is doing something that is known, when new learning is unnecessary. It's like doing something "with your eyes closed."

She looked at the chairs around the table. "I am unworthy," she said again. Then she looked down at her feet. She was wearing slippers—dark green with black on the side. She had bought these slippers when the "glass" were unavailable at Loehmann's.

"I am unworthy—" she said then looking back up at the kitchen, the counters, the chairs, the table, the bare tree in the yard outside.

"I didn't hear you," Stein said.

"I am unworthy—" she said, and then said in a voice that no one heard, not even she—

Chapter 39

Glass Slippers

WE HAD DRIVEN TO LOEHMANN'S. I SAT IN THE FRONT SEAT PLAYING with my soldiers as my mother drove. When we got there, my mother turned to me, "Richard, I have to go to that store, right over there." It was just across the street. "I want you to stay in the car. Will you do that for me?"

"I want to go with you," I said.

"If no one is sitting in the car, I'll get a ticket. I'll just be a few minutes. Please."

I was five. We were in downtown Brooklyn. I didn't know how to drive (I learned, as I've said, when I was six).

"I want to go with you."

"Richard, I'll get a ticket."

"I want to go with you."

I went with my mother into Loehmann's. I held her hand. After she bought two dresses, as we were walking toward the store exit, she saw the slippers—the dark green slippers with black on the side. She picked one up, looked at it. Then she turned to me, "If you were Prince Charming, would you marry a girl in this slipper?"

I stared at the slipper.

"Like in Cinderella," my mother added.

"Cinderella's were glass," I said.

My mother thought about that. Then she turned to the saleslady, "Do you have my size in glass?"

The saleslady shook her head. "They are on back order, I'm afraid."

My mother smiled at the saleslady. "As you can see, I've come with my very own prince," she said putting her arm around me, "So I'll take these, even though they aren't made of glass."

"Excellent choice, Your Majesty," the saleslady said. And they both laughed even though I didn't know why.

When we got back to the car, right there on the windshield. "What's that?" I asked.

"It's a ticket," she said, folding it into her purse.

"For what?" I asked.

"A pumpkin," she said.

"Know what this is?" I asked Michael Starr, putting my finger on the map. Michael Starr shrugged. "It's Florida," I said.

"Big deal," Michael Starr said.

"I'm going to Florida," I said, and then I said, "On a train!"

Alan Fisher walked up. "You wanna know what this is?" I asked pointing again at the map. "It's Florida," I said.

"Big deal," Alan Fisher said because that's what he heard Michael Starr say.

I had never been to Florida. I had never been on a train. I had never been out of Brooklyn.

"Children, take your seats," Miss Oberfeld said.

We sat down. Miss Oberfeld stood up. "Today we are going to continue our study of maps. Who can tell me what a map is?"

Alan Fisher raised his hand.

"Yes, Alan?"

I hated Alan Fisher. I still do. Even so, it never made sense that he didn't tell what me and Michael Starr had done. At any minute, I kept expecting the police to break into school and take me to a prison where I would spend the rest of my life. After all, Michael

Starr and I had set the fire. I had taken Mr. Palowski's hose. I was the one who ran through his yard. I was the one who had trampled some of his stupid flowers.

"Yes, Alan?" Miss Oberfeld said.

"A map is a big piece of paper with lots of colors," Alan Fisher said, feeling very proud of himself. As if he knew everything there was to know, even though he didn't know where Florida was. Even thought I was the one going to Florida, even though—

"Very good, Alan. Can anyone say more about maps—"

I hated Alan Fisher. I hated him even before I knew that Alan Fisher's father was my dentist.

"Richard?"

"What?"

"Did you want to tell us more about maps?"

"Me?"

"Yes, Richard. You."

"Florida," I said.

"What about Florida?" Miss Oberfeld asked.

I looked at the map. "It's on the map," I said. "It's orange."

"Yes, that's true. Florida on our map is orange," Miss Oberfeld said. "What else can you tell us about Florida?"

"It's that way," I said pointing behind me.

"The ability of many animals to find their way back to their nests over large distances would appear to be based on some type of mapping system."[1]

"Can you tell us a bit more?"

"Well, Florida is there," I said again, pointing behind me toward Sheepshead Bay. "Next to Lundy's."

"Florida is behind you—next to Lundy's?"

"And there are fish," I added for clarification.

"Fish?"

"Yup."

Alan Fisher raised his hand. Alan Fisher kept waving his hand.

It's why I didn't feel so bad when I thought that Alan Fisher was going to be sent to prison for the rest of his life for a fire he didn't set. I didn't feel bad because he deserved to spend the rest of his life in prison for being a teacher's pet. "Ow, ow, ow," like he knew all the answers. I closed my eyes and just wished the police would come right into the classroom at P.S. 195, right then and there, and take Alan Fisher away and put him in prison for the rest of his—

"What is it Alan?"

"Florida is *not* next to Lundy's," he said like he was the smartest kid in the class. "There's a gas station next to Lundy's. I know it because it's where my father buys gas."

I hated Alan Fisher.

"I see," Miss Oberfeld said. "Routes can be about places—the relation between two places. Like we are here in the class and Sheepshead Bay is over there." She pointed to Sheepshead Bay. "Lundy's is next to a garage where Alan Fisher's father buys gas. But that's not what a map is. That's what a route—that's what a path is. If you cross the street from Lundy's, there is a gas station."

"Where my father buys gas."

"Yes, where Alan's father buys gas. But a map is something more."

"Maps were viewed as sets of connected places which provided the traveler with a large choice of possible paths between any two points in the environment. . . . Routes unlike maps, were seen as inflexibly leading from one point to another and easily disrupted by alterations of relevant cues."[2]

The stroke of brilliance came in 1971 when O'Keefe and Dostrovsky showed that the hippocampus, a collection of neurons in the medial temporal lobe, was essential if a mammal, for example a rat or a dog or a man or even Alan Fisher, were going to construct a cognitive map in its head. "These findings suggest that the hippocampus provides the rest of the brain with a spatial reference map."[3]

Routes are fixed. Maps are flexible. O'Keefe and Dostrovsky's work demonstrated that the hippocampus was critical to the internal construction of space.

"I live over there," Alan Fisher said pointing out the window. "I live in the biggest house on the block."

"Yes," Miss Oberfeld said, "You live over there—in the biggest house. But what is the location of your house?"

"When you go out the school doors, then down the steps you go that way," he said pointing out the window, "until you get to the first really big tree," Alan Fisher said, "and then you go that way some more until you see the biggest house, and that's how you get to my house."

"I see. But would those instructions help us if we wanted to get to your house let's say from Lundy's. Not from school?"

"Yes, because it's the biggest house on the block. That's how you'd find it," Alan Fisher said.

"The biggest house is key to your map," Miss Oberfeld said.

"Yup," Alan Fisher said. "Because my father is a dentist."

"I see," Miss Oberfeld said.

"Space plays a role in all our behavior. We live in it, move through it, explore it, defend it. Yet . . . we find it extraordinarily difficult to come to grips with space."[4]

"The biggest house because your father is a dentist is how we find your house," Miss Oberfeld said.

"Yup," Alan Fisher said.

"Unlike other senses, space is not analyzed by a specialized sensory organ."[5] We have receptors for light, sound, touch, pain, taste, smell. But there are no receptors for space. The mammalian sense of space is constructed. It is constructed in the hippocampus.

"If you stand on a chair, you can see my house. That's how big my house is," Alan Fisher said, standing on his chair.

"Alan, please sit down," Miss Oberfeld said.

When stressed, that is to say when the hippocampal system's ability to make "maps" is compromised, an animal relies on the remaining extra-hippocampal systems, which do not integrate perceptions into maps but provide specific paths. So a rat with hippocampal damage will use its senses individually. If it can see the destination, if it can smell the piece of cheese, if it can feel its way with its whiskers, the rat with hippocampal damage will use these inputs individually to establish as best as it can where it is and where it is going. It will establish a path, but without a functioning hippocampus, it cannot establish a map.

The individual senses can thus establish mono-sensory "paths." And if these paths are taken a sufficient number of times, the paths are set down in the dorsal-striatum as habit.

"What is the relation of your house, let's say, to the ocean?"

"That's easy," Alan Fisher said, "When you go out of my house, you turn toward the big tree in the yard. But it's not the big tree at the end of the block. The big tree in my yard is even bigger. And if you go to that tree, and turn that way, you'll see the ocean if it's not foggy," Alan Fisher said.

"So when you get to the tree, you go that way," Miss Oberfeld said indicating with her arm, "but what if something were to happen to that tree, what if the tree were to fall?"

"Why would the tree fall?" Alan Fisher asked. "It's the biggest tree on the block." Alan Fisher said as confident as a rat with hippocampal damage.

"I see," Miss Oberfeld said, "The tree won't fall."

"Nope," Alan Fisher said.

"Does anyone see anything wrong with a map that says, 'when you get to the biggest tree, go that way?'" Miss Oberfeld indicating "that way" with her right hand.

We all looked at each other. Michael Starr was staring at Marcia's chair to see if a puddle might form underneath. I was looking out the window waiting for snow.

"What if the tree *were* to fall," Miss Oberfeld said. "What if the tree weren't there?"

"But it is," Alan Fisher said.

"Neurobehavioral evidence supports the existence of at least two anatomically distinct 'memory systems' in the mammalian brain—"

The bell rang.

"—A 'cognitive' memory system dependent on the hippocampus that integrates sensation and memory from multiple systems—"

"And that's what I do every day," Alan Fisher said.

"—and a 'stimulus-response/habit' memory system that depends on repetition, on habit that develops in the dorsolateral striatum over time."[6]

"Right," Miss Oberfeld said, "that's what you do every day. A path is for 'every day.' A path is like a habit. It takes time. It doesn't change."

"Yup," Alan Fisher said even though he had no idea what Miss Oberfeld meant.

"But a map has many possible 'paths'—not the same path every day. It can be used as a guide to different places. A map can be used to change the path. But the path cannot be used to change the map. The path doesn't change."

"Like going to Lundy's."

"Yes," Miss Oberfeld said, "like going to Lundy's. So girls and boys, tomorrow, we will talk more about maps and paths and the tree in Alan Fisher's yard."

Miss Oberfeld went to her desk. She looked tired, but still she was smiling. "That's all for today." I loved Miss Oberfeld.

I got my coat. I got my hat. I walked toward the back and stopped in front of the map. I was looking for the tree in front of Alan Fisher's yard. I couldn't find it.

The hippocampus integrates input from multiple systems. In the human, the hippocampus has developed "optional strategies for placing items in the map, manipulating those that are already there, and relating different segments of the map to each other. . . . Items in the map can be moved from one location to another, generating new configurations which provide information about possible actions. Not necessarily about actions that had been taken. But about actions that might be taken. The possibility of action, opens time to the future."[7]

By "opening time to the future," the hippocampus opens to the possibility of story.

I walked out the classroom. I walked down the hall. There was a clock on the wall. I knew how to read clocks. That was easy. The little hand was on the side. The big hand was on top.

My mother went to the cupboard. She took two chocolate chip cookies from the box, and put them on a plate. She poured a glass of milk. She left them on the table. She did what she always did before I came home from school. It was a habit.

Then she did something that she never did. She counted. She counted the chairs at the table.

There were four. She left the kitchen and walked to the hall.

The dorsal striatum registers past action—and offers a singular path. The hippocampus registers multiple courses of action—and offers a map. The one repeats what had been, a habit. The other offers what could be, a choice. And by offering choice, the hippocampus offers story.

"The sequential firing of hippocampal cell assemblies during retrieval of a past event could trigger activation of prefrontal cortical cell assemblies representing actions and goals that are relevant to the current context."[8]

Cell assemblies as a result of hippocampal activity are activated, which allows the prefrontal cortex, the part of the brain that makes choices in the moment, to make a choice based on prior learning, current opportunities, and future possibility. It's the part of the brain that takes "Once upon a time—" and then offers choices as to what might happen next.

I walked down the hall to the stairs that led to the street.

My mother walked down the hall to the center of the house.

I stared down at the door.

She looked up the stairs.

In depression, the increased levels of corticotropin-releasing factor and cortisol are damaging to the prefrontal cortex and hippocampus. Thinking becomes rigid as networks come into play. Paths replace maps. Habits replace choice. Routines are fixed. Affect is locked. Freedom is lost. Subcortical systems take over. The dorsal-striatum. The insular cortex. The cingulate cortex. The amygdala. Reflexive, habit based systems come to the fore as reflective opportunities are lost.

There was only one thought in my mother's head. Only one path. Only one choice. There was no map.

I pulled my jacket tight round my neck. "I hate Alan Fisher," was my only thought as I put on my cap.

I walked up Hampton Avenue. I made a snowball and threw it at the stop sign on the corner of Exeter Street. I missed. Still, I kept thinking, "When I grow up, I'm going to be a baseball player. I'm going to be—"

"Hey kid—"

I made another snow ball and threw again at the sign.

"Hey kid—" this fourth grader said as he walked over from the vacant lot that Michael Starr and I had set on fire.

"Hey—?"

I turned to the fourth grader.

"—you missed," he said.

"I wasn't trying," I lied.

The fourth grade kid stood there, smiling the way only a fourth grade kid can. "You're lying," he said.

The hippocampus is like an advanced form of Chinese checkers where input from multiple sensory systems can be moved, integrated, rearranged. Unlike neurons in a sensory system, hippocampal neurons are responding to more than one source. Hippocampal neurons are responding to collective activity from multiple inputs—sight, sound, pain, smell, touch, taste—from interior and exterior—perception and memory, present and past. It can imagine the future.

"Hey kid!"

I made another snowball.

"Hey—I am talking to you."

The integration of input in relation to space is the basis for the creation of a cognitive map. The integration of input in relation to time is the basis for the creation of story. The hippocampus is critical to the integration of space and time—and thus to story.

"Hey kid!"

It's a bad idea to get into a snowball fight with a kid in the fourth grade when you're in the first. They're bigger. They throw harder. If you try to run away, they grab your hat, toss it to the ground, and then dare you to come back.

I threw the snowball at the sign. I hit it! It was the best shot that I had ever—

"I hit it!" I said turning around, and as I did—

The kid grabbed my hat—

"Hey, that's my hat!"

—and just walked down the street.

"That's my hat!"

"Come and get it," he said, taking a step toward me. I took a step back.

My mother started up the stairs. She went to the landing, entered her room. She took off her robe. She sat down at her desk, searched for paper, choosing the first piece she found—an envelope, addressed to—

David D Brockman

169 Falmouth Street

Brooklyn, NY D34 CH

—with a return address in the upper right corner, that listed only a room.

"Room 600," it read.

The three-cent stamp had been canceled on December 3rd. She opened the seams of the envelope, laid it flat. She took a pencil, and began to write.

"This letter is a very difficult one to write and a terrible thing for a husband and children to have to read. But I feel it is the only way out. The only choice I have left. I have lost the ability—"

The next words she wrote along the margin because she had run out of space.

"—to give happiness."

She turned the envelope over and wrote more.

"And since one must give happiness to be happy, I have lost the ability to be happy within myself. Please try to find the happiness I have lost. Mommy feels she can never make happiness for any of you—"

She didn't read what she had written. She just continued to write—

"I have lost the ability to give happiness." She added three words, "I have lost—" then stopped writing. She crossed out those last three words.

She went to her closet. She looked at herself in the mirror, at this woman wearing slippers, a slip and a bra. Then she turned to the closet. She went through her clothes until she found the dress with the dark and light green pattern. Its sleeves were long. Its collar high. The neck low. She held the dress against her chest. It was the dress she had worn to her daughter's wedding. She had been told that she looked beautiful in that dress. She couldn't remember by whom. All she remembered was that someone had said, "You look beautiful, Ruth." She had no idea what that person meant. All she knew was that the person was not telling the truth.

She turned and looked again in the mirror and saw the woman holding the dress. And indeed she saw that the dress looked beautiful. The kind of dress one might take into the grave like the paisley tie that Uncle Manny would take two years later, into his. Maybe that's what they had been talking about—"the dress looks beautiful, Ruth." Maybe that's what they meant.

"Hey kid—"

She undid the zipper. Stepped into the dress—the green dress with the dark and light green pattern, the dress with long sleeves, high collar, low neck.

She glanced back at the desk. At the envelope. She realized that she had more to say. She picked up the pencil. "Room 600," she thought, now remembering that was the number of the room in Nuremberg where war criminals had been tried, convicted, sentenced. Something she had learned from a program she had seen on TV—"Room 600"—she nodded as she lowered her eyes—

"Hey you—"

—to the letter on the desk as if she knew for the first time where it was from, why it had been sent. The message it conveyed.

"Hey, I am talking to you—"

She folded the envelope, lay it on the table.

"Hey—!"

And suddenly she knew. Knowing took away doubt. Took away fear. Gave the strength to do what she now knew she had to do. "I bring no happiness. I bring no joy."

"I am unworthy," she wrote.

"Hey kid—"

She folded the envelope, then broke the pencil in two.

"I am unworthy of love."

"Hey I am talking to you."

She turned.

"Hey kid—"

She caught sight of herself in the mirror.

I stared at my hat in the hand of the fourth grade kid.

"That's my hat."

"Come and get it."

She walked into the hall, down the stairs, past the grandfather clock with the phases of the moon.

Cortisol rose like the tide.

"Come and get it," the fourth grade kid said again as he crossed the street to the vacant lot where he tossed my hat to the snow.

She opened the door to the cellar.

"Come and get it," he said, packing a snowball hard.

"Hello, I am Dave Garroway—"

"Come and get it."

The TV played.

"—and this is *Wide Wide World*, where today you're going to get a slice of the wide, wide world through television."

She walked down the stairs.

"Today you'll be with cowboys in Texas, fishermen in Gloucester, steelworkers in Cleveland—"

She took the laundry off the line, folded the sheets and towels into separate piles. She freed one end of the line the way she had for my party when I was six.

"Come and get it," the kid yelled as I stood out of range.

"You see our stage is the world, our scenery, Mother Nature. Our lights the Sun."

I stared at my hat.

She circled the rope round the pipe.

"Bipolar depression has the highest rate of suicide of any psychiatric disorder—"

She made a noose.

"Rates of completed suicide appear to be as high as 15 times the rates among the general population and four times higher than rates among patients with recurrent major depression."[9]

She tested the rope.

"I am unworthy," she said.

"Of what?" Stein asked leaning back in his chair.

The level of corticotropin-releasing factor and cortisol are persistently elevated, causing the loss of dendritic processes and death of neurons in the hippocampus and prefrontal cortex. With time this accelerates, leading to the behavioral progression from simple depression to agitated depression to psychotic depression to the point where the sense of despair becomes a conviction, worthlessness a fact.

"Come and get it."

She stared at the wall where her finger had been rubbing the plaster.

"Of what?" he repeated.

"I, I—" she said, barely a whisper.

"I see," he said.

But he didn't.

For many, suicide is the only choice. Suicide becomes the thing that one must do in order to rid the world of one who is so—

"I didn't hear you."

"—unworthy—"

"Unworthy—?"

"Hey kid—?"

She took one of the chairs stacked against the wall, one of the folding chairs my father used Thursday nights for pinochle.

"But you're not going to be sitting still," Dave Garroway went on—

She positioned the chair under the noose.

"—you will ride with our cameras on a cable car in San Francisco, you will fly over the Mississippi."

"Hey kid—"

"Take off your hat."

"Come and get it."

"You will swing high over Texas, and you will do all these things live—which means that they're happening at this very moment."

"Hey kid—"

She looked over her shoulder to see who had spoken.

257

"We found that subjects who had reported feelings of worthlessness or guilt were most likely to have psychotic features."[10]

"You too scared to come get your hat?" the fourth grade kid asked.

"I'm not wearing a hat," she said.

"I'm not scared," I said as the kid just stood there, fingering a snowball, standing over my hat. The one with an "M." The one from Sid.

"Come and get it," the kid grinned.

She took a step toward the chair.

I took a step towards my hat.

"There's no film on this show. We have seventy-three TV cameras, 40,000 miles of telephone line, and about 1,800 technicians, and me, your host Dave Garroway."

And when I reached down to pick up my hat, he threw the snowball as hard as he could right at my head.

I saw stars.

I almost fell. I didn't cry.

She stepped up onto the chair, first with her right foot then her left.

"Didn't you come with a hat?"

"Stupid hat," the kid said as he walked away laughing.

"I'm not wearing a hat," she said softly as she moved her head through the noose.

She shifted her weight.

The rope found a groove between her larynx and throat.

I had my hat.

She looked over her shoulder—

"Katherine—!"

"There, there," Katherine said.

And then I started to cry.

"Yes," my mother said, "Yes, I had a hat."

"He had a hat!"

I had my hat!

"There, there," Katherine said.

"I owe you so much," my mother said.

Katherine smiled, reaching out with her hand.

"Oh Katherine, Katherine, I am so happy to see you" my mother said, looking first over one shoulder then the other for Katherine, and as she did, her right foot slipped from the chair. The foot dangled, kicked, swung in the air. She grabbed for the rope. She tried to call for—

"Kath—"

but the noose tightened, crushing her throat and spine at cervical vertebrae two and—

"And all that will be happening right here, right now, live on Wide Wide—"

I ran down Hampton Avenue. I didn't go through Mr. Palowski's yard. I didn't want to go to jail. I wanted to go home. I wanted my mommy. I rubbed my head. I had my hat. And then I remembered I was going on a train. I was going to Florida!

I turned onto Falmouth Street. I ran and ran. I opened the door. I took off my boots. I hung up my coat. "Mommy?" I hung up my hat. "Mommy?" I knew she was home. She was always there when I got home from school. I went into the kitchen. I was going to Florida! On a train! "Mommy?" My head still hurt and then I saw the plate of cookies. I dried my tears. I took a cookie. Chocolate chip. There were two. I started to feel better.

"Mommy?"

I went up to her room. The door was open. I took a bite of the cookie. "Mommy?" I went inside. I went to her dresser. I poked through her desk looking for pennies, nickels, dimes. I took a dime and a quarter. I wasn't supposed to do that. There was an envelope on the desk.

I went downstairs. I took another cookie. I wasn't supposed to do that either, but I couldn't find my mother, and I was hungry. I took a bite. I saw the glass. I drank some of the milk. I looked around the kitchen. Something was wrong. I couldn't figure out what. "Mommy," I called. I counted the chairs. There were four. Then I saw the fifth chair all by itself against the wall. I put the chair back next to the table.

I went into the hall. "Mommy?" I took another bite of cookie. The cellar door was open. I stood there. It's not supposed to be open.

Maybe that's where she was. In the cellar. Doing the wash. Getting ready for Florida. We were going to Florida. We were going on a train. Maybe that's where she was.

"Mommy?"

"The brain is a relatively plastic organ whose final structure and function are determined by a complex interplay of genetic and environmental factors."[11]

I walked to the landing at the top of the stairs. I called down,

"The activity of forebrain norepinephrine has been hypothesized to be part of a mechanism that effectively focuses attention onto salient events in threatening or demanding situations."[12]

"Mommy?"

"The rat pup when separated from its mother has an immediate response consisting of high rates of "distress" calling accompanied by agitated pivoting, sniffing, and exploratory behavior with high levels of self-grooming."[13]

"Mommy?"

"Catecholamine concentrations rise. The hypothalamic-pituitary-adrenal axis is activated resulting in elevated cortisol. Pups become behaviorally hyperresponsive."[14]

As I walked down the steps, I counted. I always counted. I didn't know why. "One, two." I stopped, and counted again. I heard the television.

"Of course something could go wrong here—quite possibly it will, but I think it's worth a try so let's begin by taking a few giant steps."

I took another step. Then I sat down. There were four more steps to the cellar floor. Four back up to the door. Four and four plus the one I was on—

"Mommy?"

"Four characteristics in traumatized children that are particularly important: strongly visualized memories. Repetitive behaviors. Trauma-specific fears. Changed attitudes about people."[15]

One of the steps was missing linoleum squares.

I finished the cookie.

"The protest signals are aimed at bringing the primary attachment figure back. They cease upon the adult's return—

"Mommy?"

"Failure to return results in despair."[16]

I kept staring at the floor.

"Mommy?"

I had counted the steps. There had always been ten. But now there were nine. That made no sense. I looked behind. Four steps. I looked below. Five. And that's when I realized that I had been wrong. That's when I realized I hadn't been staring at the cellar floor. That's when I realized—

"Memories of the trauma tend to be experienced as fragments—as visual images, olfactory, auditory, or kinesthetic sensations."[17]

—a slipper.

A green with black on the side slipper was lying right there on the cellar floor. It was as if nothing else existed except that slipper. It was as if that slipper were a magical slipper that had magical power and stories to tell—the way Cinderella told stories, the way Babar told stories, the way my mother told stories. And all I had to do was keep staring at that slipper and I would have a story. My very own story. All I had to do was keep staring, keep counting. All I had to do—

And then I stopped staring.

And then I stopped counting.

And then I looked up.

I don't remember standing. I don't remember walking to the

cellar floor. I remember an ironing board. I remember an overturned chair. I remember slippers—one on the ground, one in the air. I remember one of the steps was missing linoleum squares.

I remember the pieces.

I don't remember the whole.

I don't remember climbing the stairs. I don't remember opening the door. I don't remember a dog. I remember the snow.

I don't remember running past the tree in the yard. I don't remember crossing the street. I don't remember cars. I remember climbing steps to a porch. I remember banging on a door. I remember banging and banging and banging and—

"It's open." I remember a voice. "It's open. It's open. Now who in the, what in the—?" And then Katie Galst opened the door, a cigarette dangling from her lips. I remember standing unable to move. "Oh Richard, Richard—"

I stood there. "I, I—"

She coughed. "What in the world—?"

"I—"

"Did your Mommy and Daddy leave you again?"

I was sobbing, trying to breathe.

"Are you asleep?"

"I—"

"Are you asleep? Are you awake?"

I stood there.

"Come in. Come in. Lord, we'll both catch the death." She ushered me in. "Now settle, calm, settle, calm, calm. Richard tell me. What is it? What did you do?"

I couldn't talk.

"What happened?"

I couldn't speak. I couldn't breathe.

"Richard—?" she said taking my face in both hands, staring into my eyes, "I want you to be honest. I know this is hard. Did you take Mr. Palowski's hose?"

"I—"

"Tell the truth." And then she said, "What's that?" indicating something I had in my hand.

I looked down.

Then Katie Galst said, "Where's Ruth? Richard, where is your mother?"

"I—"

"Where is she? Where is she?"

"I—"

"Where is your mother?"

"She went away."

"She what?"

"On a train. She, she—"

"On a train—?"

"To Florida," I said.

"That's okay. That's all right," Katie Galst said.

"She went to Florida," I said and then I burst into tears.

"Yes, you just. You, you. There." Then she said, "You just stay right there. Don't you move. I'll be right back. Don't you move. You just stay right there!"

She pulled on her shoes, threw on a coat, took a last drag on her Camel cigarette.

"Don't move," she said, as she went out leaving me staring at the door like a dog.

I didn't move.

"The child's dissociation in the midst of terror involves numbing, avoidance, compliance, restricted affect. . . . If early trauma is experienced as psychic catastrophe, then dissociation is a "detachment from an unbearable situation," "the escape where there is no escape," a "last resort strategy."[18]

I kept staring at the door, but all I saw was an ironing board, an overturned chair, slippers—one on the floor, one floating in air. There were no sounds. There were no words. There was no map, indicating where I had been, where I was, or where I should go. There was only a path that led to a dead end.

"In mammals, the autonomic nervous system response to challenge follows a phylogenic hierarchy, starting with the newest structures and, when all else fails, reverting to the most primitive structural system."[19]

"When all else fails," these vestiges take over. "When all else fails," vestiges of the reptilian nervous system that were carried over as part of phylogenetic inheritance take over. When all else fails, vestiges of the reptilian parasympathetic nervous system take over. Breathing slows. Heart rate falls. Sensation implodes. "When all else fails," vestiges of the reptilian parasympathetic nervous system reduce a mammal to the point where it behaves as if it were a toad.

"Prolonged parasympathetic activation explains the lengthy void of awareness."[20]

And then I heard sirens. I heard police. I heard shouts. And like the rush of water after the collapse of a dam, my sympathetic nervous system came rushing back.

I started to breathe. My heart rate jumped. I knew where I was.

I saw Katie Galst come through the door.

She just stood.

"Are they going to arrest me?" I asked, suddenly able to speak.

"No," she said. "No one's going to arrest you"

"Why are they here?"

"Come over here." She held me. "Oh God. Richard, your mother—"

"She, she went away. She went away—on a train. To Florida. I saw."

Katie sat down in her La-Z-Boy chair. "Richard," she said facing me square. She touched my hair, held my head, as tears fell down her face, her lips, her mouth. "Richard, your mother is not on a train," Katie Galst said.

I was crying, spitting, drooling out snot. "I saw—" I said.

Katie Galst kept holding me close as if the only thing she wanted me to see were her eyes. As if the only thing she wanted me to hear was her voice.

"Richard, your mother didn't go on a train—"

The room started to spin.

"I saw. I saw—"

Katie Galst looked at me, held me, both of us streaked with spittle and fear. "What did you see? Tell me." She shook me a little as if to shake the vision from my head, then asked again, this time softer, as if asking for an answer she did not want to hear.

"The surgeon Herbert William Page in 1883, in discussing 'railway spine,' was one of the first to suggest that in the cases in which accident victims lacked actual physical injuries but still manifested symptoms, there must be a *psychological* origin, brought on by the overwhelming terror or fright and feelings of helplessness."[21]

"The suddenness of the event . . . the helplessness of escape gives rise to emotions which in themselves are quite sufficient to produce shock and all this quite irrespective of the extent or importance of bodily injury."[22]

"Child, what did you see?" Katie Galst asked again.

"Blood," I said, "I saw blood."

Chapter 40

What Did You See? Take One

THE CAUSE OF DEATH IN HANGING DEPENDS ON THE CONDITION related to the event. When the body is released from a relatively high position, the main cause of death is trauma to the upper cervical spine—the classic hangman's fracture with severe subluxation of C2–C3 crushing the spinal cord and disrupting the vertebral arteries. Death is by asphyxiation. The face loses color and will appear white.

In the absence of fracture and dislocation, occlusion of blood vessels becomes the main cause of death. Obstruction of the venous drainage of the brain via occlusion of the internal jugular veins leads to cerebral edema and then cerebral ischemia. The face will typically become engorged and cyanotic. There will be the classic signs of strangulation, petechiae, the little blood marks on the face and in the eyes from burst blood capillaries. The tongue may protrude. Sphincters will relax spontaneously and urine and feces will be evacuated.

Chapter 41

What Did You See? Take Two

ALL EXTERNAL SENSORY INPUT TO THE CENTRAL NERVOUS SYSTEM, except for smell, goes to the thalamus, a part of the diencephalon, the brain's wheel house if you will. In the context of vision, input goes to a part of the thalamus called the lateral geniculate body, before it is relayed to the visual (occipital) cortex for further processing.

To fully "see" something, visual information must be processed. There are multiple processing layers in the visual cortex. Processing—across many layers of neurons—and thus across many synapses—takes time.

But the thalamus does not input visual stimuli only to the visual cortex. Input is also sent from the thalamus directly to the amygdala, which is part of the limbic brain. Perception is assigned its emotional tone by the amygdala. These perceptions are then coordinated with more general experience, and especially memory, by integration with input at the hippocampus.

The amygdala thus receives perceptual input from two general sources: first from the thalamus—a direct pathway from the sense organs, and second from the cerebral cortex which will have processed the visual input before sending it on to the amygdala for emotional processing.

The former direct pathway gets to the amygdala more quickly, but without much input as to what had been perceived. The latter reaches the amygdala more slowly, but with more detail provided by cortical processing.

Because of these direct projections to the amygdala, some perceptions reach the amygdala before perception can be said to have reached thought. Because there are fewer synapses, the projections from the thalamus to the amygdala arrive before processed projections from the cortex reach the amygdala.

"What did you see?"

In certain traumatic circumstances one would thus be reacting to perception before one had fully registered what had been perceived.

"Traumatic events produce profound and lasting changes in physiological arousal, emotion, cognition, and memory. Traumatic events may sever these normally integrated functions from one another. The traumatized person may experience intense emotion but without clear memory of the event."[1]

"What did you see?"

In the *Principles of Psychology* (1890), William James wrote that "involuntary attention"—a perception that calls attention to itself—is aroused by "big things, bright things, moving things, or blood."[2]

Biologically there are two principal neurotransmitters—dopamine and noradrenaline—that focus the demands for attention in the prefrontal cortex (particularly in the dorsolateral prefrontal cortex), and which then facilitate integration in the hippocampus. But in the traumatic state, these "demands" provoke massive surges of dopamine and noradrenaline in the context of increased levels of cortisol. As a result attention is "focused" in the extreme so that details may be registered without context.

"What did you see?"

An ironing board, an overturned chair, slippers—one on the floor, one floating in air.

"Severe stress with its accompanying increase in corticosteroid levels can result in a suppression of hippocampal function." Without the hippocampus providing the contextual map, trauma is often remembered isolated in space and time. "Many are aware of the fragments of trauma, but are unable to recall specifics and put them into an autobiographical context."[3]

"What did you see?"

The call to "attention" generated by "big things, bright things, moving things" directs attention from the thalamus to the sensory areas of the neocortex (vision, hearing, touch, taste) and then to the hippocampus for integration with past and ongoing sensation and experience, that is to say with memory. "Big things, bright things, moving things" are recognized in the neocortex and then contextualized in the hippocampus.

But the call to attention generated by "blood," that is to say by overwhelming trauma, takes a different path. The sympathetic nervous system (SNS) goes on high alert. The hypothalamic-pituitary-adrenal (HPA) axis is activated to the full. Levels of noradrenaline and cortisol surge. Primitive brain stem responses are initiated. The normal integrative functions of the neocortex and the hippocampus are sacrificed as incoming percepts from the thalamus go directly to the amygdala where emotional tone is assigned. This leads to quicker, habituated responses from subcortical areas of motor control.

"A high degree of activation of the amygdala and related structures can generate emotional responses and sensory impressions that are based on fragments of information rather than on full-blown perceptions of objects and events."[4]

Neither the cortex nor the hippocampus are fully engaged in the response to overwhelming trauma. Priority was not given to the accuracy of assessment. Priority was given to the speed of assessment.

"What did you see?"

"Blood," I said.

"I saw blood."

And when all is lost, when there is nothing to be done, when the high alert systems have failed—

"I, I—"

—there is then a shift from high arousal, to collapse.

"I—"

The activation of the sympathetic nervous system (fight/flight) is turned off. The parasympathetic nervous system surges—going from "relax/restore" to "freeze-dissociate." Like a reptile in the grasp of a cat, heart rate falls, breathing slows almost to a stop, metabolism drops, core body temperature falls—

"I—"

Katie Galst stood with one hand steadying herself on her La-Z-Boy chair. With the other, she reached for the pack of Camel cigarettes that was always in the pocket of her dull orange smock. "Oh Richard," she said. "My angel boy."

Her dull orange smock smelled of tobacco, laundry, macaroni and dust, but oddly it also had the smell of love. The smell, like a salt, brought part of me back.

"I—"

She stood there holding me in her hands.

"I want to see Mommy."

"Richard—" She returned the pack of cigarettes to her smock.

"I want to see Mommy."

She took my hand. "Come with me."

We walked through the hall. We stood there as she stared straight ahead at the door. She said nothing until she said, "I know. I know you want to see your mommy."

Then she opened the door of her house.

"When you open the door of my house," Alan Fisher said, "you turn this way," he said, raising one arm, "toward the big tree in the yard. And if you go to the big tree and turn that way," raising the other arm, "then you'll see the ocean if it's not foggy."

I stared into the light. My brain was flooded with noradrenaline, dopamine, cortisol—the high water marks of fear. I started to breathe. My parasympathetic nervous system was relaxing its grip.

"Taken together, the findings suggest a possible relationship between emotional state . . . and the relative use of multiple memory systems."

I had no map. There was only one path. It was flooded with fear.

"Increasing levels of emotional arousal, at least to a particular threshold, may selectively impair "cognitive" memory function, and thereby favor the use of "habit" memory systems."[5]

We stepped through the door and into the late afternoon. The sun was low. The air was cold. We turned toward the big tree in the yard. There was snow on the ground. There were cars on the street. There were police. I saw my father's Cadillac car. I heard the crunch of snow. I looked up.

I was standing next to Katie Galst.

I knew where I was. I didn't know where I was.

I saw my house. I had no house.

My father came near. He reached out his hand.

I saw the pieces. There was no thread.

"Richard," he said.

I felt for Katie Galst's coat the way a rat with hippocampal damage feels for the wall.

Chapter 42
Troubled Sleep Take Two

I HARDLY ATE. I HARDLY SLEPT. I NEEDED COMFORT, AND THE ONE I needed hovered just out of reach just over my bed. I lay there staring up as she stared down. When I slept, I had dreams. Mostly, I didn't sleep.

I went for walks.

I walked down Hampton Avenue until I got to a large tree. Then I turned to the left until I came to another large tree. It was the tree in front of Alan Fisher's house. It was indeed a very big house. There had been a storm. A limb had broken off. I walked past the tree toward the ocean and the shore. I saw a woman walking across the sand. She was wearing a green dress. I called to her. She reached back with her hand as she turned toward me.

I bolted awake.

"Mommy!" I screamed.

I was in my room. I was in my bed.

Car lights passed on the ceiling overhead.

I didn't scream because my mother was dead—

"Richard—?" a voice called.

—I screamed because I was alive.

My father came into my room.

"Are you all right?" he asked.

"Yes," I nodded. "No," I said. I didn't know what I felt. I felt for my arm.

"Was it a dream?"

I shook my head.

He sat down on the bed. He said that he understood, but he didn't say what or why. "Are you all right?" he repeated.

I nodded. I had lost control of my days. I had lost control of my dreams. My arm was numb. I had lost control of my arm.

"Dreams occurring in traumatic neuroses have the characteristic of repeatedly bringing the patient back into the situation of his accident, a situation from which he wakes up in another fright."

"Did you have a dream?"

"This astonishes people far too little,"[1] Freud said.

In order to assimilate an experience into memory, we must attach it to a context we have heard or in some way, already know. We understand events in terms of events we have already known or understood.

I looked at my father, this man who in some ways I hardly knew. "Can you read a story?" I asked.

"Yes of course," he said. Then he asked, "What would you like?"

"Babar."

For a listener to understand means to map the speaker's stories onto one's own so that the story comes within a context at least partially known.

"Your favorite—wasn't it? That's what she said. I remember she read to you almost every—" Car lights climbed the walls then crossed overhead.

"Where's the book?" he asked.

I pointed to the shelf.

He got the book, handed it to me, touched my head, then said, "Babar will help you sleep."

I held the book, my favorite book.

But what if it is a story that cannot be comprehended? What if it is a story that cannot be told?

"Goodnight," he said.

Car lights climbed the walls then crossed the ceiling overhead.

I held the book in my hands.

"Post-traumatic stress disorder reflects the direct imposition on the mind of the unavoidable reality of horrific events, the taking over of the mind psychically and neurobiologically by an event that it cannot control . . . a break in the mind's experience of time."[4]

My father never talked to me about Mother—about his wife, my mother, about how she lived, loved, mothered, died. He never talked to me about her. It was an impossible story for me to absorb, and what was happening all around made it clear that it was not a story that could be told.

"The future is no longer continuous with the past."[5]

"I told our story. It was, you see, a story that could be told" (*Hiroshima, mon Amour*).

My father made it clear to me that the story I am telling you now was not a story that could be told, not a story I was allowed to breathe. It was not a story that ever happened.

"Mommy!" I called to the snow. To the tree in front of Alan Fisher's yard. To Sheepshead Bay. To the gulls. To the fish. To the beach where I had seen her walking in my sleep—or was I walking in hers?

The Chinese philosopher Zhuang Zhou "dreamed that he was a butterfly, and on waking up, he did not know whether he was a man who had had a dream he was a butterfly, or a butterfly who was now dreaming he was a man."[6]

I called out quietly so that no one would hear.

Suicide takes a life, and then it takes a voice.

For a while I couldn't talk.

Kids stared at me. Miss Oberfeld asked if I were okay. More than anything I wanted to hear her ask, "Richard, what's the capital of

Alabama?" I didn't know. I just wanted to hear her ask. And finally, one day, I head Miss Oberfeld ask, "Richard, what's the capital of Alabama?"

"I want a dog," were the first words that came out of my mouth.

Chapter 43

A Dog

ONE WEEK LATER, SIX AFTER MY MOTHER, JOLIE AND SID TOOK ME TO the Bideawee Home.

There were enclosures made of wire and concrete. One for puppies. One for small dogs. A third where the dogs were bigger than wolves.

As I walked down the row, the dogs would start barking. Each dog seemed to understand that if it weren't chosen, it would be killed. I was overwhelmed. I was afraid of the dogs that were bigger than wolves.

"Richard, come over here," Sid called. "Over here."

I turned around. He was standing next to one of the kennels. A brown and white mutt stood with her front paws on the gate, licking Sid's fingers.

I stood next to Sid. "Put your fingers through," he said. I stuck my fingers through the fence. She licked my fingers.

We called her Ginger.

The scientists Amorapanth, LeDoux, and Nader studied the effect of action on fear.[1] They conditioned rats to fear the sound of a bell (the conditioned stimulus, CS) that was followed by shock to their feet (the unconditioned stimulus, US).

What they discovered was that if the rat were given the opportunity to escape the shock, it changed how the memory was registered in the animal's brain—specifically where in the amygdala the memory was stored. Thus when the bell sounded (the CS) indicating the impending shock (the US), if the animal had the chance to escape through an action of its own (running through a side door that opened in the experimental enclosure), then the memory of the conditioned fear (the sound of the bell) was registered differently than if the animal were not given (or did not recognize) the opportunity to take action and thereby escape.

When the animal had the opportunity to escape, the memory circuit did not go directly to the central nucleus of the amygdala, the outflow tract from the amygdala that connects a learned fear to an instinctive response (in the case of the rat, the immobilization or "freeze" response). When the animal learned that there was an opportunity to escape—that there was an action it could take—the memory was laid down in a different circuit (through the basal nucleus of the amygdala) which leads to motor circuits in the dorsal striatum rather than to immobilization circuits.

"By engaging these alternative pathways, passive fear responding is replaced with an active coping strategy. This diversion of information . . . and the learning that takes place, does not occur if the rat remains passive."[2]

The animal had to have taken an action in order for the motor pathway to be engaged. Taking an action in response to fear (leaving the original box and crossing into the adjacent box) was critical to whether the memory reinforced a passive immobilization response activated in the brain stem or an active motor response that went to the dorsal striatum. Taking an action reinforced action. Remaining passive reinforced immobilization.

The response to the event affected where the memory was stored and predicted future responses. An active initial response was critical to future behavior.

I was given a dog. Her name was Ginger.

I fed Ginger. I walked Ginger. I bathed Ginger. Ginger slept on my bed. I read to Ginger—Babar, Bambi, Old Yeller. I loved Ginger. She was my dog.

And just as I had rescued her from a passive fear response at the kennel, she had rescued me. She took care of me. I took care of her. There was an active response to what I had witnessed, to the trauma of unspeakable loss. My dog, Ginger, had helped to shift my response (from the central nucleus of the amygdala—immobilization—to the basal nucleus of the amygdala—action). It was a huge gift that we each gave to the other without either one aware that gifts had been exchanged.

Two weeks after Ginger came home, my father and I took Ginger for a walk. My father felt it was time to let her off the leash. "It's too soon," I said.

"She's a good dog," my father insisted as he let her off leash, "she won't run away."

She started to run.

"Ginger! " I called. "Ginger!"

She ran. I tried to catch her. "Ginger!"

We went from block to block. "Ginger!" "Ginger!"

"We'll find her. Don't worry," my father said.

I burst into tears. She was gone.

We walked home. My father walked ahead. I walked behind. We never held hands. We never hugged. There was no such thing as tenderness between my father and me.

"Stop crying," he said.

It was all bootstraps.

"Stop crying."

Bootstraps.

I stopped crying.

When we got home, Ginger was sitting on the stoop at the back door. Though only there a few weeks, she knew the neighborhood. She knew the house. She knew where she was. Her hippocampus was first rate. It had already made a really good map.

Chapter 44

The School Bus

WHEN FOLK DON'T DIE RIGHT, THEY HAUNT.
Traditional saying.

A few days later, a school bus stopped outside our house. That was weird. I never took a bus to school. I just ran through Mr. Palowski's yard.

What's a school bus doing here?

It honked. I went to the window. The driver waved. I ran to the closet. I closed the door. I hid on the floor. "What's a school bus doing here?" I asked my shoes, my socks, my toys, my dog, "What's a school bus—?"

I heard my father call, "Richard!" And then just like that, it came to me. He wanted us to leave. He wanted to move away. My sisters had already moved out. And now he wanted me—

The school bus.

Right then and there I knew his plan and vowed that I would never leave. And if he tried to make me, I would chain myself to the fence. I knew my mother was dead, that she had left on a train, and I knew she would return and when she did, I knew that she would return to a place she knew. This place. This house. This street. Like the tree in Alan Fisher's yard she knew the path—and I would be here waiting. I knew what she would do.

The dead come back. It's what they do. They know the path. The dead don't need a map. "Mommy!" I yelled but not loud. They had a path.

"Richard?"

And then the closet door opened.

"What are you doing in there?" my father asked.

I stared at the floor. I didn't want him to see me crying. I didn't want him to see that I had figured his plan. I didn't want him to know—

"Richard. Come out of there."

"What's a school bus doing here?"

And then I heard the horn again.

And then I started to cry even though I had vowed—

"It's gone," he said. And then he left. Leaving me in the closet. "It's gone." Like I said I lost time. I lost place. My hippocampus stopped making maps.

"We understand events in terms of events we have already understood."

Memories build on one another. Memory starts with species memory—the memory that comes hard wired into every creature's DNA. Learned memory builds on that—implicit, associative, somatic, and finally episodic memory. In order to assimilate an experience into memory, it attaches onto antecedent memory.

Overwhelming traumatic memory is different. It stands alone. It lies outside of experience and thus outside memory and outside of time. Traumatic perception has no antecedents. It has no map. It only has the path on which it came. Stuck outside of time, place, story—it stands alone.

The connections between the prefrontal cortex and the hippocampus are critical to the establishment of a personal sense of past, present, and future. This communication between the prefrontal cortex and the hippocampus is the system that mediates a personal sense of time. This sense of self and consciousness of self "affords individuals the possibility to apprehend their subjective experiences throughout time and to perceive the present moment as both a continuation of their past and as a prelude to their future. We consider this the most highly evolved form of consciousness and think of it as the Jamesian 'stream of consciousness,' which provides a fluid link from the individual's past, through the present, to the future, and back again."[1]

Trauma disrupts time. "What causes trauma is a shock that is in fact a break in the mind's experience of time."[2] What is "broken" more than anything is the hippocampal ability to piece together the fabric of past, present, and future. A break in hippocampal function—a break in the experience of memory—is a break in "relational processing," a break in the experience of time.

By disrupting the synthesis of past, present, and future, trauma disrupts story. Trauma disrupts continuity. Trauma disrupts who you are.

And then I saw it—right there on the floor. My book!

And when I saw it, the words started to play in my head, "In the great forest a little elephant is born." And as I listened to the words, I ripped the page from the book. "His name is Babar." I read another page. "His mother loves him very much." Then another and another and—

"Babar is riding happily on his mother's back." Page after page until I had ripped out every page but one. "Babar," I yelled to save him because I knew what came next. I knew the book by heart, I knew—

"Babar . . ."

You better go. You better run. You better—

And then I heard,

"A wicked hunter hidden behind some bushes—"

I looked up—

My mother was standing with her back leaning against the wall. I read the next page, "The hunter shoots at Babar and his mother." She kept staring at me. "The hunter kills Babar's mother!"

She was wearing the green dress, a slipper, a necklace round her neck.

"The monkey hides. Birds fly," she said.

It was her. She was standing right there.

There is a long list of things that can bring an experience back to life. Oddly, death is one.

"What are you doing here?" I asked.

"Reading you a story. Your favorite. Your father was never much of a reader," she said, taking the book from my hands.

"What does Babar do?" I asked.

"He cries," she said.

"Then what does he do?"

"I thought you knew," she said.

"I did," I said, "I knew before—"

"He takes a balloon," she said. "He takes a balloon and flies off," she said, tossing the book to the floor.

In a paper dealing with "childhood amnesia," Katherine Nelson challenged Freud's core theory of repression.

She argued that "childhood amnesia" was not the result of the repression of the forbidden sexual wish—like seeing your mother step naked into the bath—but rather it had to do with the way memory itself is structured, and how that structure changes as the child matures.

Nelson argued that the antecedents of early memory are individual percepts. It is only with time, and with "socialization and the impact of language" that memory organizes these "percepts" into "chunks." "Chunking"—the union of "individual percepts" is a critical function of the hippocampus—and a critical element of recall. Chunking leads to narrative coherence. Narrative coherence strengthens memory.

But the evolution of autobiographical memory—the assembly of "chunks"—is not a solitary process. Autobiographical memory depends on a child's emotional engagement with the mother (or mother surrogate). The mother focuses her child's attention, noradrenaline. Attention establishes value, the nucleus accumbens. Value creates salience. Salience releases dopamine from the midbrain. Increase dopamine released from the midbrain into the prefrontal cortex, and the hippocampus organizes perceptions into "chunks" the way an editor organizes clips of films into scenes. Perceptions brought to the hippocampus are then joined to other perceptions, which are then "chunked" to create story.

Chunking begins with the mother's smile, her voice, her gaze, her fears, her focus—which the child then makes his own. The child borrows, then learns, how to "chunk." Dopamine acting at the hippocampus connects ongoing instants of a continuous present and binds them into chunks that have past, present, and future—and thus "chunks" are no longer instances of the perpetual present, chunks are percepts linked over time. Narrative.

"The hippocampus forms memories that integrate events into a larger, coherent narrative. By bridging the divide between distant events, the hippocampus may support a narrative-level architecture for memory."[3] Memory "chunked" by narrative coherence is much more powerful than the memory of isolated perceptions. The mammalian brain evolved to remember chunks of narrative—bookended by noradrenaline and dopamine—much better than to remember isolated fragments of the ongoing present.

"Children learn to engage in talk about the past, guided at first by parents who construct a narrative around the bits and pieces contributed by the child."[4] What starts as individual bits evolves into "chunks," which evolves into linked memories, which evolves into story.

And just as the rat uses the hippocampus to construct a map, the human uses the hippocampus to create a story. And just as a rat with hippocampal damage loses its sense of space, a human with hippocampal damage loses his sense of story.

The rat loses place.

The human loses place, then time, then story. Then self.

And just as the infant depends on the mother for the regulation of basic physiology, the child depends on the mother for the regulation of basic story. And should the mother be unavailable, story suffers. And should the mother turn on her child, then the story turns on itself.

"Who are you?" she asked as she stood up.

"Richard," I said. "I'm your son."

"I have a train to catch," she said, arranging the necklace that hung round her neck.

"Will you come back?"

She looked at me sitting cross legged on the floor. She squatted down. "Like I said—" She looked at me long and hard. "I have a train to catch."

Chapter 45

Pennsylvania Station

A WEEK LATER WE WERE IN PENNSYLVANIA STATION—MY TWO SISTERS, my brand-new brother Sid, my father, and me. We were going to Florida. We were going on a train!

Pennsylvania Station was the biggest thing I'd ever seen. Massive columns. Marble walls. Ceilings that went to the sky. People moving this way and that. Men shining shoes. Men with hammers. Men with hard hats that said "Turner" right there on the side.

"Who's Turner?" I asked.

My father didn't say.

"What are they doing?"

"They're tearing it down," he said.

"What?"

"The Station."

"Why?"

"Richard, come on."

"Why does Turner want to tear it down?"

My father didn't say.

"Who's Turner?" I asked again.

"You ask too many questions," he said.

And then I looked up.

Clocks!

I saw clocks—clocks hanging from chains, clocks on the walls, and alongside each clock there were two women—one wearing clothes, the other not. I kept staring at the one who wasn't wearing any—

"Richard—?"

People rushed to their trains.

The only other time I had seen a woman like that was when my mother dropped her robe before she stepped into the bath. I couldn't get my eyes to let go.

"Richard," he said taking my hand, "You could get lost."

And then I heard from far off,

"Richard."

I looked around.

The mystical experience has many possible sources—sensory deprivation, prayer, fasting, meditation, psilocybin, overwhelming awe, near death itself tends to recall—

"Richard," I heard a woman's voice.

"Richard," my father said, "You could get lost."

—and when I heard that I realized why I was lost. I realized she was my map.

"For an infant or child the presence of the mother is a signal of safety and thus her loss is a loss of safety if not the frank kiss of death."[1]

"She's here," I thought, looking to see where she might be.

"The crisis at the core of many traumatic narratives—often emerges as an urgent question. Is the trauma the encounter with death or the ongoing experience of having survived?"[2]

"And if she is here, then I'm not lost."

"Richard."

I looked right and left. I looked at the walls. I looked at the stairs. I looked at the men shining shoes. Then I looked up at the woman draped over the side of the clock—the one who wasn't wearing any clothes. Her eyes were closed. Her breasts were bare.

"Richard."

I stared.

"Richard—"

I reached up.

"—come on," my father said grabbing my hand.

"She's here," I tried to explain, but then I heard,

"The Florida Special! Now boarding track 29—making station stops at—"

I was getting on a train! I was going to—

"Newark, Philadelphia, Wilmington—"

"—Florida!"

"Where's Florida?"

"There," I said pointing behind me—

"—Baltimore, Washington, Richmond, Fayetteville, Florence—"

"—next to Lundy's."

But maybe I was wrong. Maybe it wasn't next to Lundy's. Maybe the world was bigger than I had imagined or dreamed.

"—Savannah, Jacksonville, Fort Lauderdale, Hollywood Beach, and Miami. The Florida Special. Track 29. All aboard. Track 29."

I was going to Florida.

"Richard."

"The Florida Special. All aboard. All aboard."

"Richard."

I turned around.

"The neural mechanisms of social buffering suggest that a specific cue from the attachment figure is sufficient to block activation of the hypothalamus which prevents activation of the stress response."

"Richard."

"Further it has been shown that maternal presence is able to block the activation of noradrenaline."[3]

"Now boarding. Track 29."

"Richard, that's our train. How many times do I have to tell you? You could get lost," my father said.

Then I heard it again. "Richard."

I stared up at the glass, at the beams, the domes, and through the domes to the sky.

"Richard." I saw her voice!

"In its most general definition, trauma describes an overwhelming experience of sudden or catastrophic events in which the response to the event occurs in the often delayed, uncontrolled repetitive appearance of hallucinations and other intrusive phenomenon."[4]

I saw her voice!

"All aboard! All aboard! The Florida Special!"

I was sure I would find her—

"All aboard!"

—in Florida!

We got on the train. I had my own seat.

"Richard, sit here," my father said. I was so excited I could barely keep still.

"Richard, just sit," my father said.

The conductor came down the aisle. He wore a suit. He wore a cap.

"Before I can say anything to you, I must know a great deal about you."

I told him I was going to Florida.

"Say whatever goes through your mind. Act as though you were a traveler—"

—because I was an adventurer,

—a traveler

"—sitting next to the window of a railway carriage . . ."

I was sitting next to the window of a railway carriage—

All aboard! All aboard!

—describing the changing views."[5]

"Richard?"

I looked up.

"I'm getting something to eat," my father said. "Want to come?"

I shook my head.

"Are you hungry?"

"Yes."

"What would you like?" my father asked.

"A BLT with mayo on toast."

"How 'bout a Coke? And some fries?"

He knew I loved fries.

"Good," my father said as he turned and walked down the aisle.

"Baltimore," the conductor called out.

"Baltimore—"

I looked out the window. There were trees. There was snow. The train was slowing down—

"The next station stop will be Baltimore."

I pressed my face to the glass.

"The mother's presence attenuates amygdala activity which has a profound influence over the child's interaction with the world."[6]

And then I saw her—

"Baltimore. Baltimore."

—standing on the station platform in—

"Baltimore."

Chapter 46

Fresh Squeezed

THE HOLLYWOOD BEACH HOTEL IS PINK AND GREEN. THERE ARE two pools and an ocean. It was the most amazing hotel that I had ever seen. It had lots of TVs. I watched *The $64,000 Question*.

"And for $32,000, what is the capital of—?"

"Montgomery," I screamed.

The man on the TV didn't know. He started to cry. They gave him a car. He kept crying. I don't think he wanted a car.

I shared a room with my father. When we arrived, there was a black trunk waiting in front of the door—Room 331. "Wow," I exclaimed. "How'd this get here?" My father put the trunk on the bed. "What's it for?"

He opened the trunk.

There were clothes, lots of clothes. He was about to close it when I saw, "My cap! That's my cap, from Sid!" My father handed it to me. I put it on my head. "How'd it get here?"

He didn't say.

I put on my cap.

My father was about to close the trunk when he paused, then took out a blouse. He stared at it, and then he brought it to his face. I watched as tears welled in his eyes. It was the only time I had seen my father cry. I got scared. "It's nothing," he said wiping them dry.

"Let's get breakfast," he said, closing the trunk. I don't think he opened the trunk ever again.

Breakfast at the Hollywood Beach Hotel was always the same—bacon, eggs, silence, and toast—and a waitress named Hazel. "My name is Hazel," she said with a smile. "Can I get you some juice? This is Florida, y'all, where the juice is fresh squeezed." She smiled even though she looked like she wasn't happy to be serving bacon, eggs, and "fresh squeezed."

"Fresh squeezed would be nice," my father said. She brought us two glasses. "Thank you," he said. "Have a fabulous time here, y'all." She said "y'all" quite a lot. A lot of people who worked at the Hollywood Beach Hotel said "y'all" as if someone had told them it was how they should talk.

Me and my father went to the buffet.

"Why don't you take some melon," he said.

"This?"

"Yes," he said putting a pink slice on my plate.

"That's not melon."

"Richard, it's melon."

Whenever he started with "Richard," I knew it was best not to talk back, but I could tell—that wasn't melon.

I took a bite. It was slimy and sweet. I spit it out. I started to say, "This isn't—" when I remembered. I left whatever it was on the plate.

He pointed at the melon. He pointed to the ocean. He talked about the beach.

"After breakfast, we can go to the beach."

He never talked about Mother. It was as if he didn't notice that she was not there, just the trunk in the room with the clothes that were packed. And her blouse. And my cap.

It wasn't as if she had died. It was as if she had never been alive.

"After you finish your melon, we can go to the beach."

"It's not melon."

"Richard—"

"Can I wear my cap to the beach?" I asked.

"In the water?"

"No, on the beach. I don't know how to swim."

"I'll teach you," he said.

"In the water?"

"I'll teach you to swim, yes—in the water."

"Oh," I said, then I said, "How did it get here?"

"What do you mean?"

"My cap—?"

"In the trunk."

"Oh," I said. Then I asked, "How'd it get in the trunk?"

"Your sister," he said. "Jolie knew you would want it."

"Oh," I said. "When did she—?"

"Richard—" he said, wiping his lips with a pink and green Hollywood Beach Hotel napkin. "Let's go to the beach. I'll teach you to swim."

"In the pool?"

"In the ocean."

"I don't know how."

"I taught you to ride a bike—"

"That was in Brooklyn."

"Well, in Florida, I'll teach you to swim."

"Wow," I said.

I had never been in a pool. I had never been in an ocean. I didn't know how to swim. "Wow!" I repeated. "Where's my suit?"

"In the trunk. Go get changed. Here's the key. I'll wait right here."

I ran all the way. The room was down a long pink-and-green corridor. Every corridor was long, pink, and green. I went down one. I ran down another. Like a mouse in a maze—

Finally I found the long pink-and-green corridor with "331" on the door.

I opened the door. The trunk was next to the bed. I opened it. I dug around and found my suit. And right there beside was the blouse—the one my father had held. The one that made him cry. I stared at the blouse.

I pulled the blouse out of the trunk and held it up in front of my face.

The windows were closed. The air was still. Nothing moved except the smell of her from the blouse to my nose into me.

"Mommy?" I whispered to her blouse.

"Scars have the power to remind us that the past was real."[1]

I waited for an answer. I waited for her voice. And then I heard,

"Good morning—"

"Mommy!"

"—today's activities include a fashion show at three, bingo at five on the promenade—"

I turned. The voice was coming from loudspeakers outside.

I put the blouse back in the trunk. And then I remembered. I was going to the beach, to the water, to the ocean. I had never been in water deeper than a bath. I put on my suit. I put on my cap.

I ran though the pink and green halls, the lobby, past all the rooms and the shops. I went back to the dining hall, where my father was finishing his second cup.

"Trauma consists not only of confronting death but of having survived, precisely, without knowing it."[2]

We walked together out the double doors, past the two pools and the promenade—

I turned to my father, "Today at five you wanna know what—?"

"Richard, come on."

We crossed the path that went up and down the Florida coast.

"How far does it go?" I asked.

"That way goes to Miami," he said pointing "that" way.

I thought about that, then turned and asked, "Does this way go to Alan Fisher's house?"

My father kind of laughed. "Yes," he said, "it probably does."

I stared at the path. There were birds.

"Are those gulls?"

"Those are pelicans."

"What's a pelican?" I asked.

"Those are," he said.

We walked to the water's edge.

I put my foot in.

I had never been in the ocean.

I didn't know how to swim.

I figured my father would teach me to swim. Or my mother would teach me to drown.

Either way I would learn.

"Are you ready?"

I looked up.

"I'll hold your cap," he said.

I handed him my cap. "Don't lose it," I said.

My father turned to the sky and said, "He had a hat." Then he laughed.

"Who's that?"

"It's a joke," he said.

I thought that maybe he had been talking to Mother.

"Don't worry," he said, "I won't lose your cap."

The water was cold. The waves were huge.

"It's cold," I said.

"It's warm," he said.

We walked a little farther in.

The waves brushed his ankles. The waves smashed my knees. We walked a little further.

"The waves are huge," I said.

"The water is calm," he said.

We walked a little further. The waves brushed his thighs. The waves crushed my chest.

The bottom gave way.

"I can't stand!"

"Give me your hand."

He took my hand.

"Put your head in."

"I can't breathe."

"Turn your head. Turn like this."

I put my head in the water and turned it like that. And when I tried to breathe, water rushed in. I coughed. "I can't—"

"Keep your head in the water except when you breathe. Then turn your head. I'll hold you up."

I could feel his hands—one on my belly, one on my back. I splashed with my arms. I kicked with my legs. I swallowed water. The salt burned. I coughed. I turned my head. I kicked. I splashed. I turned. I thought I would drown and then I realized he wasn't holding me. I realized my feet couldn't touch down. I realized I was in over my head. And then I realized, I could breathe. Then I realized I could swim.

I could swim!

My father was beside me. Through the silence and pain. Through the loss. Through the smell of her in the blouse. He was smiling.

"You're swimming," he said.

"I'm swimming," I said.

He opened his arms and held me to his chest.

I was crying. He was smiling.

The memory held me and my father. The memory held like a crab. It was the best memory we ever held, ever had.

I don't think my father and I loved each other like that ever before. Ever since.

He was smiling. I was swimming.

The water held me.

Bootstraps.

The water lifted me up.

Bootstraps.

I was swimming.

Chapter 47

Vows

"DO YOU TAKE THIS WOMAN, TO BE YOUR LAWFULLY WEDDED WIFE, TO have and to hold, to love and to cherish till death do you part?"

My father married another woman less than two years after Mother's death.

My sister Susan slashed her wrists while we were at the Hollywood Beach Hotel. It wasn't a suicide attempt. She didn't cut very deep. It was her reaction to Mother's betrayal. She bled all over the pink-and-green Hollywood Beach Hotel towels and sheets.

Six months later, Susan went off with a teacher from Cornell, a writer named Carl Eisenberg. She had taken his class on mythology. They were together on some Greek island with 350 extras on loan from the Greek army to film Eisenberg's version of *The Iliad*. Eisenberg had spent over $100,000 of his own money for a movie he would never complete in order to impress my sister because he adored her ignoring the fact that he was gay. "Love isn't about sex," he said—but as everyone except Eisenberg seemed to know, love is about sex unless you're a kid—and of course unless you happen to be under the influence of Freud, for whom everything was about sex. "Now I know your motive—"[1] Freud excitedly declared to a young woman he was treating about the same age as my sister. Freudian motives were always bedrocked on sex.

My sister Susan never came home after that—not for years and years and years—bedrocked on sex. For a long while she lived at the Chelsea Hotel—sometimes alone, sometimes with men. Never with Eisenberg. She never came back.

Jolie's marriage to Sid ended in Tijuana, where she was having an affair with her Mexican lawyer, a man named Rodriquez who, though happily married and the father of four, was gobsmacked by his gorgeous young American client before the ink on the "*documentos de divorcio*" was dry.

After several nights in Mexican heat, Jolie returned to New York. She moved in with my father and me, doing her best to double as mother and wife. That went on for over a year until one day, Father came home with news that he had proposed to another woman, that he would take a second wife, a "step wife."

No one was ready for what he brought home.

It was as if my father had chosen a woman who had nothing in common with Mother. It was as if he had chosen a woman whose only real love was for cheekbones, eyelashes, mirrors, and breasts. It was as if he had chosen a woman who lived for seduction but had no desire for sex. It was as if he had chosen a woman whose primary task was to help him deny that Mother had lived.

She wore hats with wide brims, gowns that were loose, gloves that were tight, heels that were high, and cleavage so deep that when she hugged me, I feared for my life.

Late at night, she would tiptoe into my room—walking on her toes was something she said that she had to do because of the arch of her foot—carrying a pint of Häagen-Dazs and a bottle of Smirnoff. "Your father and I had a fight," she explained as she lay down beside me. "Would you like some?" she asked.

My father married, I am convinced, because he wanted to bury Mother—and he would do this by marrying a woman who didn't want a husband so much as an immaculately begotten nine-year-old son.

A few years later, the doorbell rang, "Is the lady of the house at home?"

"Who are you?" I asked.

I was on the cusp of thirteen. The woman at the door seemed a lot older. I later found out she was twenty-four.

"How old are you?" I asked.

"A man never asks a woman her age," Carmel said. That was her name, "Carmel."

For the next several months, I spent as much time as I could with Carmel. When I wasn't at school, I'd follow her as she dusted. My father's step wife complained she was a terrible maid. When I told this to Carmel, she agreed, then offered a piece of advice,

"Be good," she instructed. "And if you can't be good, be careful. And if you can't be careful, wear a 'proph.'"

"What's a 'proph'?"

"When you're older," Carmel said.

One night when my parents were out, I went to Carmel's door. I sat down and stared. I heard her TV. I heard her laugh. Then I heard her say, "Maybe what I did was wrong, but there was no sin. So just bless me. Bless me. God damn it, You should just —"

"Bless her!" I said—the words just popped out.

"Richard—?" she called. "—is that you?" I froze.

"Richard?"

"Yes?"

"What are you doing?"

"Listening," I said.

"It would be easier for you to hear from this side of the door," she said.

I stood there. "Richard—?" I didn't know what to do. "Richard, when a girl invites you to her room," Carmel said without saying more.

"What?" I asked.

"You do as she says."

I opened the door.

Carmel was lying in bed. There was a portrait of Jesus. The window was cracked. A candle flickered.

"Richard?"

"What?"

"Do you have something to say?"

"Yes."

"What?"

"My father's step wife said I shouldn't be spending so much time with you."

"Is that what she said?"

"Yes."

"And what do you think?"

"I like spending time with you."

"Come here," she said patting the bed. "Some rules are made to be broken."

I took a step.

"Take off your shoes."

I took off my shoes.

"Lie on my bed."

Carmel pulled back the sheet. She was wearing a nightgown, socks, and a scarf.

I lay on her bed.

"Let's spoon," she said.

I knew what it was, but I was a little bit scared.

"Lie with your back to my chest."

As I lay down, I began to feel something move—

"Just rest," she said.

I wasn't entirely sure what it was.

"Just rest," she said.

I felt the warmth of her breath, the soft of her breast, her arm on my chest.

"Close your eyes."

I did as she said.

"Just rest."

My breathing calmed. My heart slowed. My parasympathetic nervous system did all the rest.

"Just rest."

Within the infant-caregiver attachment system, the primary caregiver holds potent reward value to the infant. . . . A less well-understood feature of the attachment figure is the caregiver's ability to reduce fear via social buffering, commonly associated with the notion of a "safe haven" . . . a network known to involve the prefrontal cortex . . . a developmental transition from dependence of the mother to independence in the preadolescent.[2]

"Just rest."

It was the first time since my mother's death that I lay close to a woman. Close enough to feel. Close enough to smell. Close enough to touch.

"Some rules are made to be broken," she said, "but some you best obey."

"Which ones?" I asked.

"Mine," she said.

"Adolescents tend to think that nobody understands them."[3]

"Just rest."

"Carmel," I said, "how long will you stay here?"

"That depends."

"On what?"

She brushed the hair from my face. "Just rest."

Oxytocin has been shown to be one of the critical mediators in the long-term effects of social integration and social support—experiences that serve as safety stimuli and modulate central and peripheral threat responses

"Just rest."

When oxytocin goes up, an animal feels safe. Heart rate and breathing go down.

"Just rest."

Her fingers played on my shoulder, my arms, my chest.

Gentle touch releases oxytocin.

"Just rest."

I had never felt so scared and so safe both at once.

"Just rest."

Two weeks later, when I got home from school, my father's step wife told me that Carmel had left.

"Where did she go?"

"She was deported."

"What does that mean?"

"It means she did something wrong."

"What?"

"I don't know."

"She would never have just leave without telling me first."

"Well, she did," my father's step wife said.

I ran to my room, slammed the door, lay on the bed.

"Richard—" my father's step wife called through the door, "Don't be mad at Carmel."

I prayed for a door with lock and key. Carmel would never do that to me.

"Would you like something to eat?" my father's step wife said. "Would you like some ice cream?"

"I'm fine."

"Okay—just let me know if you change your—"

"Fine."

Years later I learned that Carmel had come to America for an abortion. I learned that she would marry a man named Kamber, a photojournalist who had covered the war in Vietnam. They would have children—a girl she would name Maeve and a boy she would name—

"Richard—"

"I'm fine."

—Richard.

"—I'm here if you need me," my father's step wife said from the other side of the door.

"I'm fine."

The door started to open.

"The view that adolescents need to separate, and discover their individuality and independence alone, is unsupported. . . . The adolescent must acquire his independence, personal identity and self-agency ('scaffolding') step by step."

"You know I'm here if you need me," she said.

"I'm fine," I said.

I stared at the ceiling waiting for the lights of a car—but my room in their home faced a wall across a narrow divide. Nothing moved through that space but the occasional pigeon, the rain, notes from a horn played two stories down and across.

"Richard—"

"I'm fine."

Carmel had been my "scaffolding." Her presence my port. Her body my warmth. Her fingers my guide.

"Richard—?"

And now I was in a room facing a wall.

I opened the door.

My father's step wife stood with a white bowl, her body as soft as —

"Häagen-Dazs," she offered.

"It is important for adolescents to know that there are parents and other caring adults in the background; that they are not entirely alone, adrift and at risk for fragmentation."[4]

Neither my father nor his step wife were "in the background" able to help me put the pieces back together again. They were not really there at all. Their inability to even acknowledge what Mother had done, that something had been broken, left me "alone, adrift, and at risk for fragmentation."

I was no longer an adventurer, the conquistador of Coney Island.

I was no longer going to Milwaukee to play baseball like Sid.

My story was unraveling. My world falling apart.

"Children are particularly vulnerable to physiological disorganization in the face of stress, and they rely principally on their caregivers."[5]

The story I now lived—and these are stories lived more than told— the story I now lived was one where I would pose a question to my dead mother and then find a way to get her to answer now that her voice had stopped coming into my head.

The question I would pose was straightforward and simple—

"Do you care enough to protect me from what you did?"

I was only partially aware that the question didn't entirely make sense, was more than a little absurd. But that didn't matter. That was the question I was asking through a story I was living. And I would get my mother to answer even if it meant risking my life.

That was the question I was asking as my father was answering another: "Do you take this woman, to be your lawfully wedded wife, to have and to hold, to love and to cherish till death do you part?"

And when he answered "I do," he buried Mother.

He saw her death as his failure, the failure of his work, the failure of "bootstraps." Her death was his shame. And in order to deny what he felt, he denied what he knew. He denied that she had been ill. He denied how she died. And then he denied what his denial was doing to me.

"Do you take this woman, to be your lawfully wedded wife, to have and to hold, to love and to cherish till death do you part?"

"I do."

And so my story, the story I told, the story I am telling you now, had changed. From that moment on, I was no longer the adventurer, the explorer, the conquistador of Coney Island.

From that moment, I was one who sought answers from the dead. From that moment, I was convinced that she could send signals through channels of "energy." All I had to do was find a way to receive them. Such channels had been found before. I wasn't the first. I would not be the last.

On a spring morning in 1892, a young cavalry officer in the German army named Hans Berger was on a training exercise when his horse spooked, reared, threw the young man to the ground directly in the path of an oncoming artillery carriage. The driver of the carriage was able to stop just in time. Berger lay on the ground, his head under the wheel, terrified but unharmed.

Many miles away Berger's sister had a premonition that something was wrong, and insisted that their father send a telegram. Years later Berger wrote, "It was a case of spontaneous telepathy in which at a time of mortal danger, and as I contemplated certain death, I transmitted my thought, while my sister, who was particularly close to me, acted as the receiver."[6]

Obsessed with the idea of how his mind had carried a signal to his sister, Berger was determined to demonstrate the physiological basis of "telepathic energy." In 1924, "experimenting on a 17 year old student who had undergone operations to remove a brain tumor, he attached two electrodes bandaged to the young man's head to a galvanometer and was able to record actual brain waves."[7] This was the first recording of the electrical activity of a human brain—on an apparatus Berger would call the electroencephalogram (EEG).

Berger's quest for "telepathic energy" was the beginning of the scientific study of the electrical activity of the human brain and other aspects of the mind that are not fully visible—an energy that Berger considered to be representative of the divine. There was something spiritual about "telepathic energy," about "mind." Berger was convinced that "telepathic energy" was a force of communication outside normal channels of time.

The Third Reich did not take kindly to Berger. He was prohibited from teaching, prohibited from research, removed from the university he loved.

He hung himself on June 1, 1941.

Time has come.

Chapter 48

Time Has Come

TIME HAS COME TODAY
Young hearts can go their way

I was alone. It was night. I was eighteen in Central Park lying in six inches of snow. I was a snow angel. Looking to my right, I saw Michael Starr. Looking to my left, I saw Michael Starr. Looking up, I saw my mother dancing on the branch of a tree next to an elephant. Hanging from the branch were pieces of time.

I was not the first to notice that lysergic acid diethylamide (LSD) and the Chambers Brothers were a good fit.

I don't care what they say

They say we don't listen anyway

"The notion that a principal property of psychedelics is their ability to reveal aspects of the mind that are normally not fully visible was and remains widely accepted among those most familiar with their effects."[1]

Time has come today

Time had come. Time was in pieces. I was in pieces of time. It made sense. Perfect sense. I spread my wings eleven times.

Time, time, time, time, time, time, time, time, time, time, time

In 1997 a group of researchers at Washington University in St. Louis conducted positron emission tomography (PET) studies of cerebral blood flow in human subjects as they performed a series of tasks. An unexpected finding was that in several areas of the cerebral cortex, blood flow decreased below its resting state when focused tasks were performed. This led to the discovery of the default mode network (DMN).

Oh the rules have changed today

"Finding a network of brain areas frequently seen to decrease its activity during attention-demanding tasks was surprising,"[2] was certainly an understatement of the researchers' amazement.

Now that time has come

There's no place to run

"Time Has Come Today" was the hit single on the debut album of the Chambers Brothers, a band known for its "psychedelic soul." I'm not sure how many times I listened to the song before dropping a cube of Domino sugar impregnated with LSD. All I knew was that my mother was dancing in a tree next to an elephant in Central Park surrounded by pieces of time.

I've been loved and put aside

I reasoned that if I were to make it out of the park without being murdered or mugged, then I had proof that she was watching over me from her perch in that tree.

As the sun rose, I walked towards it, until I got to Fifth Avenue. Then I turned down Fifth until I got to 57th Street. Even in my "slightly" altered state, I knew where I was.

I stood staring up at the word "Breakfast" spelled out in black and white tiles. I was at the Horn & Hardart Automat.

I stood there trying to decide between a bowl of oatmeal and a plate of fries, when a young woman approached and asked if I had change for a dollar. I pulled loose change from my pocket. She carefully picked four quarters from my palm, then moved to the section with the word "Pies" spelled out overhead where she inserted three. A window popped open. She reached in.

She moved to a table.

I followed her.

"Excuse me—"

She looked up, smiled, slid a quarter across, "Be an angel. Coffee."

"You owe me a dollar."

"Milk, two sugars."

I picked up the quarter.

"Over there," she pointed.

Below the sign, "Coffee," there was a dolphin-head spout and a slot. I inserted the quarter into the slot, pulled the handle. Coffee flowed out from the dolphin's mouth. There was a pitcher with milk.

I went back to the table.

"Two sugars?"

I walked back. Then returned with—

"Bernadette," she said, offering her left hand as she stirred the sugar with a spoon in her right.

"You owe me a dollar," I said.

"You get hit by a bus?"

"I just gave you—"

"You look like shit."

"I overslept."

"Who are you?"

"Just a kid."

She opened her purse, "Here," she said, offering a comb.

She finished her coffee. "Come with me."

"Where?"

She took out a tube of lip gloss—like the pie, cherry red.

"How do I look?"

"Pretty."

"Smiley," she said.

I followed her out of the Automat and along 57th Street as we walked a few blocks to the studios of the National Broadcasting Company, which were a few feet farther west and thus that much "closer to LA" according to Bernadette—Bernadette Smiley—that was her name.

"He's with me," she said as she blew a kiss to security. The elevator took us to ten.

The overhead labels of "Pies," "Coffee," and "Breakfast," were replaced by one huge "Frost." Gaffers, electricians, cameras, and grips all parted like a biblical sea for Bernadette. "Where is he?" she asked. "In the cave," was the reply as each member of the crew expertly navigated his or her way through the labyrinth of wires, dollies, barn doors, and spots.

"Don't stand in his light," she said as she waved to George, the key grip, on a ladder with duct tape in his teeth and a barn door in his grasp. "He's touchy that way."

"Do you work here?" I asked as she ushered me to the back of the hall. "Do you know him?"

Everyone knew David Frost. Frost had been a very big deal having interviewed prime ministers, presidents, The Beatles, the rising and falling, Nixon, the Pope, who knows maybe even the Dead.

"Is he here?"

"Richard, just sit," she said as she directed me to a canvas chair at the back of the hall. "I'll be right back." She walked to the other side of the hall and disappeared through a door, past a sign that read, "Do not enter."

The acid was wearing off. My focus restoring. Colors stopped talking. Pieces of time had been reduced from eleven to four. The two Michael Starrs had merged into one and walked off. My mother no longer danced in Central Park. I thought about dropping a little more—"two sugars" was the thought that entered my mind through a straw through a hole in the back of my head—when Bernadette returned tucking in her blouse, smacking her lips, rubbing her gums. She put her purse on the table, took out a comb, ran it through her hair. Rummaged some more. "Here's your dollar," she said handing me a five.

I watched as she reapplied gloss, cherry red. "I'm an actress," she said. "You—? No. You're 'a kid.'" She put the gloss back in her purse, "So what do you think?"

"Pretty," I said.

"You too," she said, running a finger over her lips as she took a long look at herself, then another at me, "Too, too."

She lived east of Tompkins Square Park at a time when no one lived east of Tompkins Square Park unless they had just arrived without friends in Newark or the Heights, were selling sex or something else soft, or had just been released from a twelve-step program with twelve incompletes. It wasn't cool to be white, skinny, and "too, too" this far east of Tompkins Square Park, especially at night. And I was—

"Hungry?"

"Not really."

"Too bad," she said as she approached some dude on a stoop wearing enough jewelry to drown a harp seal.

"My treat," she said after a brief exchange.

She lived in a walk-up. Five flights. I followed close behind her short dress, long legs.

When I came to, I was lying in a tub, a far East "tub in kitchen," tub. The water was warm. My clothes on the floor. There was a note. "I'm at the dentist. Wait."

Later that day or later some other East Village night, I asked Bernadette where she'd like to go to get something to eat. "I'm vegetarian," she explained, then suggested, "Hamburger Heaven." It was an odd choice, but in her defense she only ate half of what was served on her plate—portions at Hamburger Heaven were huge.

Later, and again time was playing hard to get, we went uptown to a place that she knew, a place "where the music is loud and the lights are low." When stoned, well-known lyrics work best. "I know a place—"

She seemed to be at one with the crowd, a crowd that was a lively mix of dealers, queens, hookers, and pimps. It was a place that she knew, a place that the police raided at a quarter past two.

I had never been to the Tombs. Back then the Manhattan House of Detention was a short walk from Criminal Courts. The Tombs, as the House was affectionately known, was built to hold five hundred. It held three times that number when I was shown to my cell.

A cell where I was the lone white kid with fifty older, darker men. I channeled Sicilian as best as I could—figuring if my intimates imagined I was "Family," I'd have a better chance of getting out with sphincters intact.

I got out two days later. "Loitering for the purpose of obtaining narcotics," "resisting arrest," "disorderly conduct" were dropped for "insufficient evidence." A picture of me appeared the next day in the *Daily News*. I am the one on page five, far to the right, looking confused and slightly off white.

I called to explain to my father that I had spent a few nights with a friend.

"I overslept."

I returned to Bernadette.

To celebrate our encounter with justice, we dropped another cube.

It was different this time. I wasn't alone. The air was hot. The music was soft. The acid was "light." The song was Havens, Richie—Woodstock.

Freedom freedom freedom freedom

Freedom freedom freedom freedom

I followed the music as it turned on a Fisher turntable. Back then, music spun.

Sometime I feel like a motherless child

"Psychedelics have been shown principally to effect the brain's serotonergic signaling system. There are 14 known serotonergic receptors. Psychedelics principally act at the 5-HT2A receptor. This receptor is known as the 'pharmacological trigger of the 'psychedelic experience.'"[3]

Sometime I feel like a motherless child

There are two principal serotonin receptors. The serotonin 1A (or 5-HT1A) receptor is the receptor where drugs like Prozac and

Zoloft act to improve mood and bring feelings of calm by increasing cortical control and "cognition" over subcortical abandon and "emotion." This is "top-down" control.

The other receptor is the serotonin 2A (5-HT2A) receptor. Psychedelic drugs like psilocybin and LSD interact with the 5-HT2A receptor to do pretty much the opposite. They diminish cortical control and "cognition" over subcortical emotion and "intuition." This shift from control to intuition, from cognition to emotion increases "uncertainty." By increasing uncertainty, the brain increases what may be "possible." The mind "expands." The unknown is welcomed. The "top" (the prefrontal cortex) lets go. The "bottom" (the limbic subcortex) takes over.

Sometime I feel like a motherless child

The default mode network is most densely expressed in the frontoparietal and temporal association areas of the brain—areas that have been shown to consume less energy during focused activities and more energy during unfocused activities.

Unfocused activities—such as daydreaming, fantasizing, meditating, REM sleep, wandering with no direction home—activate the default mode network (the DMN).

Freedom freedom freedom freedom

The serotonin 2A (5-HT2A) receptor increases the brain's default mode network, increasing what has been described as the brain's "entropy," a state opening to uncertainty.

Freedom freedom freedom freedom

Why, you might ask, would the brain welcome uncertainty?

Sometimes I feel like I'm almost gone

There are times when one feels like one is "almost gone." Times when everything one has done has failed. Times when there seems to be no direction home.

Uncertainty can open to the unexpected. To the never before thought or imagined. To a new path. A new direction home.

Sometimes I feel like I'm almost gone

Which may be what meditation, fantasy, daydreaming, entropy, REM sleep, psychedelics, and 5-HT2A receptor stimulation offer.

"One possible interpretation is that serotonin works to relax prior assumptions so as to weaken perseverative/habitual responding. This relaxation of prior assumptions may be done to facilitate new learning, in conditions where prior assumptions become counterproductive and/or when environmental conditions are so volatile and change-able that heightened flexibility and exploration become optimal—"

A long, long, long way from my home

Clap your hands

"The significant pro-plasticity effects of serotonin were ascribed to increased signaling at the excitatory serotonin 2A receptor sub-type . . . where the influence of prior beliefs is relaxed so that new learning can occur."[4]

That is to say, where greater uncertainty is accepted in the hope of discovering something unforeseen and valuable in the unexpected.

Clap your hands

Which can open a path to change.

Clap your hands

Path to change.

Clap your hands

Clap your hands

Clap your hands

Uncertainty can open to change.

I got a telephone in my bosom

And I can call him from my heart

But you have to be able to accept the new path, the new map. You have to be able to accept uncertainty. And at least in theory, that is what the activation of the 5-HT2A receptor does. It opens to the possibility of something new by loosening the hold of the 5-HT1A receptor on something old, on what had until then, been the tried and the true. When top- down control of the cortex recedes (certainty), bottom-up possibility of the subcortex emerges (uncertainty).

I got a telephone in my bosom
And I can call him from my heart
I was lying next to a woman. As I turned toward her, she moved toward me. She circled around me as if I were her Adam and she were my Eve. I took the apple she had brought, and sucked on it as if it were a breast. As if it were a penis. As if it were a snake.

"The serotonin 2A receptors that appear to be the key trigger for the psychedelic experience have their densest expression in high-level cortical regions belonging to the default-mode network . . ."[5]

The snake/apple/penis/breast spun into cotton candy—
When I need my brother brother
—a fortune teller handed me a spool of cotton candy as she opened my palm—
When I need my mother mother
"*El destino es el destino*" she exclaimed.
Hey yeah hey yeah hey yeah hey
Then the snake coiled round my arm—
Freedom freedom freedom freedom
No longer Eve, now my Mother coming up out of the bath, but not her bath, the "tub in kitchen" bath where I had been the night before with Bernadette, who had left a note saying she was going to the dentist because she had an ache in her heart that only a dentist could fix—
Freedom freedom freedom freedom
"Lysergic acid diethylamide (LSD) has been shown to markedly increase visual cortical blood flow especially in the primary visual cortex (V1) which has been strongly correlated with reports of visual hallucinations."[6]
Visual hallucinations start with input from the retina to the lateral geniculate body of the thalamus from which it is relayed to sequences of neurons layered in the visual cortex of the occipital lobe.
There was a bowl of apples on the nightstand by the bed. There were roaches on the floor. Bernadette snored. I figured I needed to

find a place where life and death crossed. I figured I needed a fortune teller who could read cotton candy.

I got a telephone in my bosom

"*Passive coping* (i.e. tolerating a source of stress) is mediated by postsynaptic 5-HT1A receptor signaling and moderated by stress moderation. . . . *Active coping* (i.e. actively addressing a source of stress) is mediated by 5-HT2A signaling and characterized by enhanced plasticity (defied as capacity for change)."[7]

I stared at the phone.

5-HT2A receptors by loosening the hold of the prefrontal cortex open the brain to uncertain calls.

Freedom freedom freedom freedom

The phone started to ring.

Two days later I went with Bernadette to a beach in Far Rockaway, Queens. It was a moonless night. The shops were closed except for a deli that offered coffee, cream, neon, and fries.

We walked down the shore. I rolled a joint. Bernadette sang to the stars. She had a trained voice. I went out on the jetty. I couldn't tell if the water was shallow or deep. I couldn't tell if the tide was coming in or out. I couldn't tell if the joint was mixed with dust or just weed. I couldn't tell if I were dissociating because of the weed, the dust, or her voice. I couldn't tell. And then I figured it out.

It was dust.

Phencyclidine—angel dust—is a dissociative anesthetic. Mind and body come apart. It's hard to know where things stop and start.[8]

I stared into the water.

I figured if my mother cared about me, she would protect me from splitting my head on the rocks if I dove off a jetty in Far Rockaway, Queens. I wasn't really sure, but I figured it was a way to find out.

"The default-mode network may be the brain's default response in times of adversity." This shift may be critical "as the level of adversity reaches a critical point."[9]

I was at "a critical point." I had to find out.

When I need my brother . . . brother.

I would dive into water . . . water.

Maybe it was shallow. Maybe it was deep. If it was deep, I would swim. And if shallow, I'd break my neck.

When I need my mother . . . mother.

Either way, I'd have an answer.

I had a plan.

By tolerating uncertainty allowance is made for the unknown.

"Do you care enough to protect me from what you did?"

I had a plan—even if it were a plan that didn't make sense. Or left me dead.

In Miss Oberfeld's class, we had drills to prepare us in the event of nuclear war. We were instructed to crawl under our desks, shut our eyes, and hold our heads between our knees.

Clap your hands

I thought about that as I stood on a rock at the end of the jetty staring into the ink dark sea swirling red, white, and blue—

Clap your hands

—from the neon on shore.

I imagined my mother.

Freedom freedom freedom freedom

I stared into water.

Sometimes I feel like a motherless child.

I wasn't sure if I were preparing for my death or going for a swim.

Sometimes I feel like a motherless child.

And then I realized, that's who I am.

I dove.

"The serotonin 2A receptors . . . have their densest expression in high-level cortical regions belonging to the default-mode network, and this network, as well as other fronto-parietal networks, have been closely implicated in consciousness regulation."[10]

"Are you all right?"

Increased excitation of the serotonin 2A receptor inhibits the activity of the default-mode network.

I got a telephone in my bosom

And I can call him up from my heart

"Are you all right?"

The inhibition of the default-mode network, the inhibition of an inhibitor, releases subcortical networks from cortical control. By diminishing cortical control, the subcortex is given greater access to "consciousness"—a term hard to define—but greater access to whatever "consciousness" is.

I got a telephone in my bosom

But consciousness is now fragmented because the normal integrative role of the cortex has been withdrawn.

And I can call him up from my heart

"Richard?"

When I need my brother, brother

Fragments of memory broke on the surface of the water.

"Are you all right?"

The red, white, and neon blue water.

I stared.

When I need my mother, mother

A figure danced on the shore.

Emotion without context is what activation of the 5-HT2A receptor provides.

"Richard?"

I couldn't tell if the dancing figure was Bernadette—or Miss Oberfeld checking on us after nuclear war.

"Are you all right?"

She waved her arms back and forth in the air.

"Are you all right? Are you all right?"

I saw an eye, a hand, a chair—

"Stress disrupts the functioning of the hippocampus . . . and leads to context-free associations which are hard to locate in space and time."[11]

"Are you all right? Are you all right?"

"Psychedelics acting through the serotonin 2A receptor by inhibiting the inhibitor, facilitate access to consciousness for these more basic subcortical centers of emotion and memory. This uncoupling of the hippocampus from cortical association areas can be disorganizing."[12]

"Richard!"

I kept staring, trying to make out whether it was my mother calling from the sky—

"Richard!"

—or Bernadette jumping up and down on the shore.

"Richard! Richard! Richard!"

"Bernadette?"

"Goddamn, who the fuck do you think it is?" she yelled.

"Where did you go?"

"Get your bony ass out of the water," she screamed. "Fucking now!"

"Bernadette," I called one more time, relieved to see it was Bernadette, holding a towel, stamping her foot, her arms opened wide—and not my mother stepping naked from the bath—

"Oedipal," an analyst would have said. "Fucking oedipal!" Bernadette would have said if only she had read Freud.

"You fucking bastard," she said wrapping me in the towel as I got to the shore.

She pressed her lips hard against mine. Her arms went round my neck, her legs round my waist. I fell to my knees, my face pressed to her crotch. She smelled like the sea. "You fucking bastard! You fucking, fucking . . ." she pushed me back forcing my shoulders into the sand. "I don't want to hear another fucking word out of you," she said unbuttoning my jeans, "not till I scream."

"Bernadette—"

With one hand she covered my mouth, "Not another word," she said looking me straight in the eye. Then she took my penis under her skirt as though it were hers. "You got that?" Maybe it was. "You got that?"

317

I lay on my back staring up at Bernadette who moved over me as her hair filled the sky.

Then she opened her eyes, and stared straight at me for a long long while. Then she smiled, "You're a good fuck—"

"Did you scream?" I asked.

"—a really good fuck," she said relaxing her full weight on my chest.

We lay like that as waves hit the jetty, neon skimmed the sea, salt filled the air.

I listened to Bernadette breathe.

I closed my eyes.

I started to sing,

As we danced in the moonlight

Whatever happened to Chopin,

Whatever happened to Mozart

Whatever happened to you?

I heard a faint sound. Tap tap. Tap, tap. I thought of Aunt Fran.

As we danced in the moonlight

Whatever happened to Chopin—

"Hey you!"

I looked over my shoulder. There was a cop standing about fifty feet away, tapping his nightstick on the rail.

"Hey!"

"Officer—?" I said.

Bernadette rolled off my chest.

"Good evening," I offered as I sat up.

"What are you doing?" he asked.

"Singing."

"What's the name of the song?"

"It doesn't have one—yet."

"Oh," he said still tapping his stick on the rail.

Then he said, "You're naked."

"We're young," I explained.

318

"Even so, you'll need pants," he said moving off. Tap, tap. Tap, tap. He didn't ask for our names.

I put on my pants.

I started singing again,

As we danced in the moonlight

Whatever happened to Chopin,

Whatever happened Mozart

Whatever happened to you?

When I got home, my father opened the door.

"Where have you been?"

"I overslept."

We sat down at the small table by the window facing the park. The housekeeper, a plump Chinese woman named Mrs. Chang, welcomed me back with coffee and fruit. "Thank you, Mrs. Chang," I said as she poured into my cup. "Goody goody coffee," she said in her unique version of the English language.

"Thank you Mrs. Chang."

"Goody, goody," she repeated, then disappeared down the hall.

My father put down the *Times*.

"So Richard," he began, "you 'overslept.'"

I nodded.

"And where were you when you 'overslept'?"

"Far Rockaway."

"Far Rockaway?"

"I was swimming."

"At night?"

"I can explain."

My father arranged for me to be seen by a psychiatrist the next day, a man who came highly recommended by a friend of a friend.

"Highly recommended," he said.

The doctor's name was Seymour Post.

Dr. Post's office was dimly lit. His skin seemed to suffer from a similar lack of light.

"Please sit down."

I sat. Dr. Post cleared his throat and then said in a voice that was hard to hear, "I had a call from an acquaintance of your father who asked if I could see you."

"See me?"

"In consultation."

"So, I'm here because of an acquaintance of my father?"

"You're here because of your behavior," he explained.

He looked at me. I looked at him. Our eyes locked. I turned away, thinking, *This is fucked up.*

"What are you thinking?"

"Nothing."

I've found that when lying it's best to be brief.

Toward the end of the hour, after a series of questions followed by long pauses, Post asked if I had any thoughts.

"No."

Then he said, "Fine."

Then I asked, "Can I leave?"

"You should be in treatment," he said.

"What for?" I asked.

He cleared his throat. He uncrossed his legs. He coughed again, then spoke in a voice that was hard to hear. I leaned forward. He leaned back.

"You've been acting out."

"What does that mean?"

"It means that rather than expressing things and trying to understand them, you're 'acting them out' in your life."

"Such as?" I wanted to know.

"Such as diving off a jetty, abusing drugs, putting your life at risk."

"I'm not trying to kill myself."

"You're putting your life at risk—with drugs, people, your 'behavior.' You take drugs to stay awake and then take more to sleep, your 'behavior' at Rockaway Beach."

"What's wrong with Rockaway Beach?" (And anyway it was Far Rockaway.)

"You're functioning at a 'borderline level' in a 'borderline state.'"

"In a what?"

"A borderline state," he repeated.

"Is that near St. Louis?" I asked, impressing myself with the spontaneity and wit.

Later that night, at dinner with my father and his step wife, he asked how it went with Dr. Post.

"Fine," I said.

"Did he make any suggestions?"

"He said I needed more sleep."

"Can you do that?"

"I'll do my best."

That seemed enough. It was, after all, a bootstraps approach.

Chapter 49

At the Corner of Norman Rockwell and Main—Take One

THE FIRST PAPER I WROTE AFTER I GOT TO WILLIAMS COLLEGE WAS returned with "Not Acceptable" written in red ink at the top.

I was stoned when I wrote the paper, stoned when I got it back. Stoned when three months later I was called to see my faculty advisor, a man named Craig Brown, to whose office I had already been twice. He taught history—"America 101." I liked Craig Brown. He had a soft, gentle voice.

"You know you're flunking out," Brown said before I had gotten halfway through the door. "And I don't like it when my students flunk out, especially where they are smart."

"Thank you."

"That wasn't a compliment," he said.

"Oh."

"It's been recommended you see a psychiatrist."

"By whom?"

"Student health."

"I don't want to see a psychiatrist."

"Then you should leave."

"Your office?"

"The college—you've been wasting our time."

"I've already seen a psychiatrist."

"It's been recommended you see a psychiatrist at the Austen Riggs Center, a doctor named Brenman."

"Brenman?"

"I'm disappointed when a promising student does everything he can to fuck up."

I looked at Brown. He looked at me. I had always thought that he was soft-spoken and shy. He handed me a card with a name, a date, a time.

"Don't be late."

"How do I get to Stockbridge?" I asked looking up from the card.

Austen Riggs is in Stockbridge, thirty miles to the south.

"There's a bus."

"You're late," Brenman said.

"I overslept."

A week later, I was in the office of Dr. Brenman, at the Austen Riggs Center in Stockbridge, Massachusetts. I had arrived an hour late for an appointment at half past three, having traveled from Williamstown, thirty miles to the north. I didn't have a car. I missed the bus. I went to the corner, the intersection of Routes 7 and 2. I stuck out my thumb.

Several cars passed, then a truck. There's a field that runs wild by the road with flowers, a church, two elms—it was like the corner of "Norman Rockwell and Main." A car rolled to a stop.

"Where are you going?" the driver asked as I got in.

"Thanks."

"Sure, where you going?"

"Stockbridge," I said.

He drove a Chevy Impala with one hand on the wheel. With the other he offered a stick of Doublemint gum.

"I don't imagine you smoke. Most of you don't." A pack of Chesterfields lay on the seat. The smell of the car and the smoke made me think of Aunt Fran.

"Pittsfield," he said, "I'm going to Pittsfield."

Pittsfield was halfway there. "But I'm done with work so I'll take you. Nothing better, just the wife and the kids. You know how it is."

I had no idea how that was. He adjusted the rearview mirror. I coughed.

"So what takes you to Stockbridge?" He looked down the road, then back at me. "You got a girl—in Stockbridge?"

No, I didn't have a girl in Stockbridge. He was smiling.

"So what you got?" he asked turning to me.

"An appointment," I said.

"Oh."

He turned back to the road.

Three crows greedily danced around a piece of squirrel. "Roadkill," he said with a smile. I nodded, "sure, what the fuck," repeated once or twice in my head. 'Roadkill.'

We were driving south on Route 7. Then he asked, "What are you feeling?" I looked at him. It was an odd question.

"You look like shit," he said. "Why don't you lie back, loosen your belt, get some rest?" He was watching me in the rearview mirror. "What time is your appointment? In Stockbridge?"

He looked at me again, gave a broad smile as he turned off 7 onto 43. He nodded.

"I know," as if he had read what I had been thinking. "Forty-three goes around Pittsfield. Longer but better," then he nodded to the road, "longer but better"—another glance, another smile. "I'll get you to your appointment—in Stockbridge."

I just looked at this middle-aged, bellied, father of two. "Have some gum," he said. "It's double good, double good,'" singing the jingle as he offered me—

"You're kind of cute."

I took a stick, put it in my mouth.

"Almost pretty," he said.

I stared straight ahead.

"Too, too —" I thought of Bernadette.

"Time sense may be altered, often with a sense of slow motion, and the experience may lose its quality of ordinary reality. The person may feel as though the event is not happening, as though observing from outside the body. These perceptual changes combine with a feeling of indifference, emotional detachment, and profound passivity."[1]

I felt almost no emotion except when in the extreme. Like losing touch or smell. Like losing the nerves the senses receive. Since my mother's death I felt most alive when risking my life. It was fucked up. But except for those times, my life was lived mostly numb.

My last night in the city, my last time I would see Bernadette, we went to the roof of her building. Roofs of tenements and the ConEd power station dominated the view. I asked her to dance.

"Richard, come sit."

I started dancing. I started singing.

As we danced in the moonlight

Whatever happened to Chopin,

Whatever happened to Mozart

"Richard, you're getting close to the edge."

Whatever happened to you?

My mother had been a good dancer. Her feet were sure. She would never let me—

"Richard!" Bernadette yelled, grabbing my arm. "Don't fucking do that!"

"So what's your name?" he asked as he turned off Route 43 onto Queechy Lake Drive. He drove a few miles farther, then pulled to the side. Stopped the car. Turned the key.

There were birds in the trees. Sun in the sky. Gum in my mouth.

He leaned over, touched my shoulders, my chest.

He undid my belt.

I chewed as the jingle played over and over in my head, "Double the pleasure, double the fun—"

"These detached states of consciousness are similar to hypnotic states. They share the features of surrender."[2]

"—with double good, double good—"

There are reasons why trauma takes control of a mind the way a virus takes control of a cell. There are reasons why trauma flattens emotion, leaving you numb. There are reasons why trauma leaves you willing to do whatever it takes to get feeling back. There are reasons why when he put his hand on my cock, I didn't react.

In 1976, twenty-five children were kidnapped from their Chowchilla, California school bus. The captors drove the children in two blackened vans and buried them alive in a truck-trailer. Two teenagers among the children were able to dig themselves out. All of the children were rescued. All of the children survived.

In a study done some five years after the kidnapping, every child suffered from one form or another of "psychic trauma." The most common symptoms were nightmares, numbness, a disordered sense of time, the belief that nothing mattered. When asked what they wanted to be when they grew up, many of the children replied that they never fantasized or made plans for the future because they expected to die young.[3]

"—with double good, double good—"

I kept humming as this man, whose name I never knew, never asked, never wanted, let's call him "John," father of two, imperfect skin, soft bellied, undid my belt, then the buttons on my Levi 501 fly, took my cock in his mouth, put his finger in my ass, all the while Queechy Lake shimmered and ducks took off seeking someplace warmer, farther south.

I looked down at his mouth round my cock. It didn't really matter. I planned to die young.

"—double good, double good, Doublemint gum."

"Time sense may be altered. . . . The person may feel as though the event is not happening . . . as though observing from outside the body. These perceptual changes combine with a feeling of indifference, emotional detachment, and profound passivity."[4]

Ducks usually make a lot of noise, but it had grown quiet on Queechy Lake.

"Traumatized people feel that they belong more to the dead—than to those still alive."[5]

We both lay in the front seat of the Chevy.

He rolled a joint. Took a drag, passed it.

"That was good," he said.

"Fuck," I replied.

"Really good."

There was a clock on the dash.

"I'm late."

"For your 'appointment'?"

"Yes."

"Let it wait."

I pulled up my pants. Buttoned the fly. I looked out the window. It seemed like most of the ducks were still there—not moving, making no noise. "Decoys," I thought.

Then I heard the first shot.

Chapter 50

Road Kill

THE CAR STOPPED IN FRONT OF THE AUSTEN RIGGS CENTER IN Stockbridge, Massachusetts. He turned to me, "Maybe I'll see you for your next 'appointment,'" he smiled. "In Stockbridge." I got out of the car. "So when is it?" he asked, driving alongside as far as the road went.

He blew his horn.

"Hey, kid—?"

The Austen Riggs Center is on Main Street. I found my way to the office of Dr. Brenman. Set back from the world, a well-maintained lawn, flowers, a place that seemed protected from pain. I rang the bell.

A woman answered.

"I'm here to see Dr. Brenman," I said. "Is this his office?"

"No," the woman smiled, "This is *her* office."

"Are you Dr. Brenman?"

"It's okay. It happens quite a lot. And you are?"

"Your three-thirty. I'm sorry. I'm late."

"Richard?"

"I overslept."

"Come in," she said as we both stood facing each other across a threshold waiting for who would say or do something next. She looked at me a long while then asked, "Are you all right? You look frightened."

There are opening moves in psychiatry just as there are opening moves in chess. That was an unusual one.

"I overslept."

She moved to the side allowing me to pass. I walked into her office.

There was a couch, several chairs, a table, a desk.

"Where should I sit?"

"Why don't you sit over there," she pointed.

"Are you—?" she asked as if picking up from where we had left off but this was the first time we met.

"What?"

"Depressed—?" she said.

"What makes you say—?"

"I don't usually—"

"I've always been—" I said, "—always felt a little depressed, a little dead, a little death."

She smiled.

"What?"

"Just something—it's French."

Her office was full of books, color, light. It seemed more like the home of a writer than the office of a shrink—

"I am going to pour myself a cup of coffee. May I pour one for you?"

"Coffee?"

—later I found out that it was.

"Sure."

"You came here from Williamstown?"

"Yes."

"You're late."

I nodded.

"I don't normally do this, but let me make a call. See what I can do."

She moved to the phone, dialed. "Montana—?" she said, "Look, I'm sorry to bother you—"

I wondered whether she was talking to a person or the state.

"—would you please get in touch with Harry." She paused, "Tell him not to wait. Thank you." She hung up the phone.

"I was able to make some time."

"Time?"

"So—"

"Time."

"Cream? Sugar?"

"Black."

She poured two cups of coffee from a fresh pot.

"Thank you," I said holding the cup in both hands like a bowl of soup. "Do you want to know why?" I asked without knowing why I asked.

"What?"

"Why I was late."

But she was right.

I didn't expect a woman.

I looked at her sipping coffee. She wasn't pretty. I was tired. I overslept.

"You said you overslept."

A middle-aged father of two. Or was it three? A few hits of weed, sticks of Doublemint gum in my mouth. I explained.

"So that's why you were late. A blow job?"

"A hand job," I corrected—wondering why I had told her any of this, wondering about my need to confess, and then lie. I stared at her, wondering about this woman thinking that maybe she wasn't so bad looking after all, almost reminded me of a girl I once—

"You look like you're thinking about me," she said. "Are you?"

"I was thinking about how I got here," I said.

The fucking witch, I thought.

"How you got here?" she repeated.

"The hand job," I explained.

"The hand job. Yes."

"Yes."

I took a long sip. *The fucking witch.*

"When you confess to a priest, you confess what you know. When you confess to an analyst, you confess what you don't know," something Freud said. Something about this woman made me want to confess.

She sipped her coffee. I finished mine. Old enough to be my mother.

She took another sip, put down the cup, looked at me long and hard. "Are you always this angry?" she asked.

"I'm not angry," I said.

There were only three emotions that I knew—numbness, anger, pain. As to which one I might be feeling, I only had a vague clue. It was a game of three card monte, a game of chance, and like most games of chance, the odds are with the dealer, the house. I was in her house. It was her deal.

"I'm not angry," I said again.

Even to me, it had the ring of a lie.

"When trust is lost, traumatized people feel that they belong more to the dead."[1]

It didn't matter. Nothing mattered.

It was all a game—even the sex, especially the sex, highway sex.

"I'm not angry," I said.

I was thinking about roadkill. "I'm sorry I was late." It was fucked up.

"Yes," she said, "you overslept."

I had a hard time with truth.

"Going through the motions of living . . . as if observing the events of daily life from a great distance. . . . Long after the event, many traumatized people feel that a part of themselves has died."[2]

She glanced at her watch. "We'll have to stop."

I stood up to leave. There were shelves of books. Winnicott, Bowlby, Erikson, Freud, Clifford Odets. She went to the bookcase, selected *Young Man Luther.* She handed me the book. "Just make sure you give it back. He means a great deal to me."

"Luther?" I asked.

"Erikson," she said.

The treatment of traumatic loss requires equal measures of psychobiology, psychotherapy, alchemy, luck.

"You trust that I'll bring it back?"

"Yes, I do," she said.

Chapter 51

The Oddball Paradigm

A WEEK LATER I WAS ON A BUS OF THE PETER PAN TRANSIT COMPANY, heading out of Williamstown, going south. Had this been Mexico, there would have been chickens and goats, but this was Massachusetts—no chickens, no goats. Just the flotsam and jetsam of the American dream heading south.

"Where to?"

"Stockbridge," I said.

"After Pittsfield," the driver said, giving me two bills after I had given him a five.

"Are the seats assigned?"

"What?"

"Assigned?"

"The kid wants to know if the seats are assigned," the driver yelled out to the three other passengers scattered round the bus. "Seats assigned?" he said, shaking his head as he pulled the handle closing the door. "New Ashford. New Ashford will be next."

I sat by the window as though I were "a traveler sitting next to the window of a railway carriage."[1] But I wasn't a traveler. I wasn't on a train. I wasn't an adventurer, a conquistador. I was just a kid on a Peter Pan bus sitting next to the window in my unassigned seat as we headed down Route 7 past the turnoff to Route 43 that led to a road and a lake where there were more decoys than ducks.

No. I wasn't a traveler. I wasn't a conquistador. Conquistadors don't get fucked.

I was a kid. I was alone. I was a kid who was alone because there was no I could trust. I had gone numb. No one mattered because I needed no one except my mother with whom I had made a pact using alchemy and the risk of life. I hadn't decided on the how, when, or where. But the promise was there, an ingredient in the bond of suicide that would make the two of us one, the way a "good enough" mother would do, as I watched my life in an ever-changing view. I was, as Dr. Post had said, "at risk," and now in Massachusetts, a highly borderline state.

"New Ashford. New Ashford," the driver called out as the bus slowed to a stop.

"You're late."

"I got lost."

"Another diversion?" she asked.

"Another hand job," I replied.

"Are you lying?"

"I guess."

"Why?"

"Does it matter?"

"Yes, as a matter of fact, it matters," Brenman said. "It matters because your indifference to truth isn't concealing a truth. It's revealing a lie." She stood up. "It helps you believe that you don't want the thing that you need."

"And just what the fuck is it I need?" I said surprised by my choice of that word.

Brenman looked at me. "A cup of coffee," she said as she stood up. "Black."

I stared at Brenman—unsure whether I was feeling hatred or love. Another little moment. Another "petit mort."

The underpinnings of psychopathology, like the underpinnings of psychotherapy, have a great deal to do with memory. For Freud, psychopathology had mostly to do with unconscious memory and in particular with unconscious wishes, dreams, unconsciously repressed sexual fantasy. "Where id was, there ego shall be," Freud famously said.

But what if psychopathology is driven not by what is forgotten or repressed. What if psychopathology is driven by what is remembered?

What if the ego has arrived, yet chaos still abounds.

Excellent wretch!

Perdition catch my soul

But I do love thee! And when I love thee not,

Chaos is come again.

Othello III 3

There are specific things that focus attention, "big things, bright things, moving things, or blood"[2] William James said. I had my share of big, bright, moving things. I had my share of blood.

Brenman went to the coffeepot, poured.

On the table was a blue-and-white can—Maxwell House. She poured two mugs. The smell of coffee filled the air.

"I'm afraid of the feeling of being afraid," a child from Chowchilla said five years after the fact.[3] Traumatic memories return. And when they do, they tend to get stronger, not weaker, each time.

In 1961 Frank Morrell published a paper describing a well-known yet perplexing clinical phenomenon. He was investigating why some patients after suffering a closed head injury went on to develop a seizure disorder long after the insult itself. Morrell argued that "such pathological events need not imply the emergence of new and uniquely different properties of neural tissue, but more likely implies particular variations on normal physiological mechanisms."[4] He was arguing that this was the normal response of neural tissue to injury.

Graham Goddard was intrigued by Morrell's work and sought to address the findings experimentally. Goddard planted electrodes in the brains of mice and delivered electrical stimulation at fixed intervals at subconvulsive thresholds—that is, at a level that did not result in a seizure. "At first the stimulation had little effect on behavior and did not cause electrographic discharge. With repetition, the response to stimulation progressively changed to include localized seizure discharge, behavioral automatisms and eventually, bilateral clonic convulsions."[5]

Goddard called this phenomenon "kindling," an experimental model in which repeated, intermittent administration of a subconvulsive electrical stimulus in neural tissue led to a progressive increase in the biochemical discharge. Kindling, Goddard argued, was the result of the strengthening of synaptic connections between neurons that occurred when a stimulus was repeated—whether it led to strengthened memory, strengthened emotion, or strengthened biochemical discharge that led to a seizure.

"It can be argued that the phenomenon described in the present note is analogous to learning. At the very least it is a relatively permanent change in behavior that depends on repeated experience."[6]

Goddard argued that kindling, the strengthening of the synaptic connection between neurons, occurred when a stimulus was repeated—whether it led to strenthened patterns of memory, strengthened patterns of behavior, or to seiure. And further, the repetitive stimulus did not have to be the electrical discharge from a deeply implanted electrode. The repetitive stimuus could be the affective discharge from a deeply implanted memory.

Goddard concluded that the phenomenon of kindling "deserves the attention of physiologists and psychologists alike."[7]

In 1979 a psychologist, H. J. Eysenck, published a paper that investigated the psychological issue that Goddard had raised. In his paper "The Conditioning Model of Neurosis," Eysenck described a process that he called "fear augmentation." Basically, he described a situation where a conditioned stimulus, such as the ringing of a bell, was followed by the unconditioned stimulus, a shock to the foot. But after the first few trials, the bell was delivered without being followed by the shock, a situation that should have led to extinction.

In other words, if the bell were rung and a mouse were shocked on the first few but not on subsequent trials, the response to the conditioned stimulus should undergo extinction. The mouse should stop exhibiting fear in response to the bell because the bell no longer predicted a shock.

But Eysenck encountered something quite different. He discovered that the response to an unreinforced stimulus (the sound of the bell not followed by shock) did not lead to extinction. Instead each time the bell was rung, the mouse's fear response increased. And thus Eysenck, "The conditioned stimulus followed by fear . . . may be sufficiently reinforcing to more than counteract the decremental effects of extinction."[7]

This was a situation analogous to what Goddard had described with repeated subthreshold electrical stimulation leading to a convulsive seizure. This was the premonition that had led Goddard to conclude that the phenomenon of kindling "deserves the attention of physiologists and psychologists alike."

Eysenck demonstrated that neural tissue indeed could be kindled (strengthened) not just by the repetitive discharge of an implanted electrode, but also by the repetitive discharge of a powerful affect. The repetition of the affect alone was enough to augment memory. Eysenck's work helped explain why some memories get stronger, not weaker, with time.

She handed me a mug of coffee.

"Good to the last drop," I said to myself.

"I didn't hear you."

"You think I'm afraid?" I asked.

"Yes," she said.

"So what am I afraid of?"

There had been significant neurobiologic data suggesting that attention is focused as a result of interactions that occur between two autonomous pathways connecting the frontal and parietal regions of the brain. These two pathways are the dorsal (upper) and the ventral

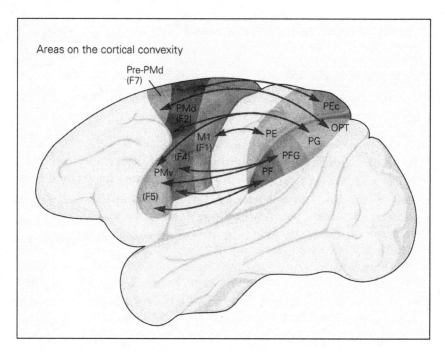

Areas on the cortical convexity

Pre-PMd
(F7)

PMd
(F2)

PEc

OPT

M1
(F1)

PE

PG

(F4)

PFG

PMv

PF

(F5)

Conscious attention is focused by multiple factors including the prefrontal cortex. The frontoparietal pathway from the visual cortex to the prefrontal cortex "holds" focus. But this hold can be shifted by the unexpected which in part is signaled by the release of the neurotransmitters dopamine and noradrenaline. When focus shifts, there is a shift from the dorsal (upper) to the ventral (lower) frontoparietal pathway. This is the "oddball" paradigm.

(lower) frontoparietal networks. The dorsal frontoparietal network coordinates "top-down" attention. This network includes direct connections to and from the prefrontal cortex, the primary auditory and visual cortices, and has direct input from the medial temporal lobes which enable the selection of sensory stimuli based on internal goals, past experience, and memory.

And so for example if one were looking for someone in a crowd who had indicated that she would be wearing a red coat, it would be the dorsal frontoparietal network that would keep one's visual cortex on the lookout for the color red. In other words, the dorsal frontoparietal network by focusing attention would be limiting perception—whether that focus be on perception from the senses or on perception based on memory. And thus by looking for someone in red, one would be less likely to see an old acquaintance passing by wearing green.

But if one did perceive the person in green, then one's attention would have shifted—and it would have been the ventral frontoparietal network that would have called attention to the friend passing by wearing green, interrupting the dorsal frontoparietal's search for red, and thus refocusing attention. This attention to the unanticipated is "bottom-up" perception and is a property of the ventral frontoparietal network which also receives input from medial temporal lobes but which has restricted access to the prefrontal cortex and thus has restricted access to working memory and "consciousness."

This shift from the dorsal to the ventral frontoparietal network is initiated by the release of dopamine and noradrenaline. This shift allows recognition of the unexpected.

But with deeply embedded, affectively driven memory, the unexpected may never be recognized. One may fail to recognize the friend in the crowd. One may fail to recognize how memory controls perception. One may fail to recognize because affectively driven memory gets stronger, not weaker, with time.

"You think I'm afraid?" I asked.

"Yes," she said.

"So what am I afraid of?"

"The oddball paradigm" is what the moment is called. "The oddball paradigm," when attention shifts in a flexible, non-traumatized brain. "Big things, bright things, moving things" shift attention, according to William James. But when the "big thing" is overwhelming trauma, when the "big thing" is "blood," the shift becomes harder to make, paradigms become fixed.

"So what am I afraid of?"

"Trust," she said.

Chapter 52

Alchemy

THE AUSTEN RIGGS CENTER IS A PSYCHIATRIC FACILITY PRIMARILY intended for residential treatment. Patients at Riggs are usually there for months at a time. Most are young adults who present with a mix of depression, suicidal ideation, underachievement. Substance abuse is a plus if you're looking to get into Riggs.

I bought a Bultaco—a Spanish twin-stroke 250cc off-road machine—from a mechanic in North Adams, Massachusetts. The bike allowed me to arrive high on speed.

"Do you have to be high?" Brenman asked.

"It's a Bultaco," I explained.

On a winding road after a soft rain, a stretch that went south from Williamstown past Mt. Greylock and the Hopper—perhaps the most beautiful road in the state—I spun out.

As the Bultaco and I went sliding along, I remember thinking this would be a good place to die. The bike ended in a brook by the road. I ended walking with a limp for two months.

"I didn't die," was pretty much what I told those who asked.

Brenman asked.

"Part of me didn't want to die."

"Which part?" she asked.

"The part that limps," was as much as I had figured out.

After leaving the session, I noticed a young woman alone on the

340

grass. She was eating an apple. I have a thing about apples—my mother's picture and all. I smiled. She smiled. I approached.

"Stephanie."

Stephanie was the daughter of an executive at General Motors, a vice president in fact. To be a patient at Riggs, you need liquid assets. Needless to say Stephanie had assets. We talked a little while, then suddenly as if just remembering, she got up. "I have to go."

"Where?" I asked.

She flicked her blond hair, "I'm off to seduce Dr. Otto," she said as if she were going to visit the Wizard of Oz. "Who's Dr. Otto?" I asked. Stephanie told me that Dr. Otto was the medical director of Austen Riggs as well as her shrink.

"Seduce?" I asked.

"Fuck," she explained. "I have an apple, and a great ass," then added, "It's a going-away present."

"Where are you going?" I asked, noticing the scars on her wrists. Females at Riggs have scars on their wrists—the way sailors have tattoos on their arms. She just smiled as she walked off. And yes, she had a great ass.

I met Stephanie several times after that—on the grass, twice in her Corvette (her father you'll recall was big at GM). A week later, I learned from Stephanie's roommate that she had been transferred to a locked unit after slitting her wrists. I was neither surprised nor upset. Mostly I missed the Corvette.

I visited her on the unit. She seemed calm, composed. She seemed at peace. I wanted to ask, "What's wrong?"

The clock on the wall read 3:45. I was already late for my appointment with Brenman. I stood up to leave, "I'll come back tomorrow."

"Don't," she replied.

"Why not?" I asked.

"Does it matter?" she said as she walked me to the unit's locked door.

We stood there for a moment like lovers. One about to leave. The other about to be left. Stephanie turned to me. "I did it," she said.

"You did what?"

She put her hands around my neck. Her eyes stared into mine. Then she smiled and said, "I fucked Dr. Otto." Then she moved closer, whispered in my ear, "And I never want to see you again," as she pushed me gently back.

The hospital door closed firmly, automatic, pneumatic.

A month later, Dr. Otto retired from Riggs.

A week later, Stephanie left for her home in Grosse Pointe.

It wasn't my finest hour.

Nor hers.

Eventually I began to accept that what had attracted me most to Stephanie were the scars on her wrists. And what had attracted her most to me were the scars on my heart. We weren't drawn to love. We were drawn to disease. "Illness attacks boundaries," a famous psychiatrist said.

Eventually I told Brenman about Stephanie. I told her everything except the bit about Dr. Otto. Like loyalty among thieves, there is loyalty among outpatients.

"She broke it off?" Brenman asked.

"Yes."

"What were your thoughts when she asked you to leave?"

"What?"

"I think you heard," Brenman said.

"I'm not sure I want to answer."

Brenman sat there, then she said, "It took you a long time to 'confess.' This happened—?"

"Three months."

"You didn't trust me?"

"I wasn't sure."

"And now?"

"The first principle of recovery is empowerment. . . . Others may offer advice, support, assistance, affection, and care, but not cure."[1]

"I'm not sure."

"That's okay. There's time."

"For what?"

"There's time," she repeated. "That's all."

"You think I've been acting out?" I asked without referencing Dr. Post.

"Yes. But acting out isn't always a symptom," she said. "Sometimes it's an attempt to figure something out."

"Like what?" I asked.

"Your story," she said.

"Memory, like belief, like all psychological phenomena, is an action: essentially, it is the action of telling a story . . ."

"My story?" I asked.

"Your story," she said.

The action of telling a story is, moreover, capable of being perfected in various ways. The teller must not only know how to do it, but must also know how to associate the happening with the other events of his life, how to put it in its place in that life history, which each one of us is perpetually building up and which for each of us is an essential element of his personality. A situation has not been satisfactorily liquidated, has not been fully assimilated, until we have put this recital in its place as one of the chapters in our personal history."

I took a hit of coffee. "This is good," I said.

"There are things I care about. Coffee. Story. Clifford Odets."

"You care about story?"

"Since your mother's suicide, you have been trying to make sense of what she did to herself, to you, what she did to your story," Brenman said, and when I said nothing, she went on, "Do I think you are 'acting out' by 'fucking' a troubled young woman who was in treatment here at Riggs? Yes I do. I wish you hadn't done that. Don't do it again. It's not good for her. It is not good for you. And so yes,

343

I think you were 'acting out.' But I don't think you were 'acting out' of disease. You were 'acting out' a question that—like a grain of sand in the flesh of an oyster—you can't quite spit out."

"A pearl?" I asked.

"Oysters make pearls," she said. "We do our best to make stories."

"Strictly speaking," Pierre Janet said, "one who retains a fixed idea of a happening cannot be said to have a 'memory' of the happening. . . . The subject is often incapable of making the recital which we speak of as a memory . . . and yet he remains confronted by a difficult situation in which he has not been able to play a satisfactory part . . . so that he continues to make efforts at adaptation."[2]

"No you're not working on a pearl—a pearl may get larger but its essence stays the same."

She stared at me. "You've been trying to make sense of something that tears at your heart."

"Like that hawk," I said, staring off.

"What hawk?"

Sunlight on the floor. Flowers on the table. A sparrow in the claws of a hawk.

"Just a hawk," I said.

A middle-aged woman. A doctor. A shrink. Visions were both coming together and breaking apart.

"I don't have a 'story,'" I said. "Not anymore."

"A story is built. Put together. It's what you were doing. It's what you're doing now—building a story from the remains of the one torn apart," Brenman said.

I shrugged.

At first glance, the problem of integration may seem quite simple. Logically it demands nothing more than that all the signals from the specialized areas be brought together, to 'report' the results of their operations to a single master cortical area. . . . But the brain has its own logic. . . . There is no cortical area to which all other cortical areas report. . . . In sum the cortex must be using a different strategy."[3]

"My story—?"

"Your story."

"What strategy does the brain use to read itself? How does the brain become a self about which it thinks?"[4]

"One's story—no matter how well crafted or built—is always a work in process. Always incomplete." Brenman watched me.

I watched her.

Then she said, "We have to stop."

I lifted the mug to my mouth, bent my head back. "Good to the last drop" came to mind. How could it not?

"I'll see you next week," Brenman said. "Be on time. I mean it."

"I will," I said. "So do I."

What was becoming clear—even to me, always late, always high on drugs, sex, speed—that this middle-aged woman, this psychologist, this shrink. She was curious about my story. She was curious about me.

"Acting-out behavior isn't always an expression of disease," Brenman had said. "Sometimes it's an attempt to understand."

I had made suicide part of how I attached, part of how I loved—a "bond" that had been part of my story ever since I saw my mother hanging, twelve inches off the cellar floor.

Turning suicide into love was my alchemy. Turning suicide into love was my curse.

I knew Stephanie was suicidal. I was drawn to her scars. The possibility that she might try to kill herself and that I might save her, kept our love, and my mother, alive. My mother had left me, but through saving Stephanie I could bring her back. Maybe I had secretly wished that she would "act out"—fuck Dr. Otto, turn this breach into the act that would propel her to make an attempt on her life—thus allowing me to save her from what I had wished. It was fucked up.

345

Acting out? Yes. Pathology? Yes. But also part of my story. A story that was becoming clear—not my finest hour. But it was clear that I would never have gotten there, never pieced it together without Brenman. And the assurance that she was there to hold it, and me, together.

I was an adolescent—both late blooming and late. I was rebelling against my elders, my parents, my nation, my "fate." I was in rebellion—a rebel who needed Brenman to contain the revolt. I needed her to keep my rebellion from tearing out my heart. I needed Brenman to hold the pieces apart and in place so they might come to light. I was both the hawk and the sparrow.

To quote a passage I've cited before, "The adolescent must acquire his independence, personal identity, and self-agency ['scaffolding'] step by step. It is important that the adolescent knows that his parents are in the background monitoring and intervening as necessary; that he is not entirely alone, adrift and at risk for potential fragmentation."[5]

Brenman had been my "scaffolding" against fragmentation and fate. It was she alone who allowed me to explore just how corrupt my story had become. It was she who had allowed the oddball paradigm to make the switch from dorsal to ventral, from the red to the green. She made it safe enough for me to see how in my courtship of death, I had drawn others in. She made it safe enough for me to see just how toxic my "preconditions for loving" had become. She made it safe.

In his twenty-three volumes of the complete psychological works of Sigmund Freud, the word "safe" appears once.

The more plainly the analyst lets it be seen that he is proof against every temptation, the more readily will he be able to extract from the situation its analytic content. The patient, whose sexual repression is of course not yet removed but merely pushed into the background, will then feel *safe* enough to allow all of her preconditions for loving, all the phantasies springing from her sexual desires, all the detailed characteristics of her state of being in love, to come to light, and from these she will herself open the way to the infantile roots of her love.[6]

This always struck me as one of the most absurd passages in all of the twenty-three volumes of *The Standard Edition of the Complete Psychological Works of Sigmund Freud*. I am sure that Brenman had read the passage. Most, if not all, analysts have. But Brenman did make it safe enough to allow all of my preconditions for loving, all the fantasies springing from my sexual desires, to come to light. She allowed me to attach to her. Just as she allowed me to see that she had made an attachment to me.

"One of the first behaviors that are seen in man and animal are behaviors directed toward attaching to an object, toward a mother or mother figure."[7]

I had felt that attachment when my "second mother" came home and took me into her arms. Then lost it when my "first mother" returned for a second time. Then I found it again with Brenman. She made it safe enough for me to attach.

"There is no such thing as a baby. There is a baby and someone."[8]

There was "someone." And it was she.

By allowing me to attach to her and by showing me that she was attached to me, she made it safe enough for me to let go.

Freud had it backward. "Safety" wasn't what I needed to form an attachment. Attachment made it safe enough for me to let go.

Attachment made it safe enough for me to get to Riggs without acting out (whatever that is), stopped most of the drugs except an occasional snort of cocaine, stopped my pursuit of women with bell-bottoms and scars, cooled my courtship of death.

Brenman had made it safe enough for me to attach to her by showing that she had made an attachment to me. There was a bond. I was not alone.

And there was coffee. The coffee was indeed very good.

Over time, my attachment to Brenman made it safe enough to reconsider the union I had made. My attachment to Brenman made it safe enough for me to accept that my mother's suicide could never be made into love. My attachment to Brenman made it safe enough for me to accept that my mother had let go of me. My attachment to Brenman made it safe enough for me to let go of her.

My attachment to Brenman made it safe enough for me to re-witness what I had witnessed when I was seven years, two months, and two days old. The stairs, the cellar, the slippers—one on the floor, one on her foot—the urine and feces dripping down her legs, her hands, her neck, her face—blue, bloated, eyes shot with blood, staring dead ahead. And one critical piece that had disappeared until Brenman had made it safe enough for me to bring it back.

As I stood staring into my mother's eyes, I wasn't mute. There was one last thing I said.

As I stood staring into her eyes, I screamed the words I had heard my father say as I lay on the floor wrapped in my blue blankie, guarding her door, a bridge that let me know that she must have known that I would be the one who would find her when I came home, that she must have known that she would not guard me the way I had tried to guard her. That her thoughts at the end were about death and death alone. That she was leaving me forever.

"You can't do this to me!"

Which forced me to accept that her suicide was not an expression of love, nor could love ever be made part of what she had done, part of what she was feeling as she put her head through the noose.

Nor could love ever be part of what I had been doing to bring her back.

"You can't do this to me," were the last words of a boy when he was seven years, two months, and two days old.

And then I ran. To the stairs. Out the door. Past the dog. Across the street. To Katie Galst. Where I stood mute. The sirens. Police.

And I knew, even then just a kid, I knew that alchemy had never turned lead into gold, and that alchemy would never turn suicide into love. I knew. Overwhelmed. Helpless. Helplessness is key to the traumatic state. I was helpless to deny what I knew.

Then I looked up.

I was not alone.

Dr. Brenman's eyes were staring into mine.

"What are you feeling?" she asked.

"Alive," I said.

There was a cup of coffee in my hand. There was a bowl of fruit on the table. Apples.

Apples had been there all along.

Chapter 53

Apples

I HAVE A PHOTOGRAPH OF MY MOTHER STANDING ON A TENNIS COURT holding her racket in one hand. An apple in the other.

I have a memory of my mother at Junior's Luncheonette. I offered her a bite of my precious BLT. She said it was mine. "All of it?" I asked.

"All of it," she replied. And when she said that, she smiled. She lifted a cup of coffee to her lips.

I have memories of my mother. I have memories of coffee. I have memories of apples. I have memories of a sparrow in the grasp of a hawk.

Complex memories, and these memories are complex, are not stored in one part of the brain. They are distributed in various areas of the cerebral cortex in neurons that are synaptically connected by the work of the hippocampus. Such a distribution is called a trace, a memory trace. I have traces of my mother. The most vivid traces I have are those when I saw her stepping naked into the bath. And when I saw her hanging from a clothesline in the cellar.

There are others. When I think of her, I can bring them to consciousness. These traces have been in my cerebral cortex for decades. Memories like these are said to be "consolidated"—that is, they are long-term memories that have been stabilized by the modification of synapses, by the mobilization of genes, by the synthesis of proteins.

There are many aspects to these memories. Just thinking about them now as I write, I can turn the image, move it from side to side, move others into my mind even though these others may not have originally been there. I can maneuver these traces the way a sculptor maneuvers clay.

One of the people who comes into that memory—who enters the trace on her own through the wormhole of coffee and Granny Smith apples—is Brenman. Margaret Brenman enters the trace—remapping time, place, strengthening a synapse here, pruning one there. That's what she did, what she does. The trace of Brenman made it safe enough to bring traces of my mother back from the dead, and to maneuver the traces the way a sculptor maneuvers clay.

But if long-term memory is stable, how can it change?

In 1968 a team of scientists led by James Misanin at Rutgers University designed a remarkable experiment, the results of which were not fully appreciated for some thirty years. But their work laid the foundation for the understanding of the dynamic and labile nature of memory and change.[1]

Misanin and his colleagues worked with rats on a Pavlovian fear response paradigm. They trained rats to fear the sound of a bell, the conditioned stimulus (CS), that indicated an impending foot shock, the unconditioned stimulus (US). After a few trials, whenever the rats would hear the bell, they would freeze—indicating that they had learned that the bell (CS) predicted foot shock (US).

After the rats had learned to fear the sound of the bell, one group of rats was given an amnestic electric discharge to the head immediately *after* the bell had been rung. The other group of rats was given an amnestic electric discharge to the head but *without* the bell (the CS) first having been rung.

What the researchers discovered was that the first group that *had received the reminder*, the bell, and were then given the amnestic electrical discharge to the head, lost the memory of the connection between the bell (the CS) and the impending foot shock (the

US). They no longer seemed to remember what they had previously learned—that the bell *predicted* foot shock. So, when they heard the bell, they continued to sniff and explore as if all were well.

The second group of rats that had *not* been given the reminder of the bell before the amnestic eclectic discharge to the head, froze when they heard the bell indicating that they had remembered that the bell predicted foot shock.

In the first group of rats, the ringing of the bell activated the memory that the rats had previously learned associating the bell (the CS) to the food shock (the US). The amnestic discharge to the rat's head then *erased the activated* memory. And so when those rats heard the bell a day later, they did not respond with fear because the memory of the connection of the bell (the CS) to the foot shock (the US) had been *erased* by the anamnestic discharge to the head.

The second group of rats that had *not* received a reminder did *not* activate the memory of the bell (the CS) to the impending foot shock (the US). Thus the memory of the bell as a predictor of impending foot shock had not been activated when they were given an anamnestic eclectic discharge to the head. These rats *did* react with fear when they subsequently heard the bell. The memory connecting the bell and the foot shock had not been erased in this second group.

What did this show?

Two huge discoveries.

First, long-term memory can be changed.

Second, in order to change long-term memory, it must become active.

These were critical insights: Stable long-term memory when reactivated is no longer stable. When reactivated, long-term memory can be strengthened, weakened, modified, erased. That is to say, long-term memory can be changed.

Misanin and his colleagues showed that memory is not set in stone. Memory is set in protein.

Protein can be changed. And when the protein of memory is changed, memory is changed.

I was staring at Brenman. I was thinking of my mother. Her image came back. I could see her.

"Retrieval (of long term memory) is usually brought about as a result of incoming environmental information with the 'memory network,' driven by that information. It follows from this that retrieval will lead to the formation of new memories made on the background of a retrieved prior experience."[2]

She came back. And when she did, Brenman was there in my vision, in my senses, in my hippocampus and neocortex. In the trace.

To mix. To mingle. These two women—neither of whom I ever called by their given names—never Ruth, never Margaret. Always Mommy. Always Dr. Brenman. Watched each other. Touched. Maybe they danced.

"To persist in a functionally useful manner, the trace must possess not only the ability to re-express the specific internal representation, but also 'retrieval handles' that permit activation by some but not other representations."[3]

Perhaps I've gone too far. It's just that as I write this I remember them together. Indeed I can see them together. Right there on the ceiling above where I write. Like when I was a kid watching the lights of the cars. I can see them, the pair of them, crossing together on the ceiling over my head. I'm not on drugs. I haven't done drugs in some thirty years. But they are both there, on this very night. On the map. I redraw.

Reconsolidation.

Reconsolidation is what it's called—when long-term memory becomes active, labile, loosens its boundaries and can be resculpted, redrawn.

Consolidation is when long-term memory is formed, when a memory that's going to stay, gets laid down by new protein synthesis that strengthens the bonds between neurons, the bonds of the synapse. It's the new protein, the growth of new synapses, and the pruning of the old—that make long term memory solid and strong.

But then something happens. When Brenman sits across from me, stares, and then asks, "What are you feeling?" and I answer, "Alive," then something has happened. Something has opened. A wormhole has opened. And when it does, old memory becomes active, alive, vulnerable. It can change. And when memory can change, the past can change.

Memory was not made to be stable. Memory is a dynamic process. From a neurobiological point of view, memory is not fixed. Memory is "an adaptive property of the nervous system" designed to use what was retrieved from the past as a result of input from the present to better predict what may come next.[4]

Memory is a wormhole, not just to the past.

Memory is also a wormhole to the future.

The past is not set in stone. The future can be foreseen.

Then I looked up.

I was not alone.

Dr. Brenman's eyes were staring into mine.

"What are you feeling?" she asked.

There was a cup of coffee in my hand. There was a bowl of fruit on the table. Apples.

Apples and coffee had been there all along.

I looked at Dr. Brenman. Tears welled in her eyes.

Tears flowed from mine.

"Alive," I said. "I feel alive."

It was something I felt for the first in a very long time.

Chapter 54

The Program

AT THE END OF THE YEAR, DR. BRENMAN LEFT STOCKBRIDGE FOR Boston, where she joined the medical faculty of the Harvard School of Medicine. A year later, I returned to New York.

It took several years before I decided to follow Dr. Brenman—not to Boston but to psychology, medicine, psychiatry, psychoanalysis. I took premed courses at night. I took the entrance exams—starting a chain of events that led from application, to medical school, internship, residency, and finally to psychoanalytic training in New York.

There was a pair of giants who taught at "the New York." "The New York Psychoanalytic Society" was called "the New York" because, as everyone there agreed, the only psychoanalytic program that was true to the core was the one we were in, "the New York." The two giants both had the initials RM. All of the candidates competed for the approval of an RM. "One RM—good. Two RMs—better"—somewhat of a bastardization of the manifesto in George Orwell's *Animal Farm*—"Four legs good. Two legs better."

Those of us studying at "the New York" were not "students." We were "candidates." We were provisional. There would be a final "reckoning" before any one of us could be ordained as a true "psychoanalyst." It was a system designed to foster competition, insecurity, mistrust. And it did.

For much of my time at "the New York," I—like my fellow candidates—sought the approval of the RMs.

Most classes were taught by example. One "candidate" read his/her "notes"—"process notes" written down during a session revealing what the "analysand" (the one on the couch) had said, and then what the "candidate" (the one in the chair) had replied. It was an opportunity for a "candidate" to be lauded or ridiculed by one of the RMs.

"Dr. Brockman seems to feel that being helpful is what analysis is about. Is that not so, Dr. Brockman?"

"Well I—"

"Dr. Brockman, as we have just heard, 'rescues' his patient, a woman who 'forgot' to come with enough money for car fare home after her session? What does that indicate?"

"Well I—"

"I wasn't asking you, Dr. Brockman. Yes, Dr. Powers, what does that indicate?" The RM asked Dr. Joanne Powers, an attractive candidate who was about to be made chief resident—an honor for which we all fought.

"It indicates that she is seeking a favor, an unconscious wish," Dr. Powers said with the confidence of someone who feels she is almost always correct. "Her wish is for rescue."

"Exactly. She is seeking the gratification of a deep oedipal wish. And Dr. Brockman seems to feel that the gratification of the patient's wish is more important than helping her to understand the meaning of the unconscious wish. Should he gratify her wish?"

"Well I—"

"I wasn't asking you, Dr. Brockman—"

In 1985 Mitchell, Osbourne, and O'Boyle published the results of a study about choice made under stress. The researchers placed a mouse in a box, the start box, at the head of a T-maze. When the door to the start box is opened, the animal is allowed to go down either arm of the T-maze. A normal mouse on successive trials will explore first one arm then the other—that is to say, the animal's curiosity will direct it to explore alternatives to see what might be found. But if the animal is placed in the start box where it is first shocked, and then the door is opened, something quite interesting happens. The animal perseverates. It continues to pick the same arm of the T-maze. That in itself is not so surprising. But they discovered something more.

They discovered that if the animal were placed in the start box of a T-maze where it was shocked, and then allowed to enter the T-maze and to choose either the left or right arm of the maze, the stressed animal would pick the same arm as on the previous trail even if it were shocked again upon entering that arm of the maze. It kept making the same choice where the shock was repeated. It did not go into the other arm to see what might happen there. A normal unstressed mouse would pick the other arm to see if the new arm offered a better, non-shock, outcome. But the stressed animal kept making the same choice despite the outcome. A stressed animal perseverates (makes the same choice) without regard to the consequences of that choice.

It took me longer than it should have to realize that I, like the stressed mouse, was making the same choice when I got to the decision phase of my "T-maze." I was continuing to seek the approval of an RM when it was becoming increasingly clear that I would never get the approval of an RM. It was becoming increasingly clear that I would never get that approval because I did not believe in what they were teaching. And it was becoming increasingly clear that no matter what I did, their goal was to defeat me. And it was becoming increasingly clear that I failed to see that.

I perseverated. I was convinced that I could win the RMs' approval even when it was clear that they saw me as a threat to be defeated because I challenged the foundations of their beliefs. But I kept seeking their approval. I kept making the same choice. I had begun in the shock box.

"Well, I–"

"I wasn't asking you, Dr. Brockman–"

And like a stressed mouse, I kept making the same choice.

The crucial difference is an animal's level of arousal when it makes the choice. . . . Though habituation (getting used to a stimulus) is usually thought to occur only to stimuli without consequences (like becoming accustomed to the touch of the shirt on one's back), the present results indicate that habituation can occur to stimuli or responses that have consequences as long as the animal is either unaware of the consequences or is aware of them but does not or cannot, use them in deciding between the available alternatives."[1]

There were consequences of my choice that I was refusing to recognize.

The stress of wanting their approval led me to perseverate like a mouse that had been shocked in the start box.

"The crucial difference is an animal's level of arousal when it makes the choice."

I was not seeing. I was not free.

"Yes, Dr. Powers, tell us what you think–"

To graduate from "the Society," you have to complete a personal analysis, called "the Training." It is a lot like basic training, only fought on your back. And just as I had been having trouble with the RMs and "the teaching," I was now having trouble with "the training."

Several months into "the training," I was lying on my back staring at the ceiling when smoke from my analyst's cigarette drifted overhead.

"What are you thinking?" he asked as he took a drag on his cigarette, leaned back in his worn leather chair, exhaled, watched the smoke, then repeated, "What are you thinking?"

I stared at the ceiling. I was thinking about my mother. A thin puff of smoke drifted above and dissolved. My hand moved toward the wall. There was another long pause.

Another puff. Another—

"What are you thinking?"

I didn't respond. I preferred being alone.

My analyst, Dr. Levin, took another drag, crossed and uncrossed his legs.

Another puff of smoke drifted like the lights of a car on the ceiling of my room at 169 Falmouth Street, a block from the ocean and two blocks from the bay.

I remembered being alone in Dr. Stein's waiting room. I remembered the machine on the floor. A machine that seemed to only make noise. I walked over to it. I pushed the switch. The noise stopped. I pushed it again. The noise came back.

"What are you thinking?"

I was thinking about a machine that sat on the floor doing nothing. I was thinking about a room in the Dime Savings Bank in Brooklyn, a room with two doors. I was thinking about my mother. I was thinking about—

"Nothing," I said.

I was thinking that there are two broad elements of any given memory. There is the content of the memory: overheard voices and a machine on the floor.

And there is the context of the memory—"a room in the Dime Savings Bank in Brooklyn, a room with two doors."

The content of the memory—overheard voices and a machine on the floor—is stored in the neocortex—the overheard voices in the auditory cortex; the sight of the machine in the visual cortex.

The pieces of memory are joined by the hippocampus through a process called cell assembly.

A machine that made noise, overheard voices—content of memory that had occurred in the context of a room with two doors.

"Exposure of a familiar context activates not only the hippocampal representation of that context, but also the memory traces of events that occurred in that context."[2]

Another puff of smoke crossed overhead. Aunt Fran was a smoker. When she drove, the car filled as if it were on fire. "Richard, get in the car."

"I'll walk," I said.

"You can't walk to the hospital."

Susan Margo was in the hospital.

"Get in."

My Aunt Fran, Uncle Manny, and my cousin Judy sat in the car. My mother was dead. Susan Margo, the one who had been the first to teach me the basics of sex—

"Richard, get in the car."

I didn't want to see Susan Margo. I didn't want to see her sick. I didn't want to get in the car.

A car rolled to a stop.

"Where are you going?" the driver asked as I got in.

"Thanks."

"Sure, where you going?"

"What are you thinking?"

The cars, the room with two doors provided the context and were stored in the hippocampus. The smoke, the smell of tobacco, memories of sex—

"Stockbridge," I said.

"Pittsfield," he said.

"Richard—?" Aunt Fran said.

—were the content all stored in the neocortex.

Tapping, tapping. Aunt Fran always tapped as she drove.

Tap, tap. Tap, tap.

Tapping his thigh as he offered me a piece of "Double good, double good—"

"What you got in Stockbridge?" he smiled. "You got a girl—in Stockbridge?"

He took a drag, exhaled. "What are you thinking?" he asked.

Smoke. I was thinking about smoke.

"Smoke," I said.

There was smoke in the car. There was smoke as he puffed on a cigarette after sucking me off, smoke in the room with two doors, smoke as I lay on the couch next to a wall. Smoke.

My neocortex was filling with smoke.

"Smoke. I'm thinking about smoke," I said.

"Memory involves a constructive process of piecing together bits and pieces of information, rather than a literal replay of the past."

Smoke was at the center, the hub.

"Memory is by no means fixed. It is a moving target, retaining a central core, shifting with reactivation and the incorporation of new information."

"I didn't hear what you said."

"In this way it serves the adaptive function of allowing an organism to bring the full weight of prior experience to bear both on current behavioral choice and on thinking about the future."[3]

In order to imagine the future, one must be able to remember the past.

"I'm thinking about smoke," I said.

He moved in his chair.

My hand moved to the wall. There were sounds that traveled across the two doors. Smoke doesn't make noise. Dreams never speak.

"Smoke?"

High on acid. High on dust. I was having trouble with smoke. I was having trouble with doors, trouble with dreams, trouble with machines that made noise. I was having trouble being on my back.

"What are you thinking?"

"Dreams. I was thinking about dreams."

He sat forward as if I had finally said something he heard.

"Dreams are never concerned with trivia," Freud said in *The Interpretation of Dreams*.

"I'm skiing down a double black diamond. Six inches of powder."
I used to ski. I used to ski a lot. I was a good skier.

I'm thinking that as I skied through the light powder, the snow kicked up a wake—a wake from a boat, a wake for the dead, awake as in unable to sleep. I'm thinking about Mary Shelley, who wanted to wake her mother, also named Mary, who had died giving birth to Mary herself.

"Six inches?"

"Six inches."

"In the dream."

"In the dream." I explain, "In the dream the wind picks up, blows snow in my eyes."

"Six inches?" he repeated.

"Six inches," I replied.

"Dreams satisfy wishes," Freud said again in *The Interpretation of Dreams*. Analysts refer to *The Interpretation of Dreams* as "chapter 7." It's code.

When asked to explain her father's rejection of the etiologic significance of real sexual trauma (the seduction theory), Anna Freud replied, "Keeping the seduction theory would mean to abandon the oedipus complex, and with it the whole importance of phantasy." Anna Freud was saying that her father abandoned what he had discovered about the significance of *real* sexual trauma in order to support the significance of *fantasized* sexual trauma—and of the unconscious wish.

Had Freud not abandoned these discoveries, she went on, "I think there would have been no psychoanalysis."[4] Anna Freud was accusing her father of denying his data in order to support his theory.

As I watched smoke pass overhead, I found myself thinking about egg creams and the words of a woman named Anna Freud and her sense that her father's science may have been spawned from a need and a lie.

I thought about skiing through six inches of powder. "It felt like I was able to fly," I said.

Dr. Levin exhaled another puff of smoke, leaned forward, cleared his throat, and then in his soft, strangely uncomforting voice, "The dream is about your desire to lay 'perfect tracks,' a metaphor for sex, and the thought that your 'six inches' are better than your father's."

I lay there watching the smoke.

After a long pause, he shifted in his seat.

My father was raised on a shtetl in Poland. There was no skiing in or near the shtetl where he lived.

"What are you thinking?"

I was thinking about dreams, perfect tracks, smoke, metaphors for sex. I was thinking about Anna Freud, who had to hide the fact that she was not in love with her father, not much oedipal fantasy there, but rather her love was for a woman—

On November 29, 1895, Freud wrote to his friend and fellow physician Wilhelm Fliess, "I no longer understand the state of mind in which I hatched the psychology; cannot conceive how I could have inflicted it on you."

He was referring to a manuscript he had written, *The Project for a Scientific Psychology*, that he had sent to Fliess. By abandoning first *The Project* and then the seduction theory, Freud was opening the door to chapter 7. "It appears to have been a kind of madness."[5]

—a wealthy American heiress named Dorothea Burlingham.

"What are you thinking?" Dr. Levin asked as he leaned back in his chair.

His question lingered in the air followed by a puff of smoke. My hand moved toward the wall. There was another long pause. Another puff. And then words overheard, "I can't. I, I, I—" more pieces of the quilt my hippocampus was knitting together and pulling apart.

He crossed and uncrossed his legs, shifted in his chair. His shoes were wingtipped. Socks, blue diamonds on black. His suit was gray. His tie was dark with bold stripes. He had full, heavy lips. He took another drag, cleared his throat, "'What can't you—?'" Flicked the ash into the tray on the table beside him. His eyes were dark, not really brown, not really gray, not really green. "What can't you do?"

"I cannot advise my colleagues too urgently to model themselves during psychoanalytic treatment on the surgeon, who puts aside all his feelings, even his human sympathy, and concentrates his mental forces on the single aim of performing the operation as skillfully as he can."[6]

"What can't you do?" uttered again this time more forcefully the way a soldier or cop, the way Freud or an analyst under the influence of—

"What can't you—?"

—because it is common knowledge that "Patients consciously and intentionally keep things back that are perfectly well known because they have not gotten over their feelings of timidity and shame."[7]

"What can't you do?" he sent into the smoke-filled air, restating what was already there.

I looked back at him.

I swung my feet to the floor.

"The session is not over," he said.

I stared.

"The session is not over," he repeated.

I stood up.

"Please lie back down."

I walked to the door.

"Do you realize what you are doing?"

I opened the first door.

"If you walk out, I will have to report this to the Committee."

"The Committee" is code for letting me know that if I walked out, he would inform the committee that I had violated the terms of the training, which would lead to expulsion from the society.

I opened the second door.

"Do you realize what you are doing?"

I walked out.

Chapter 55

Cinderella

TEN YEARS EARLIER, TEN YEARS BEFORE I WALKED OUT OF DR. LEVIN'S office, I took the slipper out of my pocket and held it in my hand.

Dr. Brenman looked at it, then looked at me.

"Is that your mother's?" she asked.

It was the slipper that she had bought at Loehman's. The slipper she had bought when there were none made of glass. The slipper that had fallen off her foot. The slipper I had picked up off the floor. The slipper I had shown to no one since showing it to Katie Galst that day I couldn't talk. The slipper that I had kept all these years. My mother's slipper.

"Yes," I said.

I looked at Dr. Brenman.

I wasn't taken to my mother's funeral. I wasn't taken to her grave. The reason being that it would have been too much for me to bear. I never understood the reason in that.

"What are you going to do with it?" she asked.

I shrugged.

She nodded, then said, "You'll figure it out."

She took a step toward me, opened her arms. I moved to her embrace.

365

It was like being held by a lover with whom you never had, nor ever would, make love.

It was our last session. The last time I would see Dr. Brenman. The only time I would say, the way maybe only a soldier gets to say, the way you get to say only once in your life, "I owe you my life."

There were tears in her eyes.

Empathy, gratitude, love.

There were tears in mine.

Chapter 56

At the Corner of Norman Rockwell and Main—Take Two

"It may be that when we know not which way to go, we have come to our real journey."

—Wendell Berry

TWENTY YEARS AFTER LEAVING DR. BRENMAN'S OFFICE, I RETURNED to the Austen Riggs Center. I walked to the entrance of what had been her office, which may also have been her home. I left a bunch of wildflowers at the door even though she had died years before. Next to the flowers, I left a book—*Young Man Luther* by Erik Erikson—a piece of her that I held on to all these years.

I got back in the car and drove north. I drove past the turn to Queechy Lake where a father of two had sucked me off. It wasn't his hand. It was his mouth. Dr. Brenman was right. I had lied about that.

I drove through Pittsfield, one of those industrial towns that never quite figured how to keep up with the times. I continued north and finally got to the crossroads of routes 7 and 2, at the corner of "Norman Rockwell and Main."

I walked into the field that runs wild with flowers. The earth was hard. The grass was brown. There were leaves on the ground. I dug a small hole with my hands.

I took the slipper out of my pocket. It was dark green with black on the sides. There were stains. Addressing the slipper opened a channel in me, maybe in her.

"Mommy," I called out.

I figured she would recognize the sound of my voice. "Can you hear me?" I called. And then I just said only louder, "Mommy!"

I waited for her reply.

The wind kicked up, rustled the earth. Memory stirred. I knew she was there. "Mommy," I said as I stood at the corner of Norman Rockwell and Main.

I held the slipper in my hands. "This is yours," I said. "It fell off your foot."

Memories joined. Time merged. Space drew into itself.

Cell assembly is the process, what that process is called when memories meet. Memory has tentacles, feelers, podia, feet. Cell assembly.

Donald Hebb spoke of something like that, how synapses join, how memories merge, but I wasn't thinking about cell assembly or Hebb, not just then, not just there at the corner or Norman Rockwell and Main where I was being pulled into time, back once again into the being of that little boy. "Mommy—" I said—

"Mommy—" I said, then "Mommy—" then "Mommy—," then—

"Mommy when you walked down to the cellar, did you pause on the fourth or fifth stair, to think who would find you? Who would be there? Who would touch you when you were cold? Mommy—" I paused, listening for her reply.

The wind was picking up.

"Mommy," I said to the green slipper with black and the stain. The slipper was worn. The stain was faded, pretty much gone. Memory was coming back, active, alive.

"Mommy—" I said, "it was me. I was the one who was there. I was the one who picked up the slipper. I was the one who—"

I looked up at the sky.

"Mommy, I was the one who touched you."

"Mommy—I, I, I—"

"I was scared. I was scared. Mommy—"

I stopped, turned away, tried to breathe.

"Mommy I was scared—"

Distant thunder rolled.

"—scared of you."

I looked up at the sky. It was starting to rain. Slow, thick drops.

"Mommy—"

I placed the green slipper with the black, in the grave. The earth was warm like a mother's touch. The clouds were thickening above.

I took out the cap, the cap that Sid had given me, the cap with the letter "M."

"And so I am burying you now with this kind of terrific little kid who would have followed you anywhere even if it meant following you to his death—which he did. He was an adventurer, a conquistador, this kind of terrific little kid—when he was seven years, two months, and two days old—"

I placed the cap in the earth next to the slipper.

I dug a little more dirt.

"Mommy—I am burying you at the crossroads of Norman Rockwell and Main. I am burying you with the boy who loved you, found you, never left you."

I held up a piece of paper.

The rain was starting. There was lightning. There was thunder. There was rain.

"After the hurricane, when I got that call. There were some pictures of you, some letters, an envelope, and one other thing."

The rain was soft. It was warm.

"There was this." I raised the piece of paper I held in my hand.

"Words. Handwritten."

I looked at the piece of paper. The wind was blowing harder.

Unsettling the earth. I was at the corner of Norman Rockwell and Main. It was getting darker. Lights were turning on.

Cars slowed as the passengers inside stared at this man standing there holding a piece of paper in his hand, rain falling, a hole in the ground, a mound of earth. A clap of thunder. Driving by they watched as he started to sing.

I started to sing,
Too-ra-loo-ra-loo-ral,
Too-ra-loo-ra-li
Too-ra-loo-ra-loo-ral,
Hush now don't you cry.
Too-ra-loo-ra-loo-ral,
Too-ra-loo-ra-li
Too-ra-loo-ra-loo-ral,
That's an Irish lullaby
Over in Killarney, many years ago
My mother sang a song to me
In tones so soft and low
Just a simple little ditty
In her good old Irish way
And I'd give the world if she could sing
That song to me this day.
"It was Katherine, the nurse, who gave it to you."
The thunder was getting closer.

With my hands, I pushed soil over the slipper. Over the cap. Over the piece of paper that Katherine had written with the words to a song,

"And I'd give the world if she could sing that song to me this day."
The smell of the earth began to rise—

I gathered stones and wild flowers and placed them on the mound.

Another clap of thunder.

—as the rain continued to fall.

Acknowledgments

There are many people whom I need to thank. These are a few.

In the beginning there was my friend, Lawrence Goldstone, who had the experience and wisdom to guide me when I was just beginning to understand that I was lost. Nancy Goldstone, who fed me in so many ways. Rita Charon, who introduced me to the narrative in medicine. Jason Brown, who shared his knowledge of the structure of story. Carl Fisher, who inspired me to write from the gut. Maryanne Chrisant, who helped me steer a first draft. Nicole Mele, who kept me on track and on time. My agent, Michael Carlisle, who had the courage to take on someone who was new—but no longer young. Michael Mungiello, who encouraged me along the way. My editor, Jeannette Seaver, whose life is an example of someone who believes in exploring new worlds. And finally, Mirra Bank who has been my life's keel.

About the Author

Richard Brockman, MD, is a clinical professor in the department of psychiatry at Columbia University and the Vagelos College of Physicians and Surgeons. He's been a visiting professor in the department of psychiatry at the University of Namibia's School of Medicine in Windhoek, Namibia. Brockman has written over forty papers published in peer review journals primarily focusing on neural science and psychiatry. His previous book, *A Map of the Mind*, has been critically acclaimed by the *New England Journal of Medicine* and the *Journal of the American Medical Association*. Brockman is the neuroscience editor for the *Journal of Psychodynamic Psychotherapy* and has served on the editorial board for *American Imago*.

His plays have been performed off- and off-off Broadway in New York, at the Fringe in London, as well as nationally and internationally. Brockman's plays have received grants from the New York State Council on the Arts and the New York Foundation for the Arts and have been finalists at the Samuel French Best Off Off Broadway Short Play Festivals, Theatre In the Raw's 12th Biennial One-Act Play Writing Contest, and the American Blues Theater's Blue Ink Festival. He has been a member of the Actors Studio playwright-directors unit, the Dramatists Guild, and a founding member of the Workshop Theater Company.

His articles have been published in the *Atlantic Monthly*, the *Los Angeles Times Magazine*, *The New York Times*, and the *Wall Street Journal*.

Endnotes

Chapter 2: "What Are You Thinking?" Take Two
1. Freud, S. "Recommendations to physicians practicing psychoanalysis." 1912 In J. Strachey (Ed. & Trans.) *The Standard Edition of the Complete Psychological Works of Sigmund Freud.* Vol 12. London: Hogarth Press.
2. Freud, S. "A Case of Hysteria." 1905 In J. Strachey (Ed. & Trans.) *The Standard Edition.* Vol 7. London: Hogarth Press.
3. Freud, S. *The Complete Letters of Sigmund Freud to Wilhelm Fliess.* In JM Masson (ed). 1985 Cambridge MA: Belknap Press p. 427.
4. Freud, S. "A Case of Hysteria." 1905 In J. Strachey (Ed. & Trans.) *The Standard Edition.* Vol 7. London: Hogarth Press.
5. Freud, S. "Observations on Transference Love." In J. Strachey (Ed. & Trans.) 1915 *The Standard Edition.* Vol 12. London: Hogarth Press.
6. Freud, S. "On Beginning the Treatment." 1913. In J. Strachey (Ed. & Trans.) *The Standard Edition.* Vol 12. London: Hogarth Press.
7. Freud, S. "Mourning and Melancholia." 1917 In J. Strachey (Ed. & Trans.) *The Standard Edition.* Vol 14 London: Hogarth Press.
8. Ibid.

Chapter 3: Herbs
1. Pavlov I. *Conditioned Reflexes.* Oxford: Oxford University Press. 1927.
2. Sullivan, R; Wilson, D; Ravel, N; Mouly, A. "Olfactory Memory Networks." *Frontiers in Behavioral Neuroscience* 2015 9(36) p. 1-6.

Chapter 4: Two Doors
1. Hebb, Donald. *The Organization of Behavior.* p. xii. New York: J Wiley & Sons 1949.
2. Ibid, p. xx.
3. Ibid, p. 62.
4. Janet, Pierre. *Psychological Healing* p.601. Eastford CT: Martino Fine 1925.

5. Seung, S; Yuste R. "Neural Networks." In *Principles of Neural Science*, edited by Kandel, Schwarttz, Jesell, Siegelbaum and Hudspeth. p. 1581–2. New York: McGraw Hill, 2013.
6. de No, RL. "Analysis of the Activity of the Chains of internuncial Neurons." *The Rockefeller Institute Journal* March 21, 1938.
7. Lashley, K.S. (1960) *The Neuropsychology of Lashley*. New York: McGraw Hill. 1960.
8. Seung, S; Yuste R "Neural Networks". In *Principles of Neural Science*, edited by Kandel, Schwarttz, Jesell, Siegelbaum and Hudspeth. p. 1591. New York: McGraw Hill, 2013.
9. Huyck, C; Passmore, P. "A Review of Cell Assemblies." *Biological Cybernetics*, 5 April 2013: 107 263–288.
10. Fuster, J; Bressler, S. "Past Makes Future: Role of Prefrontal Cortex in Prediction" *Journal of Cognitive Neuroscience*, 2015 p. 639–654.

Chapter 5: What Comes Next
1. Seung, S; Yuste R. "Neural Networks." In *Principles of Neural Science*, edited by Kandel, Schwarttz, Jesell, Siegelbaum and Hudspeth. p. 1594. New York: McGraw Hill. 2013.
2. Fuster, J. *The Prefrontal Cortex*, 1997 New York: Lippincott.

Chapter 7: The Big Orange
1. de Brunhoff, Jean. *The Story of Babar*, New York: Random House, 1933.
2. Zhang, Tie-Yuun; Meaney, Michael. "Epigenetics and Environmental Regulation of the Genome and its Function. *Annual Review of Psychology*, 2010. 61: 439–66.

Chapter 8: Troubled Sleep
1. Aserinsky, E. and Kleitman, N. "Regularly occurring periods of eye motility, and concurrent phenomena, during sleep." *Science* vol 118. September 4, '53 vol 118. Issue 3062 p. 273–274.
2. Rodriquez,C; Foldvary-Schaefer, N. "Clinical Neurophysiology of NREM Parasomnias." *Handbook of Clinical Neurology*, 2019, 161: 397–410.
3. Ibid.

Chapter 9: A Knock on the Door
1. Winnicott, D. "Transition Objects and Transitional Phenomena." *International Journal of Psychoanalysis*, 1953. vol 34(2). p. 91.
2. Ibid, p. 92.
3. Sullivan, R. "Developing a Sense of Safety," *Annals of the New York Academy of Science*, 2003 vol 1008: 122–131.
4. Winnicott, D. "Transition objects and transitional phenomena." *International Journal of Psychoanalysis* vol 34 part 2, 1953 p. 89.

5. Sullivan, R. "Developing a Sense of Safety" *Annals of the New York Academy of Science* 2003, 1008: 122–131.

Chapter 10: His Mother's Voice
1. Hofer, M; Sullivan, R. "Toward a Neurobiology of Attachment" 2008 *Handbook of Developmental Cognition*. Edited by C Nelson, M Luciana. Cambridge: MIT Press.
2. Winnicott, D. *The Maturational Process and the Facilitating Environment*. 1976, London: Hogarth Press. Footnote, p. 39.
3. Polan. HJ; Hofer, M. "Psychobiological Origins of Infant Attachment and its Role in Development". P. 117–132. In *Handbook of Attachment*. Edited by J. Cassidy and P. Shaver. New York: Guildford Press. 2016.
4. Field, T. "The Effects of Mother's Physical and Emotional Unavailability on Emotion Regulation," 1994. *Monographs of the Society for Research in Child Development* p. 208–227 New York: Wiley.

Chapter 12: Paternity
1. Stortelder, F; Ploegmakers-Burg, M. "Adolescence and the Reorganization of Infant Development," 2010 *Journal of American Academy of Dynamic Psychiatry* 38(3) p. 503–532.
2. Fuster J. "Network Memory." *Trends in Neuroscience*, 1997 10: 451–9.
3. Lashley, K.S., *The neuropsychology of Lashley*, Edited by Beach, Hebb, Morgan, Nissen. p. 26. New York: McGraw Hill. 1960.
4. Fuster, J. "Cortex and Memory: Emergence of a New Paradigm." 2009 *Journal of Cognitive Neuroscience*. 21: 11 p. 2047–2072.

Chapter 13: So When You Were Born
1. Harlow HF; Harlow MK. "The Affectional systems." Edited by Schreir, Harlow, Stonitz *Behavior of Nonhuman Primates*. p. 289. New York: Academic Press 1965.
2. Ibid, p. 288.
3. Mantis, I; Mercuri, M; Stack, D; Field, T. "Depressed and non-Depressed Mothers' Touching During Interactions with their Infants," 2019 *Developmental Cognitive Neuroscience*.
4. Miklowitz, D; Johnson, S. "The Psychopathology and Treatment of Bipolar Disorder," *Annual Review of Clinical Psychology* 2006 2: 199–233.

Chapter 15: Cortisol
1. Martin, J. *Neuroanatomy Text and Atlas*. P. 419. New York: McGraw Hill. 1996.
2. Conradt, E; Adkins, D; Crowell, S; Monk, C; Kobor, M. "An Epigenetic Pathway to Investigating Associations Between Prenatal Exposure to Maternal Mood Disorder and Newborn Neurobehavior." 2018 *Developmental Psychopathology* 30(3) p. 881–890.

3. Ibid.
4. Hoffman, C. "Stress, the Placenta, and Fetal Programming of Behavior: Gene's First Encounter with the Environment." 2016 *American Journal of Psychiatry*. 173: 7 p. 655-657.
5. Macguire, J; McCormack, C; Monk, C. "Neurobiology of Maternal Mental Illnesss." In *Handbook of Clinical Neurology*, 2020 vol 171 New York: Elsevier p. 97-117.
6. Tronick, E; Hunter, RG. "Waddington, Dynamic Systems, and Epigenetics," *Frontiers in Behavioral Neuroscience* June 2016: 10 p. 6.

Chapter 16: The Epigenotype
1. Waddinton, C. "The Epigenotype." 1942 *Endeavor* p. 18-20.
2. Meaney, M. "Epigenetics and the Biological Definition of Gene X Environment Interactions." *Child Development* 2010 81: 1 p. 41-79.
3. Tronick, E: Hunter, R. "Waddington, Dynamic Systems, and Epigenetics." *Frontiers in Behavioral Neuroscience* June 2016 Article 107 p. 1-6.
4. Polan, HJ; Hofer, M. "Psychobiological Origins of Infant Attachment and its Role in Development." In *Handbook of Attachment* edited by J. Cassidy and P. Shaver. New York: Guildford Press. 2016, p. 117-132.
5. Ibid.
6. Harlow HF; Harlow MK. "The Affectional systems." Edited by Schreir, Harlow, Stonitz. *Behavior of Nonhuman Primates*. p. 289. New York: Academic Press 1965.
7. Blumberg, M; Spencer, J; Shenk, D. "How We Develop—Developmental Systems and the Emergence of Complex Behaviors." 2017 *Interdisciplinary Review of Cognitive Science* vol 8 (1-2).
8. Darwin, C. *The Origin of Species*. 1859 New York: Modern Library p. 374.
9. Porges, SH. *The Polyvagal Theory*. 2011 New York: Norton p. 15.
10. Macguire, J; McCormack, C; Monk, C. "Neurobiology of Maternal Mental Illness." In *Handbook of Clinical Neurology* 2020 vol 171 New York: Elsevier p. 97-117.
11. Zhang, TY; Caldji, C; Diorio J; Turecki, G; Meaney, M. "The Epigenetics of Parental Effects" in *Epigenetic Regulation in the Nervous System* ed by Sweatt, Meaney, Nestler, Akbarian. New York: Academic Press. 2013 p. 85-118.
12. Macguire, J; McCormack, C; Monk, C. "Neurobiology of Maternal Mental Illness." In *Handbook of Clinical Neurology* 2020 vol 171 New York: Elsevier p. 97-117.

Chapter 18: Bacon and Eggs—Take One
1. Henshaw, C. "Maternal Suicide" In J Cockburn (ed) and M Pawson (ed) *Psychological Challenges in Obstetrics and Gynecology*, 2007 London: Springer-Verlog. p. 158.
2. Monk, C; Spicer, J; Champagne, F. "Linking Prenatal Maternal Adversity

to Developmental Outcomes" in *Development and Psychopathology* 2012 (24) p. 1361–1376.

3. O'Hara, M; McCabe, J. "Postpartum Depression: Current Status and Future Directions. 2013 *Annual Review of Clinical Psychology* 9: 379–407.

4. Paris, R; Bolton, R; Weinberg, K. "Postpartum Depression, Suicidality, and Mother–infant interactions." *Archives of Women's Mental Health.* 2009 12: 309–321.

5. Macguire, J; McCormack, C; Monk, C. "Neurobiology of Maternal Mental Illness." In *Handbook of Clinical Neurology* 2020 vol 171 New York: Elsevier p. 97–117.

Chapter 19: Bacon and Eggs—Take Two

1. Tronick, E.; Weinberg, K. "Depressed Mothers and Infants" *Postpartum Depression and Child Development* (ed by L Murray and P. Cooper) 1997 New York: Guilford Press. p. 57.

2. Hofer, M. "The Psychobiology of Early Attachment." *Clinical Neuroscience Research* vol 4 2005 p. 291–300.

3. Paris, R; Bolton, R; Weinberg, K. "Postpartum Depression, Suicidality, and Mother–infant interactions." *Archives of Women's Mental Health.* 2009 12: 309–321.

4. Tronick, E.; Weinberg, K. "Depressed Mothers and Infants" *Postpartum Depression and Child Development* Edited by L Murray and P. Cooper. 1997 New York: Guilford Press.

5. p. 66–67.

6. Sullivan, RM. "Attachment Figure's Regulation of Infant Brain and Behavior." *Psychodynamic Psychiatry* 2017 45 (4) p. 475–498.

7. Sullivan, R. "Developing a Sense of Safety" *Annals of the New York Academy of Science* 2003 vol 1008: 122–131.

8. Salten, Felix. *Bambi.* Trans by Jack Zipes. Princeton: Princeton University Press. 2022.

Chapter 20: The Still Face

1. Freud, S. "Civilization and its Discontent." In J. Strachey (Ed. & Trans.) *The Standard Edition.* 1930. Vol 21. London: Hogarth Press.

2. Freud, S. "Inhibitions, Symptoms, and Anxieties." In J. Strachey (Ed. & Trans.) *The Standard Edition.* 1926. Vol 20. London: Hogarth Press.

3. Darwin, Charles. *The Expression of the Emotions in Man and Animals.* 1872 Chicago: University of Chicago Press.

4. Freud, S. *The Complete Letters of Sigmund Freud to Wilhelm Fliess.* JM Masson (ed) Cambridge MA: Belknap. Press, 1985. p. 230.

5. Sullivan, RM. "Attachment Figure's Regulation of Infant Brain and Behavior." *Psychodynamic Psychiatry* 2017 45(4) p. 475–498.

6. Schore, A. "The Neurobiology of Attachment and Early Personality

Organization." 2002 *Journal of Prenatal and Perinatal Attachment*. 16: 3. p. 249-263.

7. Chambers J. "The Neurobiology of Attachment," *Psychodynamic Psychiatry* 2017 45 (4) 542-63.
8. Tronick, E.; Weinberg, K. "Depressed Mothers and Infants," *Postpartum Depression and Child Development*, Ed by L Murray and P. Cooper. 1997 New York: Guilford Press. p. 66.
9. Bowlby J. "Violence in the Family as a Disorder of Attachment and Caregiving Systems," *American Journal of Psychoanalysis* 44(1) 1661-74.
10. Harlow, H. "Love in Infant Monkeys," *Scientific American* 200: 6 p. 68-75. 1959.
11. Tronick, E.; Weinberg, K. "Depressed Mothers and Infants," *Postpartum Depression and Child Development* (ed by L Murray and P. Cooper). 1997 New York: Guilford Press. p. 57.
12. Ibid, p. 68.
13. Ibid, p. 76.
14. van der Kolk, B. "The Traumatic Spectrum," *Journal of Traumatic Stress* 1(3) p. 273-290. 1988.
15. Tronick, E.; Weinberg, K. "Depressed Mothers and Infants" *Postpartum Depression and Child Development* (ed by L Murray and P. Cooper) 1997 New York: Guilford Press. p. 73.
16. Field, T; Reite, M. "The Psychobiology of Attachment and Separation: A Summary" 1985. New York. Academic Press.
17. Porcerelli, J; Huth-Bocks, A; Huprich, S; Richardson, L. "Defense Mechanisms of Pregnant Mothers Predict Attachment Security in their Toddlers." 2016 *American Journal of Psychiatry* 173: 2 p. 138ff.

Chapter 21: Electric Eels
1. Wright, B. "An Historical Review of Electroconvulsive Therapy." *Jefferson Journal of Psychiatry* 1990 vol 8 issue 2. p. 68-74.

Chapter 22: Holding Her Hand
1. Pope, C; Mazmanian, D. "Breastfeeding and Postpartum Depression," 2016 *Depression Research and Treatment* p. 1-9.

Chapter 23: America
1. Macguire, J; McCormack, C; Monk, C. "Neurobiology of Maternal Mental Illness." In *Handbook of Clinical Neurology* 2020 vol 171 New York: Elsevier p. 97-117.

Chapter 24: Another Mother
1. Penney, D. Stastny, P. *The Lives They Left Behind*, 2008 New York: Bellevue Literary Press.

2. Squire, L; Kandel, E. *Memory From Mind to Molecules* 1999 New York: Scientific American Library. p. 85.
3. Lisanby, S; Maddox, J; Prudic, J. "The Effects of ECT on Memory." 2000 *Archives of General Psychiatry* 57(6) p. 581-590.
4. Harms, E. "The Efficacy of Electroconvulsive Therapy." June 1955 *American Journal of Psychiatry*. 111(12) p. 933-4.
5. Hofer, M. "The Psychobiology of Early Attachment." *Clinical Neuroscience Research* vol 4 2005 p. 291-300.

Chapter 25: He Had a Hat

1. Wakshiak, A; Weinstock, M. "Neonatal handling reverses behavioral abnormalities in rats induced by prenatal stress." *Physiology and Behavior* 1990 48: 289-292.

Chapter 26: Two Mothers—Take One

1. Levine, S; Haltmeyer, G; Kara, G; Denenberg V; "Physiological and Behavioral Effects of Infant Stimulation." 1967 *Physiology and Behavior* vol 2 p. 57-8.
2. Kaffman, A; Meaney, M. "Neurodevelopmental Sequelae of Postnatal Maternal Care in Rodents." 2007 *Journal of Child Psychology and Psychiatry* 48: 3/4 p. 224-244.
3. Tronick, E; Hunter, R. "Waddington, Dynamic Systems and Epigenetics. 2016 *Frontiers in Behavioral Neuroscience* Article 107 p. 31ff.
4. Zhang, Tie-Yuun; Meaney, Michael. "Epigenetics and Environmental Regulation of the Genome and its Function." *Annual Review of Psychology* 2010. 61: 439-66.
5. Meaney, M. "Epigenetics and the Biological Definition of Gene X Environment Interactions." *Child Development* 2010 81: 1 p. 41-79.
6. Ibid.

Chapter 27: Two Mothers—Take Two

1. Champagne, F; Meaney, M. "Stress During Gestation," 2006 *Biological Psychiatry* 59: 1227-1235.
2. Meaney, M. "Epigenetics and the Biological Definition of Gene X Environment Interactions." *Child Development* 2010 81: 1 p. 41-79.
3. Ibid.
4. Szyf, M; McGowan, P; Meaney, M; "The Social Environment and the Epigenome". *Environmental and Molecular Mutations* 2008 49: 46-60
5. Meaney, M. "Epigenetics and the Biological Definition of Gene X Environment Interactions." *Child Development* 2010 81: 1 p. 41-79.
6. Champagne, F; Meaney, M. "Stress During Gestation," 2006 *Biological Psychiatry* 59: 1227-1235.
7. Miguel, P; Pereira, L; Silveira, P; Meaney. "Early Environmental Influences on the Development of Children's Brain Structure and Function." *Developmental Medicine and Child Neurology* 2019 61: 1127-33.

8. Sacks, O. "The Power of Music." *Brain* 2006 129 p. 2528–2532.

Chapter 28: The Pneumogastric

1. Darwin, C. *The Expression of the Emotions in Man and Animals.* 1872 Chicago: University of Chicago Press. p. 69.
2. Freud, S. *The Complete Letters of Sigmund Freud to Wilhelm Fliess.* Ed. JM Masson, Cambridge MA: Belknap. Press, 1985 p. 155.
3. Freud, S. In J. Strachey Ed. & Trans. *The Standard Edition.* Vol 16. London: Hogarth Press. p. 393.
4. Freud A; Burlingham. D. *War and Children.* 1943 New York: Medical War Books.
5. Schore, A. "Relational Trauma and the Developing Right Brain" *Neurobiology of Attachment* p. 19–47.
6. Sacks, O. *Musicophilia,* 2008 New York: Knopf p. xii, 15.

Chapter 29: Happy Birthday

1. Hofer, M. "On the Nature and Consequences of Early Loss." *Psychosomatic Medicine* 1996 p. 570–581.
2. Panksep, J; Biven, L. *The Archeology of Mind,* 2012 New York: Norton p. 314.
3. Hofer, M. "On the Nature and Consequences of Early Loss." *Psychosomatic Medicine* 1996 p. 570–581.
4. Salten, Felix. *Bambi.* Jack Zipes translation. Princeton: Princeton University Press. 2022.
5. Hofer, M. "Early Relationships as Regulators of Infant Physiology and Behavior." *Acta Paediatric* Sup. lement 397: 9–18. 1984.
6. Debiec, J; Sullivan, R. "Neurobiology of Safety and Threat Learning in Infancy." *Neurobiology of Learning and Memory* Oct 2016.

Chapter 30: Fire

1. Stortelder, F; Ploegmakers-Burg, M. A "Adolescence and the Reorganization of Infant Development," 2010 *Journal of American Academy of Dynamic Psychiatry* 38(3) p. 503–532.
2. Citri, A; Malenka, R. "Synaptic Plasticity," *Neuropsychopharmacology* 2008 33: 18–41.
3. Champagne, Meaney. *Biological Psychiatry* 2006 p. 1233.
4. Beck, CT. "The Effects of Postpartum Depression on Child Development." *Archives of Psychiatric Nursing.* 1998 (12) 1 p. 12.
5. Robinson-Drummer, P; Opendak, M; Blomkvist, A; Chan, S: Sullivan, R et al. Infant Trauma Alters Social Buffering of Threat Learning." *Frontiers in Behavioral Neuroscience* 2019 (13) p. 1–14.
6. Sullivan, R; Wilson, D; Ravel, N; Mouly, A. "Olfactory Memory Networks." *Frontiers in Behavioral Neuroscience* 2015 9(36) p. 1–6.
7. Robinson-Drummer, P; Opendak, M; Blomkvist, A; Chan, S; Sullivan,

R, et al. Infant Trauma Alters Social Buffering of Threat Learning." *Frontiers in Behavioral Neuroscience* 2019 (13) p. 1–14.
8. Ibid.

Chapter 31: Where Proper Memory Starts
1. van der Kolk, B. "Trauma and Memory" in *Traumatic Stress* (ed) van der Kolk, McFarlane, Weisaeth. 1996 New York: Guildford Press. p. 279–302.

Chapter 32: Castration Anxiety
1. Freud, S. "A Case of Hysteria." 1905 In J. Strachey (Ed. & Trans.) *The Standard Edition*. Vol 7. London: Hogarth Press.
2. Freud, S. "Introductory Lectures on Psychoanalysis." 1916–17 In J. Strachey (Ed. & Trans.) *The Standard Edition*. Vol. 16 London: Hogarth Press.
3. Ibid.

Chapter 34: Do Not Enter
1. Kandel, E. *In Search of Memory*. 2006 New York: Norton. p. 10.
2. Freud, S. *The Complete Letters of Sigmund Freud to Wilhelm Fliess*. Ed. by JM Masson. 1985 Cambridge MA: Belknap. Press p. 398.
3. O'Keefe, J; Nadel, L. *The Hippocampus as a Cognitive Map*. 1978 Oxford: Clarendon Press. p. 385.
4. Ibid.
5. Tulving, E; Donaldson "Episodic and Semantic Memory" in *The Organization of Memory* Academic Press 1972 p. 387.
6. Ibid, p. 386.
7. Tulving, E. "Episodic Memory: From Mind to Brain." *Annual Review of Psychology* 2002 53: 1–25.
8. Wheeler, M; Stuss, D; Tulving, E. "Toward a Theory of Episodic Memory," *Psychological Bulletin* 1997 121 (3) 331–354.
9. O'Keefe, J; Nadel, L. *The Hippocampus as a Cognitive Map*. 1978 Oxford: Clarendon Press.
10. Ibid.
11. Eichenbaum, H; Cohen, N "Can we Reconcile the Declarative Memory and Spatial Navigation on Hippocampal Function?" *Neuron* 2014 83 Aug 20 p. 764–770.
12. Tulving, E. "Episodic Memeory: From Mind to Brain." *Annual Review of Psychology* 2002 53: 1–25.

Chapter 35: Papier-mâché
1. Gottlieb, RM. "Maurice Sendak's Trilogy," *Psychoanalytic Study of the Child* 2008 68: 186–217.
2. Siegel, D. Cognition, Memory and Dissociation. *Child and Adolescent Psychiatric Clinics of North America* 5(2) 1996 p. 514.

Chapter 36: Tying the Knot

1. Kandel, E. *In Search of Memory* 2006 New York: Norton. p. 359

Chapter 37: Guarding

1. Ohayon, M; Schatzberg, A. "Prevalence of Depressive Episodes with Psychotic Features in the General Population." 2002 *American Journal of Psychiatry.* 159: 1855–1861.
2. Freud, S. "New Introductory Lectures on Psychoanalysis." In J. Strachey (Ed. & Trans.) *The Standard Edition.* 1938. Vol 14 London: Hogarth Press.

Chapter 38: Sickness Pain

1. Eisenberger, N. "Social Pain and the Brain." 2015 *Annual Review of Psychology* 66: 601–29.
2. Packard, M; Goodman, J. "Factors that Influence the Relative Use of Multiple Memory Systems." 2013 *Hippocampus* 23: 1044–52.

Chapter 39: Glass Slippers

1. O'Keefe, J and Nadel, L. *The Hippocampus as a Cognitive Map.* 1978 Oxford: Clarendon Press. p. 63.
2. Ibid, p. 89.
3. O'Keefe, J; Dostrovsky, J. "The Hippocampus as a Spatial Map." 1971 *Brain Research* 171–175.
4. O'Keefe, J and Nadel, L. *The Hippocampus as a Cognitive Map.* 1978 Oxford: Clarendon Press p. 5.
5. Kandel, E. *In Search of Memory* 2006 New York: Norton. p. 305.
6. Packard, M; Goodman, J. "Factors that Influence the Relative Use of Multiple Memory Systems." *Hippocampus* 23: 1044–52 2013.
7. O'Keefe, J and Nadel, L. *The Hippocampus as a Cognitive Map.* 1978 Oxford: Clarendon Press p. 385.
8. Ranganth, C. "Time, Memory, and the Legacy of Howard Eichenbaum" 2019 *Hippocampus* 29: 146–161.
9. Miklowitz, D; Johnson, S. "The Psychopathology and Treatment of Bipolar Disorder" *Annual Review of Clinical Psychology* 2006 2: 199–233.
10. Ohayon, M; Schatzberg, A. "Prevalence of Depressive Episodes with Psychotic Features in the General Population." 2002 *American Journal of Psychiatry.* 159: 1855–61.
11. Lipschitz, D; Rasmusson, A; Southwick, S. "Childhood Posttraumatic Stress Disorder." 1998 *Psychiatric Annals* 28(8). p. 452–456.
12. Koob, G. "Corticotropin-Releasing Factor, Norepinephrine, and Stress" 1999. *Biological Psychiatry,* 46(9) p. 1167–1680.
13. Hofer, M. "On the Nature and Consequences of Early Loss." *Psychosomatic Medicine* 1996 p. 570–581.

14. Hofer, M. "Early Social Relationships: a Psychobiologist's view." *Child Development* 1987 58: 633–647. p. 641.
15. Terr, LC. "Childhood Traumas: Outline and Overview." *American Journal of Psychiatry.* 1991 148(1) p. 12.
16. van der Kolk, B. "The Traumatic Spectrum." *Journal of Traumatic Stress* 1(3) p. 273–290. 1988.
17. van der Kolk. "Trauma and Memory." *Psychiatry and Clinical Neurosciences* 1998 Supplement S97–S109.
18. Schore, A. "Modern Attachment Theory." *APA Handbook of Trauma Psychology* vol 1 SN Gold (ed) 2017 396.
19. Porges, SH. *The Polyvagal Theory.* 2011 New York: Norton p. 155.
20. Schore, A. "Modern Attachment Theory." *APA Handbook of Trauma Psychology* vol 1 SN Gold (ed) 2017 396–397.
21. Figley, C; Ellis, A; Reuther, B; Gold, S. "The Study of Trauma." *The APA Handbook of Trauma Psychology* vol 1 SN Gold (ed) 2017 p. 1–11.
22. Page, HW. *Injuries of the Spine and Spinal Cord and Nervous Shock* Philadelphia: Blackson and Son 1883 p. 148.

Chapter 41: What Did You See? Take Two
1. Herman, JL. *Trauma and Recovery.* 1992 New York: Basic Books. p. 33.
2. Kandel, E. *In Search of Memory.* 2006 New York: Norton. p. 313.
3. van der Kolk, B. "The Traumatic Spectrum." *Journal of Traumatic Stress* 1(3) p. 273–290. 1988.
4. van der Kolk, B. "Trauma and Memory," in *Traumatic Stress* (ed) van der Kolk, McFarlane, Weisaeth. 1996 New York: Guildford Press. p. 279–302.
5. Packard, M; Wingard, J "Amygdala and 'Emotional' Modulation of the Relative Use of Memory Systems," *Neurobiology of Learning and Memory* 2004 84: 243–252.

Chapter 42: Troubled Sleep Take Two
1. Freud, S. "Beyond the Pleasure Principle." 1920 In J. Strachey (Ed. & Trans.) *The Standard Edition.* Vol 18. London: Hogarth Press.
2. Caruth, C. *Unclaimed Experience,* Baltimore: Johns Hopkins University Press. 1996 p. 59, 63.
3. Ibid, p. 15.
4. Borges, J. *The Craft of Verse,* 2000 Cambridge: Harvard University Press. p. 29.
5. Caruth, C. *Unclaimed Experience,* Baltimore: Johns Hopkins University Press. 1996 p. 63.
6. Ibid, p. 45.

Chapter 43: A Dog
1. Amorapanth, P; LeDoux, J; Nader, K. "Different Lateral Amygdala Outputs," *Nature Neuroscience* 2000 3: 1 p. 74–80.

2. LeDoux, J; Gorman, J. "A Call to Action: Overcoming Anxiety Through Active Coping," *American Journal of Psychiatry* 2001. 158: 12 p. 1953–1955.

Chapter 44: The School Bus
1. Wheeler, M; Stuss, D; Tulving, E. "Toward a Theory of Episodic Memory" *Psychological Bulletin* 1997 121 (3) 331–354.
2. Caruth, C. *Unclaimed Experience* Baltimore: Johns Hopkins University Press. 1996 p. 63.
3. Cohn-Sheehy, B; Delarazan, A; Reagh, Z; Crivelli-Decker, J; Ranganath, C. "The Hippocampus Constructs Narrative Memories Across Distant Events." 2021 *Current Biology* 31(22) p. 4935–4945.
4. Nelson, K. "The Psychological and Social Origins of Autobiographical Memory." *Psychological Science* 1993 (4)1 p. 7–12.

Chapter 45: Pennsylvania Station
1. Sullivan, RM. "Attachment Figure's Regulation of Infant Brain and Behavior." *Psychodynamic Psychiatry* 2017 45(4) p. 475–498.
2. Caruth, C. *Unclaimed Experience*, Baltimore: Johns Hopkins University Press. 1996 p. 7.
3. Sullivan, RM. "Attachment Figure's Regulation of Infant Brain and Behavior." *Psychodynamic Psychiatry* 2017 45(4) p. 475–498.
4. Caruth, C. *Unclaimed Experience*, Baltimore: Johns Hopkins University Press. 1996 p. 11–12
5. Freud, S (1913) "On Beginning the Treatment." In J. Strachey (Ed. & Trans.) *The Standard Edition*. Vol 12. London: Hogarth Press.
6. Sullivan, RM. "Attachment Figure's Regulation of Infant Brain and Behavior." *Psychodynamic Psychiatry* 2017 45(4) p. 475–498.

Chapter 46: Fresh Squeezed
1. Caruth, C. *Unclaimed Experience*, Baltimore: Johns Hopkins University Press. 1996 p. 56.
2. Ibid.

Chapter 47: Vows
1. Freud, S. "A Case of Hysteria." 1905 In J. Strachey (Ed. & Trans.) *The Standard Edition*. Vol 7. London: Hogarth Press.
2. Robinson-Drummer, P; Opendak, M; Blomkvist, A; Chan, S; Sullivan, R, et al. "Infant Trauma Alters Social Buffering of Threat Learning." *Frontiers in Behavioral Neuroscience* 2019 (13) p. 1–14.
3. Stortelder, F; Ploegmakers-Burg, M. A "Adolescence and the Reorganization of Infant Development" 2010 *Journal of American Academy of Dynamic Psychiatry* 38(3) p. 503–532.
4. Carter, S. "The Role of Oxytocin and Vasopressin in Attachment." 2017 *Psychodynamic Psychiatry* 45(4) p. 499–518.

5. Stortelder, F; Ploegmakers-Burg, M. "Adolescence and the Reorganization of Infant Development," 2010 *Journal of American Academy of Dynamic Psychiatry* 38(3) p. 503–532.
6. van der Kolk, B. "The Traumatic Spectrum." *Journal of Traumatic Stress* 1988. 1(3) p. 273–290.
7. Millett, D. "Hans Berger: From Psychic Energy to the EEG," 2001 *Perspectives in Biology and Medicine* 44(4).
8. Craddock, J. "Hans Berger," *Encyclopedia of World Biography* 2015 vol 35. London: Gale Publishing. P. 55–57.

Chapter 48: Time Has Come

1. Carhart-Harris, R. "The Entropic Brain," 2018 *Neuropharmacology* 142: 167–178.
2. Raichle, M. "The Brain's Default Mode Network," 2015 *Annual Review of Neuroscience* 38: 433–47.
3. Carhart-Harris, R. "Serotonin, Psychedelics, and Psychiatry." 2018 *World Psychiatry* 17: 3 p. 358–359.
4. Carhart-Harris, R. "The Entropic Brain," 2018 *Neuropharmacology* 142: 167–178.
5. Ibid, p. 175.
6. Carhart-Harris, R; Muthukumaraswamy, S; Roseman, L; Nutt, D. *"Neural Correlates of the LSD Experience."* PNAS April 26 2016 113: 17 p. 4853–4858.
7. Carhart-Harris, R; Nutt, D. "Serotonin and the Brain: a Tale of Two Receptors," 2017 *Journal of Psychopharmacology* 31: 9 1091–1120.
8. NA Anis, SC Berry, NR Burton D Lodge "Dissociative anesthetics" 1983. *British Journal of Pharmacology* volume 79 p. 565–75.
9. Carhart-Harris, R; Nutt, D. "Serotonin and the Brain: a Tale of Two Receptors," 2017 *Journal of Psychopharmacology* 31: 9 1091–1120.
10. Carhart-Harris, R. "The Entropic Brain," 2018 *Neuropharmacology* 142: 167–178.
11. van der Kolk, B. "The Traumatic Spectrum." *Journal of Traumatic Stress* 1(3) p. 273–290. 1988.
12. Carhart-Harris, R. "The Entropic Brain," 2018 *Neuropharmacology* 142: 167–178.

Chapter 49: At the Corner of Norman Rockwell and Main—Take One

1. Herman, JL. *Trauma and Recovery*. 1992 New York: Basic Books. p. 43.
2. Ibid.
3. Terr, LC. "Chowchilla Revisited," *American Journal of Psychiatry* 1983 140: 12 p. 1543–50.
4. Herman, JL. *Trauma and Recovery*. 1992 New York: Basic Books. p. 43.
5. Ibid, p. 52.

Chapter 50: Road Kill
1. Herman, JL. *Trauma and Recovery.* 1992 New York: Basic Books. p. 5.
2. Ibid, p. 48–49.

Chapter 51: The Oddball Paradigm
1. Freud, S. (1913) "On Beginning the Treatment." In J. Strachey (Ed. & Trans.) *The Standard Edition.* Vol 12. London: Hogarth Press.
2. James, W. *The Works of William James.* Ed by F. Burkhardt and F. Bowers. Cambridge: Harvard University Press. 1890 vol 1.
3. Terr, L. "Chowchilla Revisited," *American Journal of Psychiatry* 1983 (140: 12) p. 1543–1550.
4. Goddard, G. "The Analysis of Avoidance Conditioning." *The Journal of Comparative Physiology and Psychology.* 1969.
5. Ibid.
6. Goddard, G. "Development of Epileptic Seizures through Brain Stimulation at Low Intensity," 1967 *Nature* 214: 1020–21.
7. Eysenck, HJ. "The conditioning model of neurosis." *Behavioral and Brain Sciences.* 1979 vol 2(2).

Chapter 52: Alchemy
1. Herman, JL. *Trauma and Recovery.* 1992 New York: Basic Books. p. 133.
2. Janet, P. *Psychological Healing,* vol 1 1925 p. 631–633. New York: Macmillan.
3. Zeki, S. *A Vision of the Brain,* 1993 Oxford: Oxford University Press.
4. Kandel, E. *In Search of Memory,* 2006 New York: Norton. p. 304.
5. Stortelder, F; Ploegmakers–Burg, M. A "Adolescence and the Reorganization of Infant Development," 2010 *Journal of American Academy of Dynamic Psychiatry* 38(3) p. 503–532.
6. Freud, S. "Observations on Transference-Love," 1915 In J. Strachey (Ed. & Trans.) *The Standard Edition.* Vol 12. London: Hogarth Press.
7. Bowlby, J. *Attachment,* 1969 New York: Basic Books p. 155.
8. Winnicott, D. *The Maturational Process and the Facilitating Environment,* 1976 London: Hogarth Press.

Chapter 53: Apples
1. Lewis, D; Misanin, J; Miller R. "Recovery of Memory Following Amnesia," 1968 *Nature* Nov 16, 1968.
2. Sara, S. "Retrieval and Reconsolidation: Toward a Neurobiology of Remembering," *Learning and Memory* 2000 7: 73–84.
3. Dudai, Y. "The Neurobiology of Consciousness." *Annual Review of Psychology* 2004 (55) p. 51–86.
4. Sara, S. "Retrieval and Reconsolidation: Toward a Neurobiology of Remembering," *Learning and Memory* 2000 7: 73–84.

Chapter 54: The Program

1. Mitchell, D; Osbourne, E; O'Boyle, M. "Habituation Under Stress." *Behavioral and Neural Biology* 1985 no 43. p. 212–217.
2. Nadel, L; Hupbach, A; Hardt, O; Gomez, R. "Episodic Memory: reconsolidation." In *Handbook of Episodic Memory,* Ed by E. Dere, Easton, Nadel, Huston. 2008 Vol 18 p. 43–56.
3. Schacter, DL; Addis, D; Buckner, R. "Remembering the Past to Imagine the Future," *Nature Reviews Neuroscience* 2007 8: 657–661.
4. Malcolm, J. *In the Freud Archives.* 1983 New York: New York Review Books.
5. Freud, S. *The Complete Letters of Sigmund Freud to Wilhelm Fliess.* Ed. JM Masson. 1985 Cambridge MA: Belknap. Press p. 152.
6. Freud, S. "Recommendations to Physicians Practicing Psychoanalysis," 1912 In J. Strachey (Ed. & Trans.) *The Standard Edition.* Vol 12. London: Hogarth Press.
7. Freud, S. "A Case of Hysteria." 1905 In J. Strachey (Ed. & Trans.) *The Standard Edition.* Vol 7. London: Hogarth Press.